RESOURCES AND HIGHER EDUCATION

RESOURCES AND HIGHER EDUCATION

Alfred Morris and John Sizer
(Editors)

John Pratt

John Fielden   Peter Knight
Richard Lewis   Maureen Woodhall
Geoffrey Sims   Peter Moore
Alan Maynard   Clive Booth

SOCIETY FOR RESEARCH INTO HIGHER EDUCATION

Research into Higher Education Monographs

The Society for Research into Higher Education,
At the University, Guildford, Surrey GU2 5XH

First published 1982

© 1982 Society for Research into Higher Education

ISBN 0 900868 90 2

Printed in England by Direct Design (Bournemouth) Ltd. Printers
Butts Pond Industrial Estate, Sturminster Newton,
Dorset DT10 1AZ

THE LEVERHULME PROGRAMME
OF
STUDY INTO THE FUTURE OF HIGHER EDUCATION

This is the eighth publication of a programme of study focusing informed opinion and recent research findings on the major strategic options likely to be available to higher education institutions and policy-making bodies in the 1980s and 1990s. The programme as a whole has been made possible by a generous grant from the Leverhulme Trust to the Society for Research into Higher Education and is entirely independent of governmental or other organizational pressure. The present monograph arises out of a specialist seminar on resources and their allocation in higher education. We are extremely grateful to Sir Kenneth Berrill, Chairman of Vickers da Costa Ltd., for his excellent chairmanship as well as for his considerable interest in the whole programme.

A fundamental question facing higher education is the extent to which consensual arrangements and assumptions that generally worked well during the long postwar period of its expansion can cope with the much more stringent conditions likely to prevail in the 1980s and 1990s. Is there sufficient common purpose amongst the various institutions and interest groups that constitute 'the higher education system' to permit the development of viable long-run policy objectives, or must higher education policy increasingly become merely the outcome of a struggle for survival and dominance among conflicting interests and ideas?

This is both a substantive and a methodological question. Substantively it will be faced squarely in the final report of the programme of study. Methodologically it will be tackled in the way the conclusions of that final report are reached.

In brief, the study is an experiment in formulating long-term strategies openly, taking into account the best available specialist knowledge about a complex system, the legitimate interests of a wide range of conflicting pressure groups, and wider public interests as perceived by disinterested individuals with no direct day-to-day involvement in higher education. The final recommendations will be the result of an iterative process in which proposals are made, then discussed, then revised, then reconsidered. Stage One is to commission research reviews by acknowledged experts in various specialist areas. Stage Two is a seminar at which others with detailed knowledge and experience of the area discuss these reviews. Stage Three is publication of the reviews together with a report of the discussion and of the policy implications highlighted by it. Stage Four is wider debate in the press and in specially convened conferences. Stage Five is reconsideration of the policy issues in the light of the wider reaction. Stage Six is the preparation of a final report. A seventh stage is of course hoped for, in which public authorities and institutions of higher education will take up the report's recommendations.

Publication of this monograph represents the conclusion of the first three stages in that part of the programme concerned with resources and their allocation in higher education.

Other volumes in the series dealt with higher education and the labour market, access to higher education, institutional change in higher education, the future of research, the arts and higher education, professionalism and flexibility in learning, and freedom or accountability for teachers.

The reports on all the seminars, together with comments on them from interested organizations and individuals, will form the basis for a final report setting out the conclusions and policy recommendations of the programme as a whole. This will be drawn up by the chairmen of the seminars and the editors of the accompanying monographs under the chairmanship of Lord Scarman and will be published in June 1983.

The scope of the SRHE Leverhulme programme is very wide. The need for a major review of higher education has been recognized by informed commentators for some time, and the financial stringency of recent years has made this need even more apparent. In its report *The Funding and Organisation of Courses in Higher Education,* the Education, Science and Arts Committee of the House of Commons commended the SRHE Leverhulme programme of study, and concluded, 'We believe that higher education is at a watershed in its development and that the time is ripe for a great national debate....' The SRHE Leverhulme programme is intended to contribute to that debate by offering both a structure within which the main issues can be considered and an assessment of the evidence on which future policy should be based.

Gareth Williams
Programme Director

FOREWORD

by Sir Kenneth Berrill

When we all gathered at the Civil Service College at Sunningdale to take part in the SRHE Leverhulme seminar on resources and their allocation my expectation was that the discussions would be important but probably dull. Important, because the alternative to adequate resources is a starvation diet which may possibly begin by stripping off surplus fat but will in the end debilitate and ruin. Important, because when resources are tight, their allocation becomes so very much more significant inside institutions, between one institution and another and between the maintained sector and the universities. Important obviously, dull probably, because the subject too easily drifts into dry arguments on accounting or on bureaucratic organization and such arguments lack the passion and interest of a seminar on say research or teaching.

In the event, as this volume shows, it was far from dull. There was a commitment to realism and a determination to face a hard future and make the best of it; coupled with an equal determination to preserve the essentials of our present higher education system.

All present accepted that the 'good old days' of the universities and polytechnics expanding more or less on their own terms had gone, probably for ever. That in future the two sectors would need to work together and be accountable in quite a different way. In this new world flexibility in resource distribution and management would need to be greatly improved if hard times were not to mean irreparable damage. A stimulating discussion leading to practical, useful conclusions.

Kenneth Berrill
Chairman

CONTENTS

INTRODUCTION AND ACKNOWLEDGEMENTS   7

SEMINAR PARTICIPANTS   9

1 BETTER THE DIRIGISTE DEVILS WE KNOW?   11
By John Sizer

Resource allocation at macro level — Student awards, loans and market mechanisms — Funding the public sector — Funding universities — Resource allocation within institutions — Salaries and conditions — Resources and the binary line — Conclusion

2 DES AND TREASURY   25
By Clive Booth

Introduction — The public expenditure process — Policy making — Levers of control — The future — Appendix: Organization of the DES

3 PRIVATIZATION AND MARKET MECHANISMS   58
By Alan Maynard

Introduction — Competing ideologies and objectives — The liberal nirvana — Privatization and loan schemes — Market realities — Incentives for suppliers — Conclusion

4 FINANCIAL SUPPORT FOR STUDENTS   81
By Maureen Woodhall

Introduction — The student grant system — Mandatory awards — Payment of fees — Parental contributions — Discretionary awards — Other support for young people — Criticisms of the present system — Student aid overseas — Lessons from abroad — Future options

5 NEW MODELS FOR FUNDING UNIVERSITIES   112
By Peter Moore

Introduction — Existing practice — Determining needs — Background — Alternative models — Comments and issues

6 RESOURCE ALLOCATION WITHIN THE PUBLIC SECTOR 124
By John Pratt

Summary — The present situation — Immediate problems — Technicalities — Problems of principle — Principles for reform — Components of a solution — A national body in a system locally administered

7 FUNDING VERSUS VALIDATING 152
By Richard Lewis

Validating bodies — The validation process — Funding bodies — The validating input to funding — Alternative relationships between funding and validating — The consequences for validating bodies — Conclusions

8 RESOURCE ALLOCATION WITHIN UNIVERSITIES 165
By Geoffrey Sims

Introduction — Government and administration — Factors in academic resource allocation — Determination of institutional shape — Approaches to resource allocation — Resource acquisition — Research funding — Conclusion — Summary

9 STRATEGIES FOR SURVIVAL 176
By John Fielden

Past and present models — Influences for change — A strategy for survival — Implications for participants

10 TERMS OF EMPLOYMENT 187
By Peter Knight

Inertia — History — Flexibility — International comparisons — Myths of employment law — What can be done? — Conclusion — Appendix: Comparative scales

11 SOME RADICAL PROPOSALS 204
By Alfred Morris

Policy analysis and the DES — Experimentation with incentives — Grants, loans and intensive courses — Allocation between sectors — Allocation within sectors — Allocation within institutions — Supply side rigidities — Conclusion — Proposals

INTRODUCTION AND ACKNOWLEDGEMENTS

This book, arising out of the SRHE Leverhulme Programme of Study into the Future of Higher Education, is the product of the seminar in the programme which took place in June 1982 at the Civil Service College in Sunningdale. A list of participants is given on page 9.

In Chapter 1, John Sizer summarizes the seminar discussions and sets out recommendations which represent the concensus view. Chapters 2 to 10 are revised versions of the papers commissioned for the seminar. The final chapter is a more personal view, that of Alfred Morris, and the proposals made there are his own.

ACKNOWLEDGEMENTS

As convenors of the SRHE Leverhulme seminar on resources and their allocation and as editors of this book, we are indebted to Sir Kenneth Berrill for his chairmanship of the seminar and for guidance when planning for it. We are grateful to the invited participants, especially those who commented on one or more of the draft chapters; and to Gareth Williams as director of the SRHE Leverhulme programme.

Special thanks are due to Betsy Breuer who was responsible for arranging the seminar, to our secretaries Maureen Salkeld and Lisa Thirlby, and to Sally Kington who supervised production of this monograph.

Finally, we should like to thank our fellow authors for agreeing to contribute to the seminar in the first place, for their helpful discussions of the subject matter and their comments on drafts of our own chapters. None of them, however, are responsible for the faults that remain; nor should they be taken as committed in any way to the opinions and recommendations, which remain our own.

Alfred Morris
John Sizer
Editors

SEMINAR PARTICIPANTS

Sir Kenneth Berrill (Chairman)
Mr Alfred Morris, Polytechnic of the South Bank (Joint Convenor)
Prof. John Sizer, Loughborough University (Joint Convenor)
Mr Colin Alves, Church of England General Synod Board of Education
Mr John Bevan, National Advisory Body for Local Authority Higher Education
Mr Richard Bird, Department of Education and Science
Prof. Tessa Blackstone, University of London Institute of Education
+ Dr Clive Booth, Plymouth Polytechnic
Mr Pat Carvill, Department of Education for Northern Ireland
Mr Geoffrey Caston, Committee of Vice-Chancellors and Principals
Prof. Keith Clayton, School of Environmental Sciences, University of East Anglia
Mr John Davies, Anglian Regional Management Centre
Dr I.M.S. Dey, The Open University
+ Mr John Fielden, Peat, Marwick, Mitchell & Co.
Mr Paul Flather, *The Times Higher Education Supplement*
Mr Richard Jameson, Department of Education and Science
+ Dr Peter Knight, Plymouth Polytechnic
+ Mr Richard Lewis, Middlesex Polytechnic
Dr Robert Lindley, Institute for Employment Research, University of Warwick
+ Mr Alan Maynard, University of York
Dr David MacDowall, The Polytechnic of North London
+ Prof. Peter Moore, London Business School
Mr E. Norris, Department of Education and Science
Mr Joslyn Owen, Devonshire Education Authority
Mr Philip Pearson, Peat, Marwick, Mitchell & Co.
+ Dr John Pratt, Centre for Institutional Studies, North East London Polytechnic
Mr Stephen Rouse, Local Authority Conditions of Service Advisory Board
Dr Hans Schütze, Centre for Educational Research and Innovation, OECD
Mr Peter Scott, *The Times Higher Education Supplement*
Mr Michael Shattock, University of Warwick
+ Prof. Geoffrey Sims, University of Sheffield
Mr Peter Slors, Ministry of Education and Science, The Netherlands
Mr Jason Tarsh, Unit for Manpower Studies, Department of Employment
Mr John Thompson, Department of Education and Science

Prof. Leslie Wagner, Department of Economics, Polytechnic of Central London
Prof. Peter Watson, The University College at Buckingham
Mr Phillip Whitehead, MP
Sir Bruce Williams, Technical Change Centre
Prof. Gareth Williams, Department of Educational Research, University of Lancaster
+ Miss Maureen Woodhall, University of London Institute of Education

---

+ Author of paper

1

BETTER THE DIRIGISTE DEVILS WE KNOW?

by John Sizer

How in future should the limited higher education cake be allocated so as to ensure it is effectively and efficiently utilized not only when the allocation process has to take account of the impact of a declining 18-year-old population, but also when society is likely to be wanting a different mix of outputs from the higher education system than at present? Should institutions become less dependent upon public funds, and to what extent should those funds flow through grants to institutions and to what extent through fees from students? Should financing mechanisms facilitate a process of contraction, adaptation and change which is determined by market forces as demographic trends impact upon demand for higher education? What should be the role of the University Grants Committee (UGC) and the National Advisory Body for Local Authority Higher Education (NAB) (and similar Irish, Scottish and Welsh bodies) in the resource allocation process? How should institutions allocate and manage their resources so as to maintain their vitality and responsiveness to the changing demands made upon them? These and many other questions and issues arise when discussing resources and their allocation. This chapter is not a comprehensive report but illustrates the discussions that led to seven resolutions being presented to the final session of the SRHE Leverhulme seminar on the subject. The recommendations in the chapter reflect the dominant views that emerged, and also accord closely with the author's views.

RESOURCE ALLOCATION AT MACRO LEVEL

Clive Booth (Chapter 2) has emphasized that in future higher education is likely to compete for resources more fiercely with other sectors of education and other types of public expenditure. It will be particularly vulnerable to Treasury attack when numbers in the 18-25 age group start to fall. Expenditure on higher education will depend not only upon the political outlook of future governments, but also, as Alfred Morris argues in Chapter 11, upon the ability of the Department of Education and Science (DES) to develop and pursue its case with the Treasury. As Booth emphasizes, the success of the spending minister in obtaining the resources necessary for his policies depends not only on his negotiating skill and political standing, but also on the effectiveness of his department's support and the political importance of his policies. Would the case for higher education be more effectively made if the Secretary of State for Education and Science formulated long-term policies for higher education and negotiated with the Treasury within the framework of these policies? Is this not preferable to short-term disjointed decrementalism?

The planning of public expenditure within the framework of short-term cash limits may be essential in the eyes of some politicians, but it is not compatible with the establishment of quantifiable policy objectives, strategies and guidelines for the effective longer-term development of higher education. However, accepting the need for long-term policies, the SRHE Leverhulme seminar also recognized the limitations of centralized planning for higher education. Therefore, within this long-term government policy framework, the seminar argued that the most appropriate planning and resource allocation process is one in which central planning and policy-making authorities respond to and co-ordinate plans and proposals initiated within institutions themselves, recognizing that realistic planning and resource allocation is an 'incremental or decremental activity' in which decisions are made essentially at the margin within a broad framework of policy goals. Would such an approach ensure that under conditions of financial stringency and declining resources macro-economic policies would not overwhelm sectoral policy issues, and that an appropriate balance would be struck between short-term 'cash limit'-led decisions and long-term policy-led decisions? One obvious danger of short-term decisions being 'cash limit'-led without proper policy analysis is a resultant 'crisis management'. A series of short-term marginal decisions may be made without full understanding of their long-term implications; large costs may be incurred subsequently which negate a large part of the original savings.

While it was recognized that ministers of all persuasions may decide, having regard to considerations which lie outside education, to restrain higher education expenditure and impose futher cuts, it was argued that the merits of policy analysis and formulation should not be neglected because of ministers' lack of use of such analyses. Given the demographic trends and the changing pattern of demands on the higher education system, there ought to be a policy for higher education, and the government at present appears to many SRHE Leverhulme seminar members not to have an overt one. There was widespread support for the following recommendation.

Recommendation 1
The government should establish and enunciate broad policies, strategies and guidelines for the higher education system, including guidance to the NAB and similar bodies and to the UGC, on the considerations to be taken into account when making decisions and recommendations to ministers concerning institutions, student numbers, subject areas, courses and allocation of resources to institutions, and to the research councils on research priorities and establishment of centres of excellence.

In debating the resolution it was recognized that assumptions underlying plans flowing from policies and strategies should also be enunciated.

How should policies and strategies be formulated, given Clive Booth's view that the ability of those in the DES administratively responsible for higher education to conduct major policy studies is limited by their relatively small numbers and lack of experience within the higher education system? The DES should have available an analytical competence in policy analysis, but should this competence be located wholly or even chiefly within the Department? Furthermore should the policy formulation process be a two-way one, with the DES and other government departments issuing scenario analyses and discussion documents and listening not only to responses from the NAB, UGC, CVCP, CDP and other interested parties, but also receiving their, and other independent analyses and proposals? Does the binary concept stand in the way of effective planning and rational allocation of resources? Should there be a Higher Education Grants Committee or a Higher Education Council? Will it suffice for the chairmen of the NAB and UGC to meet regularly, as proposed by Bruce Williams (1981), to discuss drafts before submitting their respective plans and an account of their discussions to the secretary of state? The SRHE Leverhulme seminar was of the view that:

Recommendation 2
The DES should seek private and public funding for the establishment of a higher education policy studies institute with an analytical capacity, which could provide a forum for promoting strategic thinking and planning, undertake independent policy studies, and provide institutions and other interested parties with a voice in deciding the principles upon which resource allocation decisions are made.

STUDENT AWARDS, LOANS AND MARKET MECHANISMS

The SRHE Leverhulme seminar was divided as to whether greater flexibility should be introduced into the student support system: ie through an appropriate combination of bursaries, grants, loans and fees, so as to move voting power towards the students in a manner which would be consistent with institutions becoming more market-oriented as well as endeavouring to be responsive to societal needs. One central issue in the debate was whether the market mechanism should be used to reduce the number of institutions as demographic trends bite, or whether the advice and decisions of the NAB and UGC are preferable. Will market mechanisms or dirigisme lead to the more effective and efficient use of scarce public resources? Given the rigidities in the system, some felt that market mechanisms might create unmanageable financial pressures and uncertainties for all institutions. Once a market in higher education had been created it would have to be controlled. Would it be sufficiently responsive to longer-term societal needs? Would standards be maintained? How would the correct balance be achieved between national needs and short-term market demands? Others argued that the adaptable, flexible and efficient institution would respond to the incentives structure created and would prosper, whilst the less efficient, sleepy institutions would be eliminated. Increased reliance on privatization and the market mechanism would allow more selective allocation of public resources to high priority areas, but would it limit the widening of access?

A small majority of seminar participants favoured no change in fees policy, whilst others favoured increases; one participant favoured fees covering 100 per cent of tuition costs. The status quo vote could be interpreted as in favour of orderly dirigisme and against higgledy-piggledy, market-dictated contraction, adaptation and change, but also as a vote against institutional autonomy! During discussion it was claimed that financial mechanisms can provide powerful incentives, provided their operation is understood and aims and objectives are clear. Many seminar members were not sure that this was the case, and were not prepared to experiement during a period of contraction, whilst others supported a partial shift. Certainly the case for increased privatization and market mechanisms is much stronger during a period of expansion. Those advocating higher fees recognized that they would have to be accompanied by appropriate resource allocation procedures within institutions which stimulated departmental flexibility and adaptability.

Whilst seminar members were divided on the question of higher fees, there was broader agreement on the question of student loans and Maureen Woodhall's recommendation was accepted (below).

Recommendation 3
Financial support to students should be by means of a combination of loans and grants.

Such a support system would be more flexible and adaptable to changing patterns of demand, and to changing labour market and economic conditions. Provided governments would allow a distribution of grants saved, it would in the long run release scarce resources to support the widening of access, part-time courses, continuing education, and emerging priority areas.

FUNDING THE PUBLIC SECTOR

A large number of institutions offer advanced and non-advanced further education courses to meet both national, regional and local needs, attracting both full-time and part-time 18-year-old and mature students on degree and diploma courses, and also offering a wide variety of professional and short courses. As a result of offering multiple services to multiple parties these institutions, like universities, attract funding from many sources. It was thought essential for sound financial management of institutions for there to be secure sources of funding to match the 'core' activity in the institution, which gives rise to a cost structure which is largely fixed in the short term. The UGC provides 'core' funding to universities. Without one or two secure sources of finance it is doubtful whether institutions could be effectively managed, but the proportion of income from 'core' funding should not be so high as to discourage entrepreneurial initiative at a time when institutions should be seeking a higher proportion of funds from non-public sources.

How should 'core' activity be defined? Should those institutions offering full-time undergraduate courses seek funding from a single source? What about the high and increasing proportion of part-time courses, and what about the relationship between AFE and N-AFE work? Should the division be between 'major' institutions with a large stake in higher education and 'minor' institutions? What about regional rationalization and collaboration between 'major' and 'minor' institutions and across the binary line? Should part-time courses be organized on a regional basis across the binary line? The consensus that emerged from the discussion suggested that polytechnics and other 'major' institutions should look to the NAB for the determination of their 'core' funding for first degree and sub-degree courses, and that part of the national pool of funding should be available to local authorities to provide funds to meet specific local and regional needs. Local authorities could also fund specific activities on a customer/contractor basis. The discussion appeared to firm up the view of many that a movement towards higher fees and market mechanisms would add additional, and possibly unmanageable, uncertainties to an already 'messy' and complex situation.

In accordance with Recommendation 1 the role of the NAB should be to call for, respond to, and co-ordinate plans and proposals initiated within institutions themselves. Whilst inter-institutional cost comparisons should provide a starting point for 'value' judgements incorporating, whenever possible, quantitative and qualitative outcome measures, they should not in themselves determine the basis of resource allocation by the NAB. Again, the question of collaboration between the NAB and the UGC arises, and also the very existence of the binary line; but could a national system be managed by a single body? Given the imperfections and complexities of the public sector, should the NAB become well established, and should the NAB and the UGC learn to talk together and develop effective liaison and co-operation before any thoughts on a Higher Education Grants Committee are pursued? Is there a role for the CNAA in assisting the NAB to evaluate and co-ordinate institutional plans and proposals? In introducing his seminar paper (Chapter 7) Richard Lewis emphasized that validating bodies cannot be, because they are not set up to be, the judgement bodies for funding agencies, a view that received substantial support.

In the light of discussion the seminar accepted a resolution which formed the basis of the following recommendation.

Recommendation 4
Whilst public sector institutions should continue to satisfy a variety of needs and attract finance from a large number of sources, it is essential for the financial stability of institutions that 'core' funding should be provided from one or two sources. The NAB, and similar Irish, Welsh and Scottish bodies, should call for, and respond to, plans and proposals from institutions and recommend allocations of 'core' block funds (being the larger part of the funds nationally available) for first degree and sub-degree courses after evaluating proposals in the context of national and regional frameworks. The LEAs should allocate a smaller part of the funds nationally available for individual authorities to fund initiatives either side of the binary line. In addition, LEAs should undertake from their own funds specific funding on a customer-contractor relationship, as well as 'topping up' with grants from their own funds if they so wish. Given the multiplicity and complexity of sources of funding (see Table 1.1), it is essential for institutions to have strong financial administration with sound resource allocation and financial control systems. Institutions should have greater freedom to veer between heads of expenditure without seeking the approval of the maintaining local authority.

FUNDING UNIVERSITIES

In introducing his paper (Chapter 5) Peter Moore emphasized that an overwhelming proportion of university income (87.5%) is received currently from the government in the form of UGC grants and student fees, and that any scenario for the future has to bear in mind the vulnerability of funding systems depending heavily on public financing. Furthermore, because of the commonality of funding mechanisms, universities are possibly not as innovative as they might be. Given the strong pressures to reduce the level of government expenditure and also the need to maintain the vitality and responsiveness of institutions during a period of a declining 18-year-old population and changing demands upon the system, there is a strong case for seeking to increase private support for universities, both to alleviate the effects of reduced government funding and also to stimulate innovation and change. Moore explores a number of alternative models for the future financing of universities, ranging from variants of the old quinquennial system to alternative ways in which more private money can be injected, combined with greater market freedom among the universities. The role of the UGC would vary significantly between the models. In discussing the models one quickly runs into the inflexibilities and rigidities in the current staffing situation, both the age distribution of staff and the nature of tenure in some universities.

Earlier discussion at the SRHE Leverhulme seminar had identified

TABLE 1.1
Possible sources of funding of higher education institutions

1. Funding for 'core' teaching from established agencies: viz UGC for the universities, DES for DG institutions, and for maintained AFE and 'AFE Pool' (under recommendations from NAB) plus any individual LEA topping-up.
2. Local authority supplementation for teaching on a trans-binary basis (funded by deduction from funds otherwise available for 'core' teaching as preceding item).
3. Local authority-funded customer-contractor remits to institutions on a trans-binary basis.
4. Short-course funding from Manpower Services Commission and from industry and commerce.
5. A proportion of home student teaching costs via fees.
6. Student fees from overseas students.
7. General research support from the agencies in 1 above.
8. Grants from the Computer Board for computing facilities.
9. Specific support for research and for postgraduate research 'training' from the research councils.
10. Fees and grants from government, industry and commerce for specific consultancy, research and services.
11. Grants specifically for innovation from the agencies in 1 above, other government departments and charities.
12. Alumni.
13. Donations to fund posts.
14. Conference and holiday lettings.
15. Catering and residence subsidies (if any) (from the agencies noted in 1 above).
16. Royalties on inventions and copyrights.
17. Profits from trading activities.
18. Investment income from endowments and use of temporary cash balances.

differences of view on the applicability of market-oriented models. The question therefore was asked: What is a reasonable rate of change and how can some of the constraints that currently inhibit adaptation and change be eased? Should we rely on the market forces or has the UGC a continuing role to play in adapting the universities to changing circumstances. Should the concept of the UGC 'core' grant be retained? Can it be left to institutions to create innovation funds to finance new developments, or should the UGC maintain a central fund for this purpose? Furthermore, could the UGC support and possibly control entrepreneurial initiatives at institutional level? Many were sceptical as to whether self-governing institutions are capable of managing contraction, adaptation and change in response to market forces. There would be resistance to closing departments, squeezing existing activities to create innovation funds, and developing and implementing a strategy to cope with the bulge in the age distribution of staff and to ensure there is a constant flow of new young blood. Redundancy and retirement must be an important part of the adjustment process, and if it were left to institutions would they make decisions in the long-term interests? Such considerations point to a continuing role for the UGC in stimulating institutions to develop plans for their future development, providing guidance, and co-ordinating the overall contraction, adaptation and change of the system, whilst at the same time preserving maximum institutional autonomy and stimulating entrepreneurial activity. The UGC would liaise with the NAB to ensure that the higher education system as a whole is responsive to national needs and priorities.

The seminar was not attracted to the radical, market-oriented models of universities but preferred to adapt a proven and widely respected UGC 'core' grant model to changing circumstances. Many preferred the dirigiste UGC devil they know to the market mechanisms devil they don't.

Consideration was given to the important question of research funding. Should the UGC continue to provide a single block grant for teaching, scholarship and research, should it give a separate grant for research, or should more money be given to the research councils with the UGC concentrating upon funding teaching and scholarship? As the SRHE Leverhulme monograph on *The Future of Research* (Oldham 1982) and the recent joint report of the ABRC and UGC (1982) have highlighted, a dual funding system runs into serious difficulties in a period of contraction and increasing financial stringency. Firstly, it may not be possible to maintain adequate research facilities in all institutions, and secondly, there are dangers in linking research funding to undergraduate numbers. When resources are scarce it is important to concentrate them in centres of strength to ensure areas of national importance are adequately supported. It may well be that some of these exist in departments where undergraduate numbers are declining significantly. If a single block grant is provided not only is there a danger that favourable staff/student ratios will be maintained at the expense of research, but also that institutions will not provide differential funding to centres of excellence. It was agreed that it is important to protect research capacity in universities and to maintain a diversity of sources of funding of research. A general view emerged that resources should not be moved to the research councils, but that the UGC should provide separate research grants with guidance to universities in response to institutional plans and proposals. Dutch and Australian systems of funding teaching and research in universities were cited as possible models. Furthermore, given that fundamental research of value is also undertaken in a number of public sector institutions, should a corresponding approach to research funding be adopted for that sector?

The resolution discussed and supported led to the following recommendation which, it was agreed, would apply equally to the NAB and the UGC.

Recommendation 5
The UGC should collaborate closely with the NAB. They should respond to plans and proposals from institutions and continue to provide selective guidance based on judgements of the relative merits of departments and subject areas. They should provide separate block grants for teaching and scholarship, and for research. The funding of research should not be linked directly to undergraduate numbers. There should be a multiplicity of sources of research funding, and specific funding should continue to be provided by the research councils. Both the UGC and the NAB should maintain a central fund to finance new developments and innovations, and to facilitate adaptation and change in the system. They should encourage efforts to increase funding from non-government sources and facilitate entrepreneurial initiatives.

The implementation of this recommendation would require the development of new systems of financial control by the NAB and the UGC. Regardless of whether the recommendation is implemented, there is an urgent need to review both the content and format of university published accounts and the Form 3 return to the UGC.

RESOURCE ALLOCATION WITHIN INSTITUTIONS
Declining student numbers and falling real income per full-time equivalent (FTE) have their sharpest impact at the institutional 'coal face', where limited resources are actually transformed into educational services. The major managerial challenge will be to maintain institutional vitality, creativity and responsiveness to changing needs when all the pressures may well be working in the opposite direction. The aim must be to manage not just for survival but for excellence. The papers by Geoffrey Sims (Chapter 8) and John Fielden (Chapter 9) are concerned with ways

of ensuring that the resource allocation process is consistent with this objective.

In introducing his paper Sims highlighted the current pressures on institutions, and the short-term struggles for survival, and emphasized the need to get back to real planning again. He argued that while in periods of expansion decentralized resource allocation processes are appropriate, in decline there is a strong case for greater central control. Institutions need to maintain a central innovation fund, and have a good policy for entrepreneurial activity.

There was some scepticism about rigid and detailed academic plans. Institutions have to get used to uncertainty. However, the greater the uncertainty the greater the need to develop strategies and long-term plans to cope with it. Should plans be prepared centrally or should participation in the planning process be maximized? The performance assessment and organizational and behavioural aspects of the planning process were emphasized and attention was drawn to papers by Sizer (1982) and Davies and Morgan (1982) in the SRHE Leverhulme monograph *Agenda for Institutional Change in Higher Education* (Wagner 1982). Planning has to be a participative, interactive process, with positive leadership from the centre. Institutions need to develop strategies for long-term resource mobility as well as for short-term survival. Agreed long-term strategies would need to be translated into detailed action plans including mission statements for academic departments and units, which define not only the role of the department but also the performance measures towards which each is striving. It is essential that the resource allocation process is consistent with the university's development plan and agreed departmental mission statements if centres of excellence are to be supported and subject area strategies implemented. In the absence of well developed plans, there is a danger that resource-allocating committees might take marginal resource allocation decisions which are not consistent with maintaining the longer-term vitality, responsiveness and creativity of the institution. Thus, decision makers within institutions must ask themselves whether their resource-allocation formulae are compatible with their long-term objectives and strategies.

In managing institutional decline and retrenchment it was recognized that university councils (using this term as in the majority of English universities) and governing bodies of public sector institutions have to play a stronger role than in the past, and that real divisions might develop between university senates/polytechnic academic boards and councils/governing bodies. The planning process has to involve the academics in the operating units, but in the end has to be centrally determined. This will shift the responsibility of resource allocation and the power towards the councils/governing bodies, but how effectively will they exercise this power given the size and membership of councils/governing bodies? Will success depend upon the willingness and determination of a few, powerful lay members of councils/governing bodies to support the vice-chancellors/ polytechnic directors?

Innovations in response to new needs and new opportunities are frequently created through the initiative of individuals. Directors, principals and vice-chancellors of institutions will have to create an environment which motivates individuals and fosters rather than frustrates such initiatives. Not only should they support staff of high ability, the performance of all staff should be reviewed regularly with a view to increasing their effectiveness. A central, within-institution innovation fund was advocated. Furthermore, institutional agreement will have to be secured for department mission statements, which recognize both the need to protect centres of excellence and that resource allocation processes cannot be based on fair shares for all. In particular, problems will arise with the dual funding system if the resource-allocation process to departments is based on student numbers. Conflict could arise between a diminishing student base and existence of an excellent research group in a department. As in the case of the NAB and UGC providing separate research grants with guidance to institutions (Recommendation 5), the establishment of a separate research budget within each institution undertaking substantial amounts of research (as recommended in the joint ABRC/UGC report (1982)) was seen as an important step in resolving such conflicts.

In discussing the stimulation of entrepreneurial activity and reduction in reliance on public funding, the need to create an appropriate structure of incentives and rewards was recognized. It was equally important to control the balance between academic and entrepreneurial activity; to exercise proper financial and managerial control over such activity; and to ensure that the desire to maximize personal and department income does not dominate the academic roles of departments. It was suggested that while institutions might be forced to employ fewer administrative staff they should be sympathetic and supportive towards the entrepreneurial role, but should also ensure that appropriate rules and procedures are observed.

In the light of this wide-ranging discussion the seminar approved a resolution that contained the following:

Recommendation 6
Institutions should recognize that under conditions of contraction, declining resources and changing needs, planning and resource allocation need to be more centralized, but should ensure that there is extensive consultation with academic departments and units. Each institution should:

    a *Develop a strategic plan, which includes a strategy for survival (short-term) and resource mobility (long-term), and include mission statements for each academic department and unit.*
    b *Ensure that its resource allocation procedures are consistent with the strategic plan and mission statements.*

c Establish a separate university research budget, and identify those departments and units whose past research performance and future potential warrants their receiving preferential treatment when allocating this budget.
  d Establish a central innovation fund to support new courses and research initiatives and to develop staff of outstanding teaching and research potential.
  e Seek to increase the share of funding from non-governmental sources, and introduce appropriate incentives to foster entrepreneurial activity, whilst ensuring that such activity is consistent with the teaching and research missions of departments and with the appropriate financial rules and procedures of the institution.
  f Recognize that the contraction and adaptation will require fewer administrative staff but of higher quality.

SALARIES AND CONDITIONS

Peter Knight's paper on salary scales and conditions of service (Chapter 10), the 'grubby area of higher education finance', stimulated a lively discussion and argument across the 'binary divide'. It did illustrate how important the employment function has become to the process of facilitating institutional adaptation and change, in ensuring a constant flow of new blood into a contracting system, in creating reasonable career prospects, in maintaining the motivation of staff when career prospects are diminished, and in implementing strategies for resource mobility within institutions. The following recommendation emerged:

Recommendation 7
Salary scales should continue to be negotiated nationally. Employers' representatives in salary and conditions of service negotiations should:

  a Recognize the need to facilitate and not inhibit institutional vitality, adaptation and change.
  b Ensure maximum flexibility is maintained so as to encourage staff mobility, and to allow a regular flow of able, young teaching and research staff to be recruited with reasonable career prospects.
  c Recognize that long salary scales are incompatible with stimulating institutional vitality.
  d Ensure that early retirement schemes are available.

RESOURCES AND THE BINARY LINE

The 'binary line' kept raising its contentious head during the SRHE Leverhulme seminar. In particular, the seminar was divided on whether a long-term policy objective should be for institutions whose primary activity is teaching full-time undergraduates drawn from a national pool of applicants to make their case for 'core' finance to a single source.

Nevertheless, this may be one of the inevitable consequences of the majority view in favour of rationalization and contraction being managed by grant-awarding bodies as opposed to market mechanisms. If full-time undergraduate numbers are to fall from approximately 350,000 in 1981/82 by about 20 per cent (70,000) by the early 1990s, the government will be forced to develop policy strategies and guidelines (Recommendation 1) as to how this contraction will be handled either side of the binary line. The application by the NAB and the UGC of the dirigiste scalpel will necessitate close collaboration on both national and regional rationalization but may create tensions. These may ultimately lead the DES to the view that a single source of funding is essential; but will the many other actors on the higher education stage agree, would it prove possible for the DES to establish a consensus in favour of change, and would legislative time be made available?

CONCLUSION

This opening chapter has attempted to summarize some of the key points raised in the wide-ranging discussions leading to the resolutions debated in the final session of the SRHE Leverhulme seminar. Overall, the seminar favoured an approach to planning and resource allocation under conditions of contraction, financial stringency and changing needs which requires a 'top down' DES/UGC/NAB statement of policies, objectives, and guidelines, 'bottom up' responses from institutions, advice to the secretary of state from the NAB and the UGC, and 'top down' decisions by him, the NAB and the UGC. If we are to have an adaptive, responsible and flexible system, it is better to have one hundred plus institutional crystal balls in the air than a single, large DES one or a NAB and UGC pair. Following agreement of plans with their funding bodies, institutions would have to ensure their resource allocation procedures were consistent with their plans and with department mission statements.

If the recommendations to reject market mechanisms in favour of the well proven, much admired UGC 'core' grant model are welcomed by institutions, they should be prepared to support the UGC and NAB through difficult times. Ministers and senior DES officials should ensure that they provide the policy guidance and appropriate time framework to allow both the NAB and the UGC, or any future trans-binary body, to undertake their daunting task within the spirit of a 'top down, bottom up, top down' model.

REFERENCES

Advisory Board for the Research Councils and University Grants Committee (1982) *Report of a Joint Working Party on the Support of Scientific Research* Cmnd 8567. London: HMSO

Davies, John L. and Morgan, Anthony W. (982) The politics of institutional change. In Wagner, Leslie (Editor) *Agenda for Institutional Change in Higher Education* Guildford: Society for Research into Higher Education

Oldham, Geoffrey (1982) The research function of higher education: conclusions and recommendations. In Oldham, Geoffrey (Editor) *The Future of Research* Guildford: Society for Research into Higher Education

Sizer, John (1982) Assessing institutional performance and progress. In Wagner, Leslie (Editor) *Agenda for Institutional Change in Higher Education* Guildford: Society for Research into Higher Education

Wagner, Leslie (Editor) *Agenda for Institutional Change in Higher Education* Guildford: Society for Research into Higher Education

Williams, Bruce (1981) Disappointed expectations: the challenge to higher education *Charles Carter Lectures 1981* University of Lancaster

2

DES AND TREASURY

by Clive Booth

INTRODUCTION
Most of the other papers for the SRHE Leverhulme seminar on resources dealt with topics which are largely 'internal' to higher education. They were concerned, for example, with mechanisms for distributing funds within higher education or with the financial support of students. By contrast, the central subjects of this contribution, the Department of Education and Science (DES) and the Treasury, operate on the complex network which links higher education and government. Since 1963 the Treasury has had no direct financial relationship with the universities.[1] It brings its influence to bear indirectly, as indeed for the most part does the DES, which pursues its higher education policy aims mainly through intermediaries — notably the UGC and local authorities.

From the Treasury's viewpoint, higher education is but a small part (2.5 per cent) of the total of public expenditure, one sub-programme among many. Total higher education expenditure forms 23 per cent of the public expenditure programme for which the Secretary of State for Education and Science is responsible and it is thus a significant but by no means dominant element of the DES budget.[2] (Current expenditure on secondary schools is about 20 per cent higher and on primary schools about 20 per cent lower.)

There are two main ways in which the DES and the Treasury are involved in resource allocation. First, and most obvious, is the annual process of determining how much public expenditure in a particular year can be devoted to higher education and how that should be distributed to institutions and students. Secondly, both departments affect resource allocation through the formulation and implementation of policy. These two processes of public expenditure planning and policy making interact; and in order to describe them it is convenient to start with public expenditure planning because it follows a tightly structured and well defined (yet steadily evolving) annual routine.

THE PUBLIC EXPENDITURE PROCESS

The Public Expenditure Survey
Until 1961, the traditional method of controlling government spending was by the annual submission of estimates by departments to the Treasury. This had several weaknesses: it was piecemeal, proceeded on a short time-scale, took little or no account of the consequences of expenditure decisions beyond the year in question, and was unrelated to the resources available.

In 1961, the Plowden Committee proposed a new system of annual public expenditure surveys covering a period of years ahead and related to prospective resources.[3] This was immediately adopted and, although subsequently changed in some details, is still in use today. It is supervised by an official committee, the Pubic Expenditure Survey Committee, whose acronym, PESC, has come to be the accepted abbreviation for the whole survey process. The committee consists of the principal finance officers of spending departments with a Treasury chairman and secretariat.[4]

PESC undertakes the annual preparation of a projection covering up to five years ahead of public expenditure divided into seventeen main programmes and including capital and current expenditure by government, local government and nationalized industries. At the centre of the PESC exercise is the projection of the costs of continuing with 'existing policies'. These policies may then have to be adjusted to fit the total of public expenditure which the Cabinet judge, on Treasury advice, can be made available.

Like painting the Forth Bridge, no sooner has one PESC cycle been completed with the publication on budget day of a public expenditure white paper, than the next cycle begins. The first step is the Treasury's submission to the Cabinet of an economic forecast which will indicate the headroom for public expenditure over the planning period of between three and five years. This forecast, from which the Cabinet will determine the broad strategy to be followed, sets the tone for the rest of the PESC cycle. The forecast will provide a general indication of the scope for expansion or the need for contraction of public expenditure. Clearly the accuracy of the forecast will determine whether the expenditure plans are firmly based or not. Over-optimism at this stage may require the plans to be cut back later.

The detailed guidelines for the PESC exercise are proposed by the Treasury and settled by the Cabinet. The Treasury acts as guardian of the guidelines and has the advantage of being both player and referee. Among the approved guidelines will be instructions — expressed in terms of percentage changes — on the preparation of options for savings or additions. Each department may have to offer packages of measures which will deliver reductions totalling, say, five and ten per cent over the period. New policies requiring extra spending may also be proposed, again up to certain specified percentage limits. In principle, this provides ministers with a series of possibilities for introducing new policies within a constrained total of public expenditure by selecting counterbalancing savings.

By the summer, PESC will have produced for Cabinet a report containing the expenditure projections and options. Although technically a report by officials, each spending minister will have seen and agreed the chapter covering his department. However, items in the final report may still be disputed between the Treasury and departments and the final report will reflect the Treasury view, leaving departments to continue to register their dissent in later negotiations.

It may take several Cabinet meetings before agreement can be reached on even the total of public expenditure for each of the financial years in question, with the fiercest argument concentrating on the financial year immediately following. (Figures for later years are always regarded as being more provisional.) The Cabinet must then turn their attention to fitting the spending plans to the total expenditure they have decided can be allowed. Because of the influence of population changes and other factors, even the continuation of existing policies may imply an increase in expenditure above the agreed limit. Moreover, ministers will often want to include new policies which have become politically urgent or which are manifesto commitments.[5]

A point is usually reached where, even after hard bargaining, the Cabinet have not succeeded in whittling down the spending plans to fall within their previously agreed total expenditure limit. They will then leave the Chief Secretary to the Treasury, sometimes accompanied by two or three non-spending ministers, to hold meetings with individual spending ministers with the object of persuading them to reduce their claims or make offsetting savings. These meetings are known as 'bilaterals'. According to Barnett:

'In practice ... the July Cabinet, fixing the total expenditure, was the crucial one. Both the Treasury and spending ministers recognised it as the key battleground, though there might be a lot of skirmishing over the division of "spoils" in the bilaterals later on. It is true that, in theory, the overall total could be increased at the October meeting, or there could be some "fudging" of the figures ... but in the main, the Prime Minister would be very firm about not allowing a re-opening of this Cabinet decision.'[6]

For a spending minister, success in Cabinet and the subsequent bilaterals will be determined by negotiating skill, the quality of briefing provided by the department, the political standing of the minister and the political importance, particularly as seen by the Cabinet and the parliamentary party, of the spending programme under attack. But the outcome may also depend on personal factors:

'More often (expenditure priorities) were decided on the strength of a particular spending minister, and the extent of the support he or she could get from the Prime Minister. In later years, when Jim Callaghan was Prime Minister, I have seen him snap the head off Shirley Williams, then Secretary of State for Education, although he was fond of her, and would usually apologise almost immediately after. But it might well be enought for her to lose her bid.'[7]

The bilaterals must be completed and the conclusions endorsed by Cabinet so that certain decisions can be announced some months in advance of the following financial year. Such announcements include the size of the rate support grant for that year, the Exchequer grant to universities and the advanced further education pool. Further details of the expenditure plans appear in the public expenditure white paper which is published on budget day, so that the public can (in principle) compare the government's intentions for the revenue raising and expenditure side by side. This may be presentionally tidy but it also means that important information is withheld from publication for between six and eight weeks. The delay does not help those outside bodies whose medium-term planning must be done in the context of the government's public expenditure plans.

Recent Developments in Public Expenditure Planning and Control
By far the most significant recent developments in PESC have been the introduction of cash limits and cash planning. Before 1976, PESC expenditure forecasts had been made at constant 'survey prices', usually the price level prevailing in November of the year preceding the PESC exercise itself. No allowance was made for inflation because it was assumed that the full repricing for inflation would be made as the plans for each year were updated and eventually embodied in parliamentary estimates and supplementary estimates. The emphasis was thus on the use of resources in volume terms. This had not been a serious problem while inflation was low but by the early 1970s there was a widening gulf between the figures on which ministers based their decisions and the cash requirements. Even so, the rationale for constant price planning had stout defenders.[8]

By 1976, the government had concluded that it ought not to fuel inflation by an open-ended commitment to finance public expenditure plans in real terms whatever the cash cost. The white paper *The Attack on Inflation* (Cmnd 6151) made it clear that 'the Government's purchases of goods and services will have to be cut back if prices rise too high.'[9] In *Cash Limits on Public Expenditure* (Cmnd 6440) the government explained that when volume programmes for the following financial year had been settled and were being translated into cash terms, an allowance would be made for price increases in setting the cash limit. The new discipline for spending departments was that 'they will not be able to rely, as they have in the past, on supplementary provision if this would take their total provision for the year beyond the cash limits'.[10]

About three quarters of central government-voted expenditure, almost all except social security payments (and student grants), are covered by cash limits. The rate support grant paid to local authorities, but not total local authority expenditure, is also cash limited.

Pliatsky, who was until 1977 a second permanent secretary responsible for the public expenditure side of the Treasury, writes:

'There can hardly have been an intention on the part of the Labour government to stick ruthlessly to the announced cash limits. The sort of idea in the air was that, if the actual increase in staff costs exceeded the allowance made for it by, say 5 per cent, cash limits could be increased, but only by something like 2 per cent.'[11]

Barnett argues that cash limits worked most effectively in the first two years (1976/77 and 1977/78) because a voluntary incomes policy was working reasonably well and the assumptions made for pay and price inflation in fixing the limits proved to be reasonably accurate.[12] Pliatsky points out that the new Conservative government, inheriting in 1979 cash limits for 1979/80 which allowed for pay increases of five per cent, carried out almost in its entirety what the outgoing government had threatened to do in part: they stuck to the cash limits.[13] Since large pay settlements had been and were being negotiated for the public services following the collapse of the informal pay policy, there was a substantial cut in most programmes in volume terms. On top of this the new government applied direct volume cuts in some planned programmes, including education, and allowed growth in others. Since 1979/80, cash limits have consistently failed to compensate for inflation.

The introduction of cash planning in the 1980 public expenditure white paper marked a further step away from planning in volume terms. Previously cash limits had been set only for the financial year immediately following. For example, the 1981 white paper gave cash limits for 1981/82 and plans for 1982/83 in constant prices.[14] The 1982 white paper contains plans for 1982/83, 1983/84 and 1984/85 all expressed in cash terms. Annual inflation for the purposes of those plans is assumed to be seven, six and five per cent for each successive year.[15]

As with previous white papers, it must be assumed that the figures for later years will be reviewed as the PESC cycle rolls forward, but the dilemma for any public body such as a local authority, university or polytechnic, is to know whether to plan on the cash figures or on the resource indicators shown in the white paper. For example, Table 2.10.1 of the white paper shows the number of teachers employed in 1982/83, 1983/84 and 1984/85 'consistent with these expenditure plans'. Are local authorities to assume that they should employ these teachers or some lower number based on the excess of expected inflation over that assumed? Similarly, the white paper refers to a loss of 10,000 teaching posts in higher education.[16] What assumptions should be made by institutions in planning this contraction?

It is one of the roles of the DES to act as a shock-absorber when such tensions arise. The Treasury must be re-assured that every effort is being made to contain forecast expenditure within the cash plans; and the local authority associations, the UGC and other bodies need to feel that the government will be flexible if, as so often before, actual inflation is significantly above the government's planning assumptions.

The Effects of Cash Limits and Cash Planning

Cash limits have introduced a very much tighter discipline into public expenditure. At the same time they have transferred the strain of adjusting to unplanned changes, especially in inflation, from the government to the institutions within the public sector. By encouraging caution cash limits have also increased the probability of underspending (except, as in the case of the local authorities, where there are important non-exchequer sources of revenue); and by making inadequate provision for inflation they have squeezed programmes in real terms.

The most obvious effect for higher education of cash limits and plans is to increase uncertainty and to muddy the waters of policy making. By espousing cash planning, the government is seen to be demonstrably less concerned with establishing quantifiable educational policy objectives or standards than their predecessors of either party. This is an important departure from the original PESC conception, which started from the assumption that the government wished to secure certain policies and would make available the necessary resources: public expenditure planning was 'policy-led'. From its early days, the present government made known its preference for 'expenditure-led' policy making, by which policies must be trimmed to fit the resources for public expenditure the government wish to make available.

The difficulties that can arise are well illustrated by recent policy on higher education. In effect, ministers wanted to make a particular cash saving in higher education within a three-year period. They were advised that cuts of the magnitude required over the time allowed would be impossible to secure by 'natural wastage' of staff: moreover, the cost of paying off redundant staff would almost certainly make unattainable the saving that was originally required. However, the commitment to stick to the theoretical savings target was so strong that these practical consequences were ignored, thereby making the plans themselves suspect and raising questions about whether and how funds for restructuring would be found.

Pliatsky, who was responsible for advising ministers on the introduction of cash limits, argues that the government will face great tensions over the shortfall between assumed and actual inflation:

> 'This does not mean that we should revert to planning public expenditure in volume terms without regard to what is happening to prices, or to providing public money to pay for inflation irrespective of the level it has reached, but it does mean that we cannot altogether jettison the concept of volume in drawing up physical programmes or disregard the concept of equity in public service pay. In the long run the workability of operating the public expenditure system entirely in cash terms will depend on progress in coping with inflation ... unless and until we can assume low inflation rates with confidence that they will actually happen, there will probably have to be some compromise between cash

planning and programming in real terms over the medium term — meaning any period longer than a single year ahead.'[17]

Bringing the Local Authorities (and Others) into PESC
During the early 1970s it became clear that there was no effective connection between the planning of current expenditure by local authorities and the assumptions made in Whitehall about local authority expenditure for PESC purposes. Sometimes the central and local plans were widely divergent. In 1975 proposals were therefore formulated for what was known at the time as 'bringing the local authorities into PESC'. A Consultative Council on Local Government Finance was created, bringing together leaders of the local authority associations and the ministers responsible for services provided wholly or partly by local government in England and Wales (education, environment, personal social services, roads and transport).

The council set up a number of expenditure steering groups consisting of civil servants and local government representatives to prepare estimates of relevant expenditure within broad guidelines that paralleled the PESC exercise, including the percentage options for additions or reductions. Thus the Expenditure Steering Group — Education (ESGE), chaired by a DES deputy secretary, acts as a sounding board for local authority opinion on the consequences of adopting various alternative expenditure plans. During the 1980 PESC cycle, for example, the local authority associations successfully appealed for some moderation of the department's proposals for reducing teacher numbers in advanced further education.

The ESGE machinery, although useful, does not commit individual local authorities to the government's plans and the combined effect of authorities' decisions can still result in significant departures from the PESC assumptions.

The University Grants Committee is not so closely involved in public expenditure planning as the local authorities, but they are invited to comment during the PESC cycle on the effects of adopting the percentage options for saving and spending and their comments are fed back to the DES for officials and ministers to consider. In 1981 the Advisory Board for the Research Councils was for the first time similarly given an opportunity to comment on the PESC options (which the government had made public) as they affected the science budget. Their views were also taken into account by the DES, which provides the secretariat for the ABRC.

Limitations of the PESC System
PESC was originally envisaged as a system of planning and control and in each of these functions difficulties were encountered. Of course no system of national planning can be precise or faultless: plans will always be 'broad brush' and will need periodic adjustment. Difficulties in achieving effective *control* over public expenditure, combined with the tendency to base plans on over-optimistic forecasts of economic growth, contributed to undermine PESC as an instrument of *planning*.

There are only two periods when PESC can be said to have fulfilled the aspirations of its founders: these were in 1961-66 when the growth assumptions embodied in the economic forecasts underlying PESC actually materialized; and in 1968-70 when controlled reductions in the total of public expenditure in real terms were achieved.

One weakness was that the rolling forward of 'existing policies' left too much scope for the surreptitious expansion of programmes: the concept of an existing policy was treated too subjectively. Moreover, the readiness of ministers to agree to new policies outside the PESC cycle without considering the expenditure consequences stored up problems for the future. Some of these weaknesses were removed in time: for example, by counting any increase above inflation in existing policies as an additional bid which might or might not succeed; and by rigidly enforcing the rule that new policies not assimilated during PESC should compete for a strictly limited contingency reserve.

Some of the lack of control was connived at by the Treasury. According to Barnett:

'Thus when Denis Healey wanted to reduce the PSBR painlessly he would ask Harold (Lever) if he could come up with what he called 'ripping wheezes' to achieve his objective. He did so to the tune of many hundreds of millions of pounds by, for example, persuading first the clearing banks and later the Trustee Savings Bank to re-finance export credit and ship building so achieving two gains by reducing both public expenditure and PSBR.'[18]

Apart from such sophisticated examples of what Barnett calls 'fiddling the figures' which inject a spurious accuracy into planning, the PESC system itself encourages over-estimating (and thus inefficiency) because it is more difficult in a later year to revise upwards the expenditure figures of a previous survey (which may require savings elsewhere) than to revise downwards (which yields savings, though they may not be redirected within the same spending area).

A more fundamental criticism of the PESC machinery is that by concentrating unduly on existing policies, it focuses attention on established doctrine and encourages only marginal reallocations of resources between programmes. There is little or no incentive to review the existing policies contained in PESC or even, indeed, to state them, except in a rather perfunctory fashion: the timetable of the cycle is too tight for anything else.

Various efforts have been made to complement PESC by more radical and systematic reappraisals of policy. This was the purpose of PARs (Programme Analysis Review) which were in vogue during the Heath Government.[19] Although departments' approaches to PARs varied, they had in common the attempt to state policy aims and objectives and the analysis of costs and benefits of alternative solutions. The Treasury and Central

Policy Review Staff were quite closely involved with departments in these exercises.

Higher education was the subject of an early PAR and, according to Pliatsky,[20] was one of the few examples of an important policy issue being put on the PAR list. The higher education PAR, although never itself published,[21] provided a basis for parts of the 1972 white paper *Education: A Framework for Expansion.*[22]

That PARs ran out of steam within a few years can be partly attributed to the complexity of the exercises themselves. They placed heavy demands on staff for prolonged periods. There is also the question whether the technocratic approach to policy making embodied in PARs was tenable in the context of government:

> 'In spite of an ambiguity as to how far PAR was meant to be concerned with the determination of policy and how far with methods of carrying it out, the PAR approach, if taken seriously, was bound to concern itself with policy implications. But policies on public expenditure cannot be divorced from the political process. To criticise the PESC system as "purely incremental" was to ignore the fact that policy reviews were regularly being carried out in response to political and economic pressures, and decisions on them were being taken on the political plane, either in parallel with or outside the technological PESC process — outside the Whitehall system altogether in the case of manifesto policies. ... The figures resulting from the political decisions were then assimilated into the PESC machine.' [23]

Higher Education and PESC

The method of planning embodied in the PESC system is one which expresses policies in terms of quantified objectives and then converts these into expenditure runs. Examples of such objectives are the Plowden targets for nursery education, the 'roofs over heads' criterion for school building, and the Robbins principle. The most important requirements for policy objectives to gain legitimacy are that they should have some underlying sense of rationality, even if untested in any scientific sense; they should be attainable over a reasonable period of time; they should have broad political appeal; and they should be timely. It may have been an accident of timing as much as the rationale, attainability or political appeal of the recommendations in the Robbins Report[24] that secured a niche for higher education in PESC plans from which it was able to withstand onslaughts on public expenditure during the late 1960s and the early 1970s.

The timeliness of Robbins was that it caught the crest of a wave of public optimism, a belief in broader educational opportunities and in education as a vehicle of social mobility. Not least, politicians of both main parties took an expansionist view of public expenditure. The Robbins committee produced a 'principle' capable of being translated in PESC terms with comparative ease. As Stuart Maclure put it: 'for a respected collection of university professors to use the moral imperative and say "courses ... *should* be available" was to stake a claim on public funds of indeterminate proportions, in a form which it rapidly became indecent to challenge.'[25] Government acceptance of the principle placed higher education expenditure for some years in an almost unassailable position in successive PESC rounds.

Higher education became perhaps the prime example of a 'policy-led' expenditure programme. The number of full-time and sandwich higher education students in Great Britain more than doubled from 192,000 in 1961/62 to 463,000 in 1971/72.

Calculating the expenditure requirements from projections of the size of the relevant age group and of the number gaining minimum entry qualifications and wishing to proceed to higher education was a deceptively simple matter; and it was on the age participation rate (APR) that the longer-term forecasting by the DES of demand for higher education foundered. While the 1972 white paper *Education: a Framework for Expansion* assumed that participation would reach 21 per cent of the relevant age group by 1981 and still be rising, in practice it peaked at 14.2 per cent in 1972/73, falling to 12.4 per cent in 1979/80 before recovering to 12.7 per cent in 1980/81 and 12.9 per cent in 1981/82, the highest level since the mid-1970s. What precisely the Robbins principle means and whether it has been abandoned are matters of controvesy.

The picture is, however, complicated by the contraction of teacher training, an important route into higher education for those with less than two GCE Advanced level passes, for whom, as a group, opportunity diminished sharply from 1972 onwards. When entrants to teacher training having less than two 'A' levels are excluded, the APR has been remarkably stable at just over 12 per cent since 1972/73.[26]

It may be that the general tendency in the last decade for projections of student demand to stay on the high side of actual numbers reflected a combination of factors: among them disillusionment among the public with education as an instrument of social improvement, and an unfulfilled expectation by the DES that policy development at secondary school level (including the raising of the school leaving age and development of comprehensive secondary education) would lead to growth in participation in higher education.

The result of the adoption of the Robbins principle by successive governments and of the chronic over-estimation of demand in projections of the APR was that government plans for higher education were capable of being trimmed back progressively as part of the general retrenchment of public expenditure in a way that, in the early stages, was relatively painless. Furthermore, the increase in the size of the age group meant that absolute demand was rising even though the APR for higher education excluding teacher training was stable. Because student numbers were expanding, albeit slowly, for much of the 70s, particularly in large public sector institutions, it was possible to increase 'efficiency' as measured by student staff ratios and cut unit costs whilst maintaining academic standards in teaching if not in research.

Table 2.1 shows how government decisions were reflected in successive white papers.

Filling in the Detail after PESC
The PESC negotiations tend to concentrate on the larger issues — the total number of students to be planned for the total public expenditure commitment. In preparing the PESC forecasts, the DES will, however, have made policy assumptions about the division of places (and thus expenditure) between the universities and the public sector, expenditure on student awards (the product of the number of students and the average value of awards), and income reaching institutions from sources other than central and local government. (The balance between tuition fee income and general support received through the UGC or local authorities is less important for PESC purposes since in theory it does not affect the total level of public expenditure on higher education.) These detailed policy issues have to be pursued after the Cabinet's final decisions have been taken. They are discussed later in this chapter.

The public expenditure white papers have not normally indicated how the total of places assumed for higher education will be divided between the university and public sectors: this is usually discussed with the UGC and the local authority associations (in ESGE). In the late 1960s and early 1970s the department assumed that growth would be biased towards the public sector, thus reflecting the original thinking underlying the 1966 white paper which favoured the development of a form of higher education different from universities.[27]

The public presentation of this policy also referred to the relative capacity of the two sectors to expand, but this was a secondary consideration. In practice, however, university growth overtook the public sector partly because of the contraction of teacher training (Table 2.2).

In 1981 the public expenditure white paper left institutions free to admit 'as many students as they can consistent with their academic judgement'.[28] The result was interesting. The UGC decided to impose restrictions on student enrolments thus limiting erosion of the 'unit of resource', although it is far from clear that this is what the DES would have wished. Meanwhile, the public sector institutions increased admissions significantly, taking advantage of the benefit of tuition fee income which in many cases must have exceeded marginal cost.

Education ministers, in spite of their public posture, tend to be ambivalent about the local authority sector's ability to act contrary to the expenditure plans. Local authority expenditure is different in kind from exchequer expenditure. Since the exchequer contribution to local authority spending is fixed, expenditure in excess of that planned (apart from

TABLE 2.1
Public expenditure white papers 1972-82

Publication date and Cmnd number (in brackets)	Target for full-time and sandwich places in GB by 1981/82: thousands	Notes based on white paper texts
Dec 72 (5178)	750	Reflected policy of *Education: A Framework for Expansion*. Large capital programme for buildings and student residence.
Dec 73 (5519)	750	Reductions in universities' recurrent grant and equipment grant could be 'accommodated without detriment to planned growth'.
Jan 75 (5879)	640	'... revised figures maintain the Robbins principle ...'. General 'slowing of demand for education' because of lower than expected trends in staying-on at 16 and number qualifying for higher education.
Feb 76 (6393)	600	'... implies some increase in competition for entry in some subjects compared with recent years'. Age participation rate expected to grow from 14% to 15%,' ... little if any scope for increasing staff numbers after 1976-77 ... capital expenditure ... severely restricted ...'.
Feb 77 (6721)	560	Tuition fees for home and overseas students to be increased sharply in 1977-78. Limitation on numbers of overseas students proposed. No increase in total number of academic staff. Continuing severe restrictions on capital expenditure.
Jan 78 (7049)	560	Assumed division between universities and public sector: universities 310,000 by 1981/82, public sector 250,000 by 1981/82. Intended that in 1978-79 the number of overseas students be reduced to about the level of 1975-76, an implied reduction of about 12% or 11,000 places.
Jan 79 (7439)	544	Downward adjustment because enrolments in 1977/78 lower than expected. APR of 13.8% by 1982-83.

DES AND TREASURY

Publication date and Cmnd number (in brackets)	Target for full-time and sandwich places by GB by 1981/82: thousands	Notes based on white paper texts
Nov 79 (7746)	No forecast	'... resources available for home students in higher education will be about the same as in 1979/80.' New overseas students expected to meet the full cost of their tuition. Capital expenditure halved.
Mar 80 (7841)	[500 implied]	Home student numbers to remain broadly constant, implying fall in admissions. Small reduction in expenditure on institutions and student support, especially in the non-university sector.
Mar 81 (8175)	No forecast	Fall in planned expenditure owing to (a) removal of subsidy to overseas students, (b) reduction in expenditure on home students, so that 'by 1983/84 institutional expenditure (net of tuition fee income) will be rather more than 8% below the level planned in Cmnd 7841'. ... 'This is likely to lead to some reduction in the number of students admitted to higher education with increased competition for places; but the Government expects institutions to admit, as they have done this year, as many students as they can consistent with their academic judgement ... the plans assume a significant tightening of standards.'
Mar 82 (8494)	[1981/82 target not applicable]	Total spending by institutions in 1984-85 expected to fall by at least 10% in real terms below 1980-81 level. Loss of 10,000 teaching posts, fall of 10% in student numbers and 13% in undergraduate admissions over the same period.

Note The actual numbers of full-time and sandwich students in higher education in GB in 1981/82 was about 500,000.

mandatory student awards and associated tuition fees) must be raised principally from the rates. Higher rate-borne expenditure, when substituted for exchequer-borne expenditure reduces the public sector borrowing requirement and the money supply. Some easing of the competition for higher education places at a time when the size of the 18-year-old age group is close to its peak may thus be available from the local authority sector. Politically this may not be a bad outcome for the government faced with the alternative of denying entry to qualified young people, many of them from social classes to whom a Conservative government looks for electoral support.

After dividing resources nationally between sectors the DES is concerned with the allocation of funds among public sector institutions. Great efforts have been made by a working party under DES chairmanship to devise an objective formula for distributing the capped advanced further education pool which will penalize the higher cost institutions while allowing for variations in subject mix. The new National Advisory Body for Local Authority Higher Education is likely to inject an element of judgement into the distribution of resources.[29] There are signs that both the NAB and the UGC will in future receive from the DES some broad indications of the considerations the government believes important for the flow of funds to institutions. Whether ministers can find guidance which is neither too platitudinous nor too specific is an open question.

TABLE 2.2
Full-time and sandwich student numbers in GB higher education (1966/67 = 100)

	Universities	Public sector	All
1966/67	100	100	100
1967/68	108	116	112
1968/69	114	129	121
1969/70	119	136	127
1970/71	123	141	132
1971/72	127	148	137
1972/73	130	152	140
1973/74	132	153	142
1974/75	136	153	144
1975/76	141	158	149
1976/77	147	157	152
1977/78	152	148	150
1978/79	156	142	149
1979/80	159	141	151
1980/81	161	142	152

POLICY MAKING

As has been explained earlier, the PESC exercise brings forward to ministers each year a report containing forecasts of expenditure on present policies and options for reductions or additions. Any Whitehall civil servant developing new policy proposals knows that they must be sufficiently worked out to be ready at that time in the spring when departments are preparing 'shopping lists' of options for ministers. If this key point is missed, the best part of a year's delay may be the penalty. 'Getting a bid into PESC' is thus all-important. Another hurdle, to be negotiated for proposals requiring legislation, is the Cabinet committee responsible for co-ordinating preparation of the Queen's Speech at the state opening of parliament. Legislation can add twelve or eighteen months to the timetable for implementing a policy.

Policy formulation itself is the business of the civil servants in the policy branches of the DES assisted by central branches: the organization of the DES is outlined in the Appendix. Policy branches work under the supervision of the most senior officials (known as heads of the office) and ministers.

All new policy proposals being developed in readiness for a PESC bid must be negotiated by spending departments with the Treasury. The DES conducts its relations with the Treasury almost exclusively through its Finance Branch. At the Treasury end, only three senior officials (an assistant secretary and two principals) are exclusively concerned with the entire DES programme. The small number of people who are thus involved in DES-Treasury discussions at official level assists communications.

Once Treasury support has been obtained, or at any rate, downright opposition avoided, policy proposals must be taken to a Cabinet committee (and thus run the gauntlet of other spending ministers). Education policy seldom reaches the level of Cabinet discussion.[30]

This is a necessarily brief resumé of the policy-making process within government. It is often not realized by outside observers that a secretary of state's room for manoeuvre is severely limited by the internal and external obstacles that must be overcome. Measures which do not have electoral appeal, the political support of the party in government and the strong support of interest groups within education are unlikely to succeed. Proposals for radical changes in higher education will be stillborn unless these conditions can be met.

By Whitehall standards, the DES is a small department. Excluding the office of Arts and Libraries, the total number of headquarters staff is less than 1,400, of whom about 150 are senior staff (principals and above). The team in HFE Branch I responsible for policy on university finance totals eight (including typist and clerks); a similar number covers advanced further education finance. DES has no local or regional administrative organization. In addition to the staff just mentioned there are 400 HM inspectors in England, about 100 of whom have responsibilities in further and higher education.

Staffing restrictions will ensure that the DES remains small unless there are dramatic changes in its functions and in government policy towards the civil service. The DES staffing target for April 1984 requires a reduction of 10 per cent below the 1981 level.[31] Some of this could be saved by the purely cosmetic device of hiving off functional units such as the UGC, whose staff could cease to count on the DES's books; but there is also real pressure to give up tasks and increase 'efficiency'.

Because of staff cuts and the growing political pressures generated by the consequences of expenditure cuts already announced, the attention which the DES can devote to particular areas of policy will decrease in the foreseeable future unless staff are concentrated in a few priority areas. Ministerial pressure will see to it that the department's staff are thinly spread, for ministers are loathe to accept that there is any area of the education service on which they cannot be fully briefed; and the rather general responsibilities placed upon them by the 1944 Education Act reinforce this view.

How New Policies Emerge

Policy changes may arise in a variety of ways. In education they commonly originate in the exchange of ideas which is constantly taking place through the network of educational interest groups, including the associations representing teachers, education officers, vice-chancellors, principals, subject specialists and so on. Sometimes the DES itself promotes discussion, as it did, for example, with *Higher Education into the 1990s*.[32] Few initiatives are nowadays taken by the DES without prolonged consultation; and the experience of the 1981 green paper[33] suggests that the outcome is not always what the DES would have hoped for.

If the DES can be said to have a self-image, it is that of a partner rather than a leader, a stimulator of debate and builder of consensus. This is partly a consequence of the decentralized education system and the length of the educational process itself. Because the education system is so large and difficult to re-orientate, the DES must take a long view and favours gradual, evolutionary change over sudden reform. This often makes outsiders impatient with the department and invites unfavourable comparisons with the Manpower Services Commission which has the enormous advantage of being able to dispense large sums using its Exchequer grant powers. Some recent Labour secretaries of state for education made bids within Whitehall for specific grant powers, but without success. Press reports suggest that the DES is now promoting proposals for a separate block grant for education.[34]

Another reason for the department's caution and its reliance on partnership is its relatively meagre in-house expertise. Apart from the teacher training specialists, few of the hundred or so HMI specializing in further and higher education came to the Inspectorate from higher education institutions; at least until recently, in-depth inspections by HMI of major public sector education institutions have been rare and apart from maintaining the advanced course approval system, HMI have concentrated their attention on non-advanced further education.

The combination of restrictions on staffing and limited in-house expertise severely inhibits the department's scope for conducting major policy studies. Two decades ago such a gap might have been filled by appointing committees of distinguished outsiders (although the consequences for DES staffing were still significant because much background material and secretariat support came from the department). A decade ago the stimulus might have come from a PAR. Both of these devices have now fallen out of favour. At the same time, pressure groups have increased and become more vociferous. The new departmental select committee system has also been perceived by many departmental staff as an additional burden and distraction.

The Role of Civil Servants
Policies originate in a variety of ways but they must at some stage be developed and implemented with the assistance of permanent officials. Civil servants are thus in a position to influence policy, and their influence usually outlasts the tenure of a secretary of state or the life of a government.[35] This raises questions which are pertinent to the role of the DES in issues of policy and resources: first, how far do individual civil servants affect policy; and secondly, do senior civil servants in the DES share a corporate view on policies towards higher education?

Boyle referred to 'a handful of civil servants ... who said what they believed with great logical and moral force. ... They can't be named but they and their colleagues and the upper reaches of the educational world would know whom I mean. They are anything but faceless in the world in which they work.' He noted 'two traditions in the Department: the social justice tradition, wanting to widen opportunity ... and the technical college tradition — education for investment, education for efficiency. They were described in the early 1960s ... by Toby Weaver, as "the dialectic within the office" — and that dialectic was quite sharp.'[36]

But Boyle regarded it as 'absolute and dangerous nonsense' to suppose that there are predetermined and static suppositions within bureaucracy '... if only because new officials are coming to positions of authority and their value judgements ... are a factor in the situation as well.'[37]

The initial formulation and later momentum of the binary policy owed much to the convictions of one senior civil servant. Crosland confessed to delivering the 1965 Woolwich speech prepared for him by the department without fully understanding or accepting the principles it contained; and he regretted not postponing such a major statement of policy although he ultimately became a committed convert to binarism.[38] In the 1972 white paper the same belief among senior officials in the need for an antidote to the anti-industrial values of the universities was manifested in the preferential growth projected for the public sector.[39]

Individual officials are not often personally identified with particular policy proposals but may be more so in future because of the new departmental select committees. Appearing before the Education, Science and Arts Committee in 1980, for example, Mr. Alan Thompson, a DES deputy secretary, canvassed his idea for a 'broad steer' from government to higher education:

> '... to translate somehow the very specific requirements of the market place into very broad subject areas, grouping them in, for example, the technologies, the sciences, the arts subjects, and the business studies subjects, and to try to work out from such messages as can be derived from the employment market a subject profile which would be a guiding principle for the institutions of higher education. If that can be done, *I personally, and I can only speak personally at this point*, would have no hesitation in thinking that this would be the kind of programme that it would be the responsibility of the Government, in one way or another, to give to the higher education system.'[40]

Adherents to the two traditions of social justice and economic efficiency identified by Boyle can still be found in the DES, but the arguments rage less fiercely. Attitudes are now more defensive. Much of the department's thinking is dominated by problems arising from the contraction of the education system at all levels caused by demographic changes and shrinking resources. Nevertheless the attitudes and values of individual senior civil servants remain an important part of the policy-making equation.

LEVERS OF CONTROL

In an earlier seminar in this series, Fowler has argued that broad policies enunciated by government for higher education have failed because 'govenment has grasped the wrong levers of control.'[41] In this section, we consider what levers have been used in the past; and in the following section how they might be used in the future. The choice of policy levers and the allocation of resources are interrelated: decisions on one tend to affect the other. It is convenient to divide the discussion into six broad areas:

a Efforts to stimulate public awareness of policy issues and muster support for new policy initiatives.
b Policies concerned mainly with questions of efficiency or financial control.
c Policies affecting the length or geographical distribution of courses.
d Policies acting upon student demand.

e   Policies on institutional structures or relationships.
f   Policies on the machinery of government.

Efforts to stimulate Public Awareness of Policy Issues
It is a prerequisite of successful policy implementation that those whose co-operation is needed should have some understanding of and preferably participation in shaping policy. To encourage informed public discussion the DES produces statistical bulletins and occasionally more extensive documents such as *Higher Education into the 1990s*.[42] The latter drew attention to the 'hump' in the size of the 18-year-old age group that would occur during the 1980s and proposed five alternative ways of adjusting the higher education system to it. Unfortunately, the fifth model (Model E) offered the hope of resource stability not available in the others: it was rather like asking a condemned man to choose between a reprieve and four alternative ways of execution. The problem was compounded by the minister launching the conference on the discussion paper who, entirely on his own initiative, expressed strong support for Model E. Because of this, there was little discussion of the other alternatives. This outcome may have been inevitable. DES officials believed at the time, and still believe, that Model E had to be included for completeness and it may yet turn out to be the pattern for the future. The debate has been partially revived by a DES consultative paper on continuing education.[43]

Since coming to power in 1979 Conservative ministers have avoided referring to *Higher Education into the 1990s* although it would have been possible to describe their policies for higher education in terms of the alternative models. Views may now be divided about whether the discussion document was worthwhile. It probably did much less to concentrate minds than the 1981 and 1982 expenditure white papers, together with the UGC's letters of 1 July 1981. In the longer term, however, the discussion document may prove to have stimulated in the higher education world a consciousness of the need to promote its interests more actively.

Policies concerned with Efficiency or Financial Control
The expansion of higher education after Robbins raised questions in the DES about the extent to which growth could be accompanied by economies of scale and increased efficiency. According to Crosland:

> '... I insisted that the universities should be made accountable to PAC. Lastly, and most important, the UGC itself was persuaded to take a much more positive line on productivity, specialisation, concentration of subjects and control of building through cost limits.
> The type of letter reaching the universities from the UGC is now much more detailed in its guidelines for expansion.'[44]

At this time (1967/68) the DES believed that Robbins had seriously underestimated the scale of expansion required to meet demand from those qualified to enter the system. The Treasury and DES were agreed that plans for expansion would have to depend in some measure on the reduction of unit costs. With this aim in view, the minister of state, Mrs Shirley Williams, initiated discussions in 1969 with university and local authority representatives. The proposals included increasing student/staff ratios from around 7:1 to perhaps 10:1 or 11:1; encouraging more students to study within reach of home; securing the more efficient use of buildings and equipment; avoiding duplication of facilities; encouraging sharing between universities and polytechnics of various services; changes in the system of student support, including the possibilities of loans; new ways of organizing the academic year; and the expansion of distance learning.[45] There was talk of developing a general plan for higher education matching provision in the universities with provision in polytechnics subject by subject and region by region. For the first time, planning for the universities would not be considered in isolation. That was the hope.

While the university interest responded with a general but guarded expression of willingness to make economies so long as academic standards were maintained, few of these proposals were actively pursued beyond the initial stages of discussion, mainly, it seems, because of the reluctance of the Committee of Vice-Chancellors and Principals (CVCP); and the DES evidently felt unable to force the pace of change in the absence of consensus. Whether the department could have been more tenacious is a good question. However, during the 1970s unit cost reductions were in the event achieved through the process of applying a general squeeze on the total of resources for higher education allocated through the PESC process rather than by specific measures.

In the public sector, rapid expansion had been encouraged by the operation of the advanced further education pool, a system which gave individual local authorities the illusion of being able to write cheques on other local authorities' bank accounts.[46] Under the auspices of the Pooling Committee, a joint body of the DES and the local authority associations, DES cost accountants developed norms for student/staff ratios on different types of course (known as 'Delany norms' after the DES accountant concerned) and public sector institutions were encouraged to work towards them. The course approval system operated by regional advisory councils and DES regional staff inspectors (HMI) was used to prevent the proliferation of under-subscribed courses. Except for colleges of education, many public sector colleges were growing very rapidly and were able to reduce unit costs as enrolments grew. This was particularly true when tight restrictions on capital expenditure after 1973 compelled them to use existing plant more intensively.

Neither the Pooling Committee nor the course approval system was designed to rationalize the public sector. The former was concerned with technical questions; the latter operated in a predominantly passive fashion. As the hopes for continued expansion faded, the DES became increasingly concerned to have a national body able to exercise more effective control over the distribution of courses in the public sector and to engage in dialogue with the UGC 'across the binary line'. The first attempt to establish a national body, based on the recommendations of the Oakes report,[47] foundered on the 1979 general election when a bill before parliament was lost.

When in opposition, the Conservatives had objected to the Oakes proposals but expressed no clear ideas about alternatives, and they were opposed in principle to the creation of 'quangos'. By late 1980, however, they were coming to accept that a new initiative was needed and they considered a series of hypothetical options ranging from complete decentralization to complete centralization. What finally emerged was a green paper offering two models,[48] one of which (creation of a new Exchequer-funded sector under a body analogous to the UGC) was clearly favoured by DES officials. Apart from the Committee of Directors of Polytechnics (CDP), the interest groups were more or less united in their opposition to this option. Both the local authority associations and the main trades unions concerned feared an erosion of their power and influence.

Threatened by a stalemate on the green paper options, and against the background of further reductions in planned higher education expenditure, the DES proposed a compromise which appeared to be closer to the local authority model than to the model they had originally favoured. It remains to be seen whether the NAB will be able to move sufficiently quickly to exercise much influence over the contraction planned for the next three years.

Policies affecting the Length or Mode of Courses
The DES can influence the distribution of resources to different types of course by conferring or withholding its support. For example, resources were made available for extending the length of the certificate of education course from two years to three in 1960; and in the 1972 white paper, *Education: A Framework for Expansion*, the government announced that the 'gap' between part-time and three-year advanced courses (which it had been partly responsible for creating in 1960) would be filled by the two-year Diploma of Higher Education (DipHE).[49]

As the experience of the DipHE has shown, DES support, extending even to inclusion of a course in the select list of those attracting a mandatory award, is not enough. The orthodox three-year degree is firmly established in the minds of employers, students and institutions as the most appropriate mode for higher education. Extension of mandatory awards to the two-year higher (national) diploma in 1975 was according to Fowler strongly opposed by the permanent secretary of the time because he thought it would be difficult to hold the line thereafter.[50] In the event, enrolments on higher diploma courses have not grown as fast as first degree courses and the DES does not seem to have had any difficulty in resisting further changes in the awards system.

There are, however, signs that the three-year degree will not go unquestioned in future. Proposals abound for biasing the distribution of resources more towards part-time courses by changing the weighting such courses receive in the calculation of full-time equivalence for pooling purposes and by changing the awards system. The DES has firmly resisted proposals for allocating resources to four-year courses, even in the arguably special case of the Finniston recommendations.[51]

Policies affecting Student Demand
The system of 90 per cent state-funded mandatory awards introduced in 1962 following the Anderson Report[52] ensured that student demand would not restrain the post-Robbins expansion. As already mentioned, the level of student demand for particular courses may be influenced by the *availablity* of mandatory awards, and the DES has been reluctant to extend the scope of these awards. The *real value* of the mandatory award itself may also affect the level of demand: although many forces were probably at work, the lack of buoyancy in student applications in the early 1970s may be partly attributable to the decline in the real value of the award, which sank to almost 80 per cent of the level recommended by Anderson.[53] Ministers may find it convenient to allow the real value of the award to deteriorate during the 1980s while demand for places exceeds supply. This serves two purposes: first, it would reduce the number wishing to enter higher education perhaps to the level where the Robbins principle could be said to be satisfied; and second, it would force students to draw on other forms of support, including commercial loans, and so achieve by gradualism what would have been difficult by a more overt attempt at changing policy.

Another way in which governments can in principle affect student demand is through tuition fees policy. The introduction of full-cost fees for overseas students has already reduced first-year enrolments in higher education by 20 per cent below the peak of 1977/78. Although bitterly opposed by higher education institutions, this has proved an effective method of stemming the growth of public expenditure on overseas students[54] in contrast to the quota policy proposed in 1977. It should be noted that the rationale for full-cost fees was based firmly in public expenditure considerations and ministers' desires not to make cuts in other, higher priority areas. It would be interesting to know whether, given the choice, higher education institutions would have preferred to find equivalent savings of £150m per annum — a cut of 6 per cent — in some other way.

The overseas student fees issue has demonstrated the difficulty of reconciling the overlapping policies of two departments. It may have been desirable for much of the support for overseas students from developing countries, who accounted for 85 per cent of all overseas students in 1979/80, to have been counted as part of the overseas aid programme. This is the practice in a number of other countries. However, if the Foreign and Commonwealth Office had accepted this principle it would have been adding to their expenditure programme and they would have had to find compensating savings in the aid programme or elsewhere. It is not surprising that they were reluctant to do so.

Tuition fees for home students have been a less emotive policy issue. Since most home students' tuition fees are paid by their LEA they are unaffected by changes in the fee level. Until recently the DES has regarded a fee pitched somewhere between 20 per cent and 30 per cent of average student costs as providing institutions with a modest source of independent income. The Select Committee proposed that it should be 30 per cent because the fee element acts 'as an important discipline to institutions in maximising their numbers each year'.[55] For precisely this reason the government decided to cut the tuition fee by almost half, from £900 pa in 1981/82 to £480 pa in 1982/83, at the same time increasing the proportion of funds allocated directly to institutions to 'assist the management of restructuring'. The reduced tuition fee will unquestionably cause institutions to review their admissions plans: this may prevent a repetition of the unanticipated growth, mainly in the public sector, which required a supplementary estimate of £75m in 1981/82 for student awards expenditure. However, the adoption of a unit costing formula for allocating the advanced further education pool will not altogether eliminate the financial attraction of the marginal student.

Policies on Institutional Structures or Relationships
By recognizing different types of institution, either administratively or by legislation, the government can exercise financial discrimination between types. This does not preclude discrimination *within* types but such discrimination tends to be more difficult to defend academically and politically.

The designation of polytechnics originated in the firm belief in the DES at the time that a strong second sector of higher education, differentiated from the universities and vocationally orientated, should be developed from local authority colleges; and that vigorous institutions would result from concentrating resources in a limited number of places. A certain vagueness about role was evident from the start and no active steps were taken to limit polytechnics to specific subject areas modes or study or levels of work: to use Fowler's metaphor, it was not that the wrong levers were grasped, it was rather that levers were left untouched.

Just as structural change provided a vehicle for expansion, so the DES has until recently contemplated such change as a means of assisting rationalization: their preferred option in the 1981 green paper[57] would have created a new direct grant sector comprising all the public sector colleges mainly engaged in higher education, and the DES would have been able to influence the balance of resources both within the new sector and between it and the colleges left outside. It remains to be seen whether the indirect method now being pursued through the National Advisory Body will prove effective.

Policies affecting the Machinery of Government
Changes in what may be broadly termed the machinery of government can have significance for resource allocation. By bringing together responsibility for the universities, public sector higher education and civil science under a single department in 1964 [58] the government created the opportunity for closer co-ordination of policies on the 'dual funding' of research. This is likely to assume great importance during a period of contraction, enabling the government, if it wishes, to go for a policy of concentrating research in a limited number of centres by safeguarding research council funds while reducing general support to higher education through the UGC and local authorities. Recent decisions to protect the science budget can be interpreted in this way.[59] Such a policy would be more difficult, but by no means impossible, for separate departments of government.

It is impossible to answer hypothetical questions about what would have happened to resources if the machinery of government had developed in other ways. But there can be reasonable certainty that the creation of the Manpower Services Commission in 1973 has had the effect of diverting some resources away from education, including higher education, in the longer term. The Treasury's role in this case has been significant, for it has supported the funding of special measures through the MSC because such expenditure is highly specific and in principle temporary.[60] Expenditure on education, by contrast, is seen as leading to a long-term commitment and not easily directed to specific purposes. The role of the MSC as a purchasing agent of government, buying services on short-term contracts from competing public and private sector suppliers, may in time extend to higher education.

THE FUTURE
Three factors in particular are likely to affect the way in which the DES and Treasury exercise their roles in future. They are: the competition for public expenditure; the political outlook of future governments; and the availability of effective policy-making machinery.

The Competition for Public Expenditure
Higher education competes for resources with other sectors of education and with other sectors of public expenditure. The expenditure requirements of the primary schools have been falling for some years because of the decline in births which occurred between 1964 and 1977. The relationship

between pupil numbers and the resources needed to maintain broadly constant standards of provision is not a simple one. However, if pupil numbers are taken as a broad proxy for expenditure requirements, the resources needed by primary schools are likely to fall slightly until the mid-1980s, recovering to their 1980 level by the early 1990s and increasing further to the turn of the century. The pattern for secondary schools shows a fall until the early 1990s with recovery thereafter.[61]

In the short term the expenditure requirement of the primary and secondary school systems will be declining but under the PESC rules this does not give the secretary of state a windfall to spend elsewhere. In the long term, the increasing requirements of the schools (and of non-advanced further education which will be used to offset youth unemployment) will discourage governments from restoring funds to higher education.

Apart from the longer-term pressure within education, the claims of other spending programmes, especially social security, law and order, employment, defence and health (where the increase in the number of the elderly is expected to create a significant growth in demand) will cause the Treasury to argue strongly for a decline in education expenditure following broadly the demographic changes mentioned above.

For these reasons, the present government will continue to resist the pleadings from the higher education system for a slower rate of contraction. The CVCP has asked for the contraction planned for the three years to 1984/85 to be spread instead over five years so that the staff savings can be found mainly be 'natural wastage'. Unless it can be shown that this will cost no more in public expenditure in *each* of the years concerned, the secretary of state must make a bid in PESC for the extra spending. Because the Treasury would resist any increase in the total for education, the secretary of state would have to find the money by making a balancing saving within the education service; and it was after rejecting such alternatives that his predecessor settled for cuts in higher education in the first place!

The Political Outlook of Future Governments
What effect will party political forces have on the future resourcing of higher education? Kogan has suggested that 'the period of opposition [is] critically important to the process of policy fashioning. In the social services, at least, years are fruitful or wasted as much in opposition as in government.'[62] Yet the political parties do not seem to engage in much realistic thinking about social priorities in general, let along higher education. According to Barnett:

> '... [the Labour government's] expenditure priorities are generally decided on often outdated, and ill considered plans made in opposition, barely thought through as to their real value, and never as to

their relative priority in social, socialist, industrial or economic terms.'[63]

Nor does the present government so far show many signs of having related policy for higher education to their broader principles of achieving national economic regeneration through increasing personal incentives, promoting competition in the market place and reducing public expenditure. It is still unclear how higher education is expected to contribute to the rebuilding of the 'trading base'.

In the present government and in future Conservative administrations ministers will be torn between suspicion of innovations that challenge the high standards of traditional teaching in conventional subject disciplines and the desire to achieve a reorientation of the education system towards values that place wealth creation and entrepreneurial activity in high esteem. At present, the rhetoric is not being translated into reform, but if it were to happen, then Conservative values might point to policies which:

i Make students more keenly aware of the financial effect of their decisions by changes in the student support system.
ii Place greater financial influence in the hands of consumers (both students and employers) whose choices would thus determine the success or demise of particular institutions and perhaps encourage a private sector.
iii Reinforce entrepreneurial behaviour among institutions by steadily reducing their funding from conventional public sources.
iv Protect selected courses in subjects considered to be of particular national importance by earmarking resources for them and associating them with more generous student grants.
v Promote productivity in higher education by creating resource incentives which favour shorter, more intensive courses.

This would be a radical programme, requiring steadfastness of purpose against fierce opposition from interest groups within higher education; and because legislation would be needed for some reforms the programme would require more than the life of a single parliament for implementation.

Future left-of-centre governments could also have an ideological interest in breaking the conventional mould of higher education, because of a conviction that it is remote and hierarchical, that its traditional values distort much of the rest of the education system and that greater social equality should be promoted through wider access. Such aspirations might be translated into plans for:

i Abolishing the binary system.
ii Replacing the present nationally-orientated system of resourcing higher education with a local or regional one.

iii Reducing or abolishing the distinction between advanced and non-advanced further education.
iv Biasing financial incentives towards part-time modes of study and towards adult and continuing education.
v Encouraging through the awards system participation by children from lower socio-economic groups.
vi Treating higher education as part of a broader programme for work-sharing by increasing opportunities for people to spend periods of time usefully outside paid employment.

This is an essentially expansionist view of the future and as such would have problems of resourcing as well as upsetting some vested interests in higher education.

Both the political programmes outlined above are radical and would place great demands on the resources of the DES, which would have to be increased. However, past experience suggests that whatever parties are in power [64] the forces opposed to change will be considerable. Blume has referred to the antipathy of public administrators in Britain towards long-term planning.[65] In Maclure's view:

'... successive British governments have felt much happier dealing with the allocation of resources — making incremental changes on the basis of immediate requirements — than engaging in dangerous thoughts about public aims and purposes or the strategic role of higher education in relation to larger social and economic policy.' [66]

Availability of effective Policy-making Machinery
This chapter has drawn attention to the quite severe limitations on the freedom of action of the DES and the limited resources at its disposal for policy formulation. The temptation to concentrate on the practical problems of scaling down the higher education system will be overwhelming and the government may want to keep a low profile, leaving the hard and unpopular decisions to the UGC and NAB. If that is so, and if those in higher education feel that more fundamental changes in the character or orientation of higher education are required, they may well be left to find their own salvation. Indeed, the SRHE Leverhulme programme of study can be seen as a response to that challenge.

At present the prospect of a more interventionist stance by the DES looks fairly remote. As one senior DES civil servant has put it in conversation with the author:

'After four decades or so of orderly planning we may now have a government who just do not believe in that, even as a means of making their own policy. You raise the question whether we can do without better machinery for promoting strategic thinking and planning;

some ministers at least may hold that this is not a fit activity for public expenditure on civil service resources ... it would be interesting to speculate what would happen if [the DES] were committed to the maximum disengagement of the government from policy-making in education.'

NOTES

1 Until 1963 the Treasury was directly responsible for government policy on university finance and the UGC advised the Chancellor of the Exchequer on the distribution of Exchequer grant to the universities and on future university development. See Bridges, The Rt. Hon Lord (1964) *The Treasury* London: George Allen & Unwin.
2 The proportions quoted here are for 1982/83 and are derived from *The Government's Expenditure Plans 1982-83 to 1984-85* (1982) Cmnd 8494; London: HMSO.
3 *Report of the Committee on the Control of Public Expenditure* (1961) Cmnd 1432; London HMSO.
4 For an extensive account of the PESC process, its place in the Whitehall bureaucracy and its relationship to parliament, see Heclo, Hugh and Wildavsky, Aaron (second edition 1981) *The Private Government of Public Money* London: Macmillan.
5 A good example of a politically urgent policy is the New Training Initiative, estimated to cost £1 billion per annum, half of it 'new money' (ie not carried forward from existing programmes). See Manpower Services Commission (1981) *A New Training Initiative. An Agenda for Action* London: MSC. A large new programme of this kind increases the pressure to find savings in related areas such as education, although parts of education, such as provision for 16-19 year-olds, may benefit.
6 Barnett, Joel (1982) *Inside the Treasury* London: André Deutsch, p.47.
7 Op. cit., p.59. A well-known example of the effect on policy and resources of ministerial relationships is the creation of the Open University, which owed much to the long-standing political understanding between the then Prime Minister, Harold Wilson, and the Joint Parliamentary Under Secretary at the DES, Jenny Lee. This ensured that resources for the OU were safeguarded in PESC in spite of the scepticism of some DES officials.
8 See, for example, Goldman, Sir Samuel (1973) *The Developing System of Expenditure Management and Control* Civil Service College Studies London: HMSO, p.39.
9 *The Attack on Inflation* (1976) Cmnd 6151; London: HMSO.
10 *Cash Limits on Public Expenditure* (1976) Cmnd 6440; London: HMSO.
11 Pliatsky, Sir Leo (1982) *Getting and Spending* Oxford: Basil Blackwell, p.174.
12 Op. cit., n.6, p.191.

13 Op. cit., n.11, p.181.
14 *The Government's Expenditure Plans 1981-82 to 1983-84* (1981) Cmnd 8175; London: HMSO.
15 Op, cit., n.3, vol.II, p.103, para.12.
16 This appears to be an increasingly unrealistic expentation, not unlike the assumptions of earlier white papers about the rate at which the number of school places would be taken out of use.
17 Op. cit., n.11, p.198.
18 O.p. cit., n.6, p.124.
19 See especially paragraph 14 and 46 of *The Reorganisation of Central Government* (1970) Cmnd 4506; London: HMSO. This white paper stated that, as a natural extension of the public expenditure survey system, there would be regular reviews of departmental policies designed to provide ministers with an opportunity to identify and discuss alternative policy options, which could then be explored in greater depth before decisions were taken on expenditure programmes. These would involve greater emphasis on the definition of objectives, and the formulation as far as possible of programmes in output terms, with ample scope for the examination of alternative programmes. There was to be 'a capacity at the centre for the assessment of policies and projects in relation to strategic objectives' in the form of a small multi-disciplinary central policy review staff (CPRS) in the Cabinet Office working for ministers collectively under the supervision of the Prime Minister.
20 See Pliatsky, op. cit., n.11, p.104.
21 A report by the Organisation for Economic Co-operation and Development (1973) *Educational Development Strategy in England and Wales* Paris: OECD refers to the role of PARs as well as giving a broader account of planning in the DES. The Tenth Report from the Expenditure Committee, Session 1975-76, *Policy Making in the Department of Education and Science,* argued that PAR reports should be published. However, the reports themselves were not published, although some material from them was incorporated in publications.
22 *Education: A Framework for Expansion* (1972) Cmnd 5174; London: HMSO.
23 Op. cit., n.11, p.104.
24 Committee on Higher Education (Chairman, Lord Robbins) (1963) *Higher Education* Cmnd 2154; London: HMSO.
25 Maclure, Stuart (1980) *Higher Education: The Philistine at the Gate?* Lecture given at the University of California, Berkeley.
26 Department of Education and Science (1980) *Trends in Entry to Full-time Higher Education* Statistical Bulletin 12/80 London: DES.
27 *A Plan for Polytechnics and Other Colleges* (1966) Cmnd 3006; London: HMSO.
28 Op. cit., n.15, p.106, para.14.

29 The announcement of the new National Advisory Board was made in a written parliamentary reply to a question from Mr C. Murphy MP on 23 December 1981. The reply gave details of the constitution and terms of reference of the advisory body which consists of a committee under ministerial chairmanship and with balanced DES and local authority representation, supervising a board under an independent chairman and with wider interest group representation.
30 For a discussion of the role of Cabinet and its committees in educational policy, see Kogan, Maurice (Editor) (1971) *The Politics of Education* Harmondsworth: Penguin Books. Anthony Crosland, who was Secretary of State for Education and Science for almost three years, never brought a higher education matter before Cabinet.
31 Department of Education and Science (1981) *Annual Report 1980* London: HMSO.
32 Department of Education and Science (1978) *Higher Education into the 1990s* A consultative document. London: DES.
33 Department of Education and Science (1981) *Higher Education in England outside the Universities: Policy, Funding and Management* A consultative document. London: DES.
34 Sir Keith backs education block *Local Government Chronicle* 7 May 1982, p.488.
35 Since 1944 the average tenure of ministers of education and secretaries of state has been just under two years.
36 See Kogan op. cit., n.30, p.84.
37 Op. cit., n.30, p.84.
38 Op. cit., n.30, p.193.
39 Op. cit., n.22, para.120, p.36.
40 House of Commons Fifth Report from the Education, Science and Arts Committee Session 1979-80 (1980) *The Funding and Organisation of Courses in Higher Education* 2, pp.21-22. London: HMSO. Italics added.
41 Fowler, G.T. (1981) *The Evolution of the Higher Education System and the Institutions within It*. Paper presented to the SRHE Leverhulme Seminar on Institutional Adaptation and Change, September 1981.
42 Op. cit., n.32.
43 Department of Education and Science (1980) *Continuing Education: Post-experience Vocational Provision for those in Employment* London: DES.
44 Op. cit., n.30, p.196.
45 *The Times* 24 March 1969, p.1.
46 For an explanation of the working of the pool, see the DES memorandum in op. cit., n.40., p.34.
47 *Report of the Working Group on the Management of Higher Education in the Maintained Sector* (1978) Cmnd 7130; London: HMSO.
48 Op. cit., n.33.

49 Op. cit., n. 22, p.32.
50 Op. cit., n. 41.
51 The DES has made no additional funds available to finance four-year enhanced engineering courses. This has not stopped some institutions from providing them. See the Finniston Report (1979) *Engineering our Future* Cmnd 7794; London: HMSO.
52 The Anderson Report (1960) *Grants to Students* Cmnd 1051; London: HMSO.
53 However, the real value of the award in 1981/82 was little different from 1970/71 (84% and 85% respectively of the 1962/63 value) yet demand in 1981/82 was buoyant. Unemployment may be an important explanatory factor.
54 *Statistical Bulletin 19/81* (1981) London: DES.
55 Op. cit., n.40, para.113, p.xlviii.
56 Op. cit., n.3, para.14, p.40.
57 Op. cit., n.33.
58 Secretary of State for Education and Science Order 1964 (SI 1964 No 490).
59 The 'protection' of the Science Budget was announced in the 1981 expenditure white paper (op. cit., n.15, para.19, p.107) and apparently continued in the 1982 white paper (op. cit., n.3, para.19, p.40).
60 See, for example, Barnett, op.cit., n.6, p.150.
61 These forecasts are derived from DES (1981) *Statistics of Education 1979. Vol 1 — Schools* London: HMSO.
62 Op. cit., n.30, p.38.
63 Op. cit., n.6, p.59.
64 I have not considered here the policies that might be adopted by a future centrist government, chiefly because there is little by way of principles still less policy statements to indicate how such a government would proceed. The SDP has a position paper on higher education presently in preparation which will presumably stimulate discussion within the SDP-Liberal alliance.
65 In his paper for a previous seminar in this SRHE Leverhulme series, Blume has observed: '... long-term thinking and planning are essential. Despite some ill-fated initiatives taken in the early '70s the culture of British public administration is opposed to such strategic thinking and planning. It is precisely the fate of these initiatives (PAR, the initially strategic role of the CPRS, many proposals of the Fulton Committee), which is indicative.' See Blume, S.S. (1982) A framework for analysis. In Oldham, G. (Editor) *The Future of Research* Guildford: Society for Research into Higher Education.
66 Op. cit., n.25.

APPENDIX

ORGANIZATION OF
THE DEPARTMENT OF EDUCATION AND SCIENCE

A simplified diagram showing the organization of the permanent staff of the DES is given on page 57. The first eight branches listed are 'policy branches'. Until 1980 responsibility for the resourcing of universities and public sector higher education lay in separate branches; and higher education and science came under separate deputy secretaries. The departmental reorganization of 1980 brought all these matters for the first time under a single deputy secretary and brought university and public sector finance within a single branch, headed by an under secretary.

At the time of writing the ministerial team consists of a secretary of state and three parliamentary under secretaries of state, one of whom has a general responsibility for higher and further education, and another for science. The 1980 reorganization has thus not been fully reflected in the allocation of junior ministers' responsibilities. The secretary of state is also assisted by two special advisers.

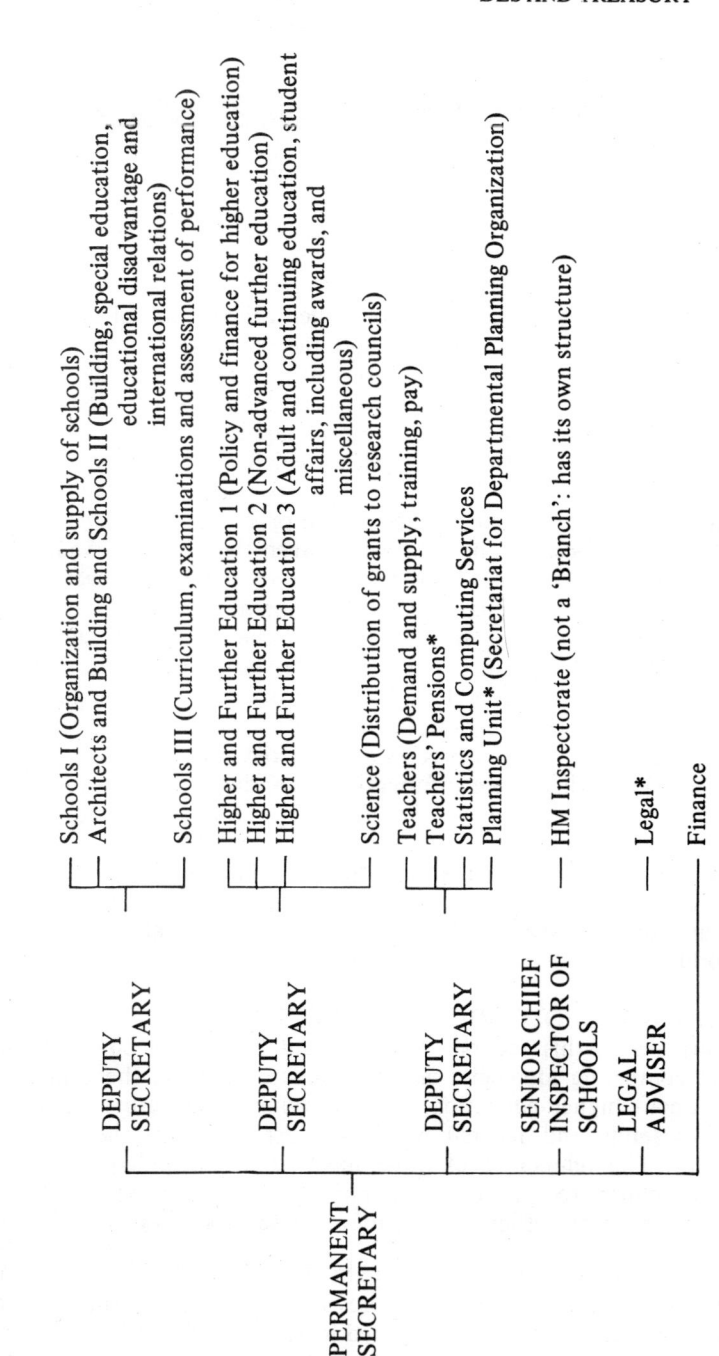

BRANCHES

PERMANENT SECRETARY
- DEPUTY SECRETARY
  - Schools I (Organization and supply of schools)
  - Architects and Building and Schools II (Building, special education, educational disadvantage and international relations)
  - Schools III (Curriculum, examinations and assessment of performance)
- DEPUTY SECRETARY
  - Higher and Further Education 1 (Policy and finance for higher education)
  - Higher and Further Education 2 (Non-advanced further education)
  - Higher and Further Education 3 (Adult and continuing education, student affairs, including awards, and miscellaneous)
  - Science (Distribution of grants to research councils)
- DEPUTY SECRETARY
  - Teachers (Demand and supply, training, pay)
  - Teachers' Pensions*
  - Statistics and Computing Services
  - Planning Unit* (Secretariat for Departmental Planning Organization)
- SENIOR CHIEF INSPECTOR OF SCHOOLS
  - HM Inspectorate (not a 'Branch': has its own structure)
- LEGAL ADVISER
  - Legal*
- Finance

* Not headed by Under Secretaries

PRIVATIZATION AND MARKET MECHANISMS

by Alan Maynard

INTRODUCTION
This chapter addresses a variety of issues arising out of proposals for privatization of higher education* and the more substantial use of the market mechanism. In the first section the nature of the competing ideologies, collective/socialist and market/liberal, which dominated the contemporary debate about the finance of higher education are explored. The second section identifies the policies which might generate the liberal nirvana, and deviances from the pure liberal paradigm are noted. The third section reviews briefly some of the specific problems associated with these liberal policy proposals. The contrast between the liberal nirvana and the reality of the market place is the concern of the fourth section. There it is argued that the debate about the liberal proposals has confused theoretical and empirical issues: most of the contested outcomes are empirical issues which can be resolved only with experimentation. In the final section a set of general problems associated with the provision of monitoring and incentive devices in higher education are reviewed. A distinction is made between process and outcome measures of performance and it is argued that more information, 'standard' setting, and financial incentives could generate greater efficiency. However, in conclusion, it is noted that the obstacles to such changes are the same as those that inhibit the working of the market and the liberal nirvana. The reality of the privatization debate is that it does not solve the basic problems which are common to all public and private higher education systems across the world.

COMPETING IDEOLOGIES AND OBJECTIVES
The purposes of this section are to set out briefly the characteristics of the two competing ideologies which dominate much of the contemporary debate about higher education, and to examine the nature of the policy objectives (ends and means) which are derived from these competing ideologies. The reluctance of those involved in the policy debate about higher education to spell out their objectives and the means which they regard as the most efficient to achieve those objectives is very marked.

---

* The term university is used throughout as a shorthand for the higher education sector. The arguments presented here apply to the whole of the higher education industry as defined in Hunter (1981).

Although the contributors to this debate are difficult to classify and categorize there appear to be two competing ideologies dominating the arguments: the liberal or market ideology and the socialist or collective ideology. The degrees to which the competing advocates adhere to these ideologies varies: ie their location on the spectrum between the two poles differs, often considerably.

The simplest way of describing these two ideologies is to describe the attitudes of their adherents to four factors: personal responsibility, social concern, freedom and equality.

LIBERAL AND SOCIALIST PARADIGMS

	Market View	Collectivist View
Personal responsibility	Personal responsibility for achievement is seen as very important, and this is weakened if people are offered unearned rewards (eg 'free' education for their children, 'free' health care or 'generous' social security benefits). Moreover, such unearned rewards weaken the motive force that assures economic well-being (eg incentives to work, to save, and to take risks) and in so doing they also undermine the moral well-being of society, because of the intimate connection between moral well-being and the personal effort to achieve.	While accepting the desirability of personal incentives to achieve, economic failure is not equated with moral depravity or social worthlessness.
Social concern	Social Darwinism dictates a seemingly cruel indifference to the fate of those who fail in the economic system. A less extreme position is that charity, preferably expressed and effected under private auspices, is the proper vehicle to meet social concern. However, charity needs to be exercised under carefully prescribed conditions: for	Private charitable action is rejected, or alternatively given a very minor supplementary role. Charity is seen as potentially dangerous morally (because it is often demeaning to the recipient and corrupting to the donor) and usually inequitable. It seems preferable to create social mechanisms that

	Market View	Collectivist View
	example, such that the potential recipient must first mobilize all his own resources, and when helped, must not be in as favourable position as those who are self-supporting (the principle of 'lesser eligibility').	create and sustain self-sufficiency, and are accessible according to precise rules concerning entitlement which are applied equitably and explicitly sanctioned by society at large.
Freedom	Freedom is to be sought as a supreme good itself. Compulsion attenuates both personal responsibility and individualistic and voluntary expressions of social concern. Centralized education planning and a large governmental role in education financing are seen as an unwarranted reduction of the freedom of parents and children as well as of education professionals. Private education is therefore viewed as a bulwark against totalitarianism. (Social security and the NHS similarly reduce the freedom of consumers and producers (insurers) and the private insurance industry is seen as a social defence against social monopoly which reduces the freedom of the individual).	Freedom is seen as the presence of real opportunities of choice, and although economic constraints are less openly coercive than political constraints, they are none the less real, and often the effective limits on choice. Freedom is not indivisible, but may be sacrificed in one respect in order to obtain greater freedom in some other. Government is not an external threat to individuals in the society, but the means by which individuals achieve greater scope for action (that is, greater real freedom).
Equality	Equality before the law is the key concept, with clear precedence being given to freedom over equality wherever the two conflict.	Since the only moral justification for using personal achievement as the basis for distributing rewards, is that everyone has equal opportunities for such achievement, then the main emphasis is on equality of opportunity, and where this cannot be assured, the moral worth of achievement is thereby

Market View	Collectivist View
	undermined. Equality is seen as an extension to the many of the freedom actually enjoyed only by the few.

These arguments have been developed in the context of health care by Donabedian (1971) and Culyer, Maynard and Williams (1982). They have been 'grist to the mill' for political philosophers for many decades. Thus Gallie (1956) discussed the liberal ideology and differentiated it from the collectivist ideology with great clarity twenty-five years ago:

> 'The kernel ideas of liberal morality, commutative justice, the meritorious individual, the moral necessity of free choice and contract (especially in economic life) and the self limiting character of good government are countered by the ideas of distributive justice, the contributing individual, freedom as essentially freedom to be not to get, and collective action in economic affairs. It is as if the parable of the talents were countered by the parable of the vineyards.'

An alternative way of categorizing the competing idoelogists is to apply the terms 'universalist' (collectivist) and 'selectivist' (liberal). Those in favour of universality seem to adhere to the following framework:

Objective Allocation of scarce education resources to those who will benefit most (benefit is usually defined in relation to effects on lifetime earnings and subjective criteria) regardless of ability and willingness to pay.
Means Public production and finance.

On the other hand those with a selectivist view point adhere to a differing set of ends (objectives) and means:

Objective Allocation of scarce education resources generally in accordance with ability and willingness to pay but usually with some constraint relating to the finance and provision of some (usually undefined) 'minimum standards' for all.
Means Private production and finance.

Because of my terms of reference I propose to be selective and not subject the collectivist ideology to detailed analysis here; such work can be carried out in a separate paper. The objective here is to analyse the characteristics of the work of the liberal ideologists in higher education. This analysis will be rigorous (the sensitive liberal might even find it harsh!) and it is to be remembered throughout that the defects in logic and evidence in the liberal case can be paralleled with equally substantial problems in the collectivist paradigm, in particular the gaps between the hypothetical and actual characteristics of the political market place.

The liberal would-be reformers of the existing higher education system have a consistent ideology whose characteristics have been developed and reiterated regularly over the last two decades. Basically these writers seek to maximize freedom above all things and regard the state as a threat to their freedom, rather than as the agent which may, according to the collectivist, develop and protect freedom. The liberals prefer freedom to equality and emphasize incentives as a mechanism by which people are encouraged to strive for labour market success and sustain economic growth. Success in the labour market determines people's access to rewards such as education, and unearned rewards, such as 'free' university education, are seen as benefits which reduce labour market incentives, individual effort, economic growth and the moral well-being of society. Social concern is best expressed, in this liberal view, conservatively and preferably privately, as charity, and benefits are best provided on the principle of less eligibility (ie all recipients of charity should get benefits less than those acquired by the self-supporting).

Obviously these paradigms are extreme polar views but this elaborate analysis of the competing ideologies is essential if the full nature of market views on higher education is to be appreciated. The differences between the liberals and the collectivists relate to the objectives of education policy and these objectives are derived from a set of normative judgements about the nature and dynamics of our society. If there is disagreement about these judgements, it is not surprising that there is argument about the alternative policies (means) preferred by the contending parties!

THE LIBERAL NIRVANA
The liberal arguments about altering the finance and provision of higher education are based on a neo-classical (Chicago) view of how markets work and how human capital is created. Becker (1964, 1975) has argued that the individual makes decisions about the quantity and quality of his human investment in relation to his perception of its marginal benefits, in terms of its effects on his lifetime earnings net of human capital production costs, and its marginal cost, in terms of the costs of financing investment. The advocacy of student loans by the liberals is seen as a means by which greater eficiency could be acquired in this market place, and at the same time, the objective of greater freedom enhanced.

Great efficiency might arise from the introduction of student loans in a variety of ways. First, if students were permitted to choose between courses and universities and alterations in choice led to changes in resource flows within and between institutions, these institutions would have an incentive to strive to produce those courses which were demanded by students. Any failure to meet student preferences would lead to lower departmental budgets if there were internal student migration, and lower institutional budgets if there were system migration.

Thus if universities and colleges were dependent on the consumers for their income, these bodies would have a greater incentive to identify with care and meet the preferences of their students. This could be seen at a macro or micro level: eg Corner and Culyer (1969) advocated the payment of piece rates for teaching. Alternatively the creation of a market in tutorials can be advocated whereby students are given tokens, they spend these tokens on the tutorial of their choice, and the tokens could be cashed by tutors. Such a mechanism would create a direct cash nexus between tutor and tutee and any failure by the tutor could be penalized by loss of students, their tokens, and some part of his income (see also Peacock and Culyer 1970).

The scope for introducing incentives to change resource allocation, hopefully in the direction of greater efficiency, seems to be significant because, as has been argued for hundreds of years, the organization of higher education seems less than satisfactory. Thus Adam Smith (1776) wrote about the teacher who is salaried and not paid by his students:

'His interest is, in this case, set as directly in opposition to his duty as is possible to set it. It is the interest of every man to live as much at his ease as he can, and if his emoluments are to be precisely the same, whether he does, or does not perform some very laborious duty, it is certainly his interest, at least as interest is vulgarly understood, either to neglect it altogether, or, if he is subject to some authority which will not suffer him to do this, to perform it in as careless and slovenly a manner as that authority will permit.' (Smith 1776, 1976, volume 2, page 760, paragraph 7)

Of the organization of colleges and universities he wrote:

'The discipline of colleges and universities is in general contrived, not for the benefit of students, but for the interest, or more properly speaking, the ease of the masters. Its object is, in all cases, to maintain the authority of the master, and whether he neglects or performs his duty, to oblige the students in all cases to behave to him as if he performed it with the greatest diligence and ability.' (Smith 1776, 1976, volume 2, page 764, paragraph 16)

These arguments set out by Smith so clearly over two hundred years ago are derived from similar value systems to those held by liberals today. The liberal argument is that the supply of education could be organized more efficiently if incentives rewarded enterprise directly via a cash nexus. Furthermore, diversity in organization which would, it is asserted, characterize the market, would sustain freedom and competition. These arguments will be subject to more detailed appraisal below.

Not only would student loans affect the supply of higher education by incentive effects, the liberals believe that there would be beneficial effects on the demand side too. Minimal regulation of the competing suppliers and the differing preferences of consumers would lead to diversity in the production of higher education, and wider access to this diversity if the loan could be spent freely by the student. Thus the process of competition introduced by the loans system would, it is argued, lead to the questioning of existing supply side structures and the evolution of alternatives which met student preferences and which might be cheaper and equally effective in transmitting knowledge. So, for instance, these curious university institutions which teach for three years but seem to use capital and labour inefficiently over long vacations and which inhibit the division of labour by academics (both within the profession and in relation to the use of co-operant factors of production) so that they are jacks of all trades (teaching, administration and research) and possibly masters of none, might be challenged by institutions offering two-year degrees and different resource-use patterns (see Ferns 1969).

If loans could be spent freely, the consumers could demand those services which met their intellectual and monetary preferences. The process of competition could sustain innovation and lead to a better matching of student preferences and producers' supply (Maynard 1975).

It is asserted by the liberals that student loan schemes would also affect beneficially the flow of information. Student preferences and supply could be better matched if the market produced more information about the merits of alternative universities and colleges, their courses, and the abilities of their faculty. The lack of property rights in the benefits of providing such information has contributed to the under-performance of existing student unions in the provision of education. If students wished to spend their resources more efficiently and they had to pay for their education, the liberals assert that 'market forces' would provide an incentive for agents to generate and sell information relevant to course choice. Such information could inform consumers and penalize inefficient producers.

The bulk of the analysis of the higher education market in general, and student loans in particular, is related primarily to supply side effects: ie incentives to be more efficient. However, as always in liberal analysis, the contributors to this debate display often implicit but clearly quite different distributional objectives. Let us review some of these differing distributional perspectives.

Peacock and Wiseman (1964) advocate that the student's higher education be financed by a loan and that the borrower should repay this loan by adding to his income tax payments, up to the age of retirement, a sum equal to a specified percentage of his taxable income. The percentage would be calculated by reference to the annual average income of graduates, the average size of families, and other factors which are not clearly specified. The objective of the repayments is to cover the government's borrowing costs: ie in this scheme the repayment rate is determined by the objective of balancing, over time, the expenditure (loans) and finance (loan repayments) of an autonomous loans fund. The authors advocate provision for the repayment of the loan at any time during the borrower's life, the sum to be repaid 'would be equal to the sum borrowed, compounded at an interest rate higher than the fund's borrowing rate, less the sum of the annual repayments already made' (Peacock and Wiseman 1964, page 37).

Clearly these proposals have some subtle redistributive effects. The advocacy of a repayment mechanism based on a percentage of taxable income through the working life cycle until retirement implies the objective of cross subsidizing low earners with high earners. Thus the high-earning doctor might subsidize the low-earning social worker. Students who fail examinations or put their knowledge to relatively poorly paid uses will pay less. Will this affect, and if so in what way, that liberal goal of providing an incentive to study? Students who decide to emigrate would repay more than the costs of funds they used (because of the inflated interest rate repayment condition) and this might affect international migration and the international division of labour. The desirability of such cross subsidization between students begs a clear statement of policy objectives.

Prest (1963, 1966) explicitly recognizes that the amount of repayment made by loan recipients could be linked to society's higher education objectives. If it wished to override market indicators such as the rate of return to higher education, the government could increase its subsidization of the sector and reduce the opportunity cost to students of community higher education. Prest advocates a similar repayment system to Peacock and Wiseman and, as he indicates, this ensures that no policy difficulties arise with the 'lame, the halt and the blind' (Prest 1966, page 22) because such potential low earners will repay less than graduates with high earnings.

Glennester, Merrett and Wilson (1968) advocate a graduate tax of a proportional nature. They propose that there be no loan but that the recipient of higher education should pay an increment for the usual income tax payments which would be collected by the PAYE system. Like the Peacock-Prest-Wiseman scheme, the graduate tax, if implemented, would cross subsidize differing earnings groups. The level of taxation is also open to debate: how much should it be and what precise equity goal is it being used to achieve?

Mishan (1973) is quite clear about the objective of his loan proposal: the student should be made to repay the full cost of the loan. Mishan is seeking to ensure that the student bears the full opportunity cost of his decision to consume the services of the higher education sector and he is generally unwilling to countenance subsidization by the government or between student groups. This view reflects the extreme (or pure!) liberal position of the decision-maker being forced to bear the full costs of his choice in a competitive market. Such an outcome, it is asserted, encourages market search, cost minimization and the efficient use of resources.

Thus the liberal nirvana in higher education generally encompasses arguments in favour of the adoption of some form of student loan system in place of the present system of grants. It is asserted that loan programmes will have beneficial effects, particularly on the efficiency with which resources are used. Distributional arguments are generally related to the observation that students are temporarily poor but in terms of their life-cycle incomes, rich. Hence it is inequitable to redistribute to those who in terms of life-cycle returns are affluent. Rather it is more equitable to create a loans market, perhaps with special arrangements because of the relative absence of collateral. However, the degree to which the various loan advocates favour full-cost loans is limited. Only Mishan (1973) appears to take this position, the rest (eg Peacock, Prest and Wiseman) seem to favour constrained types of scheme which favour the poor at the expense of the rich. Whilst such collectivist tendencies may be approved by many it begs the question of whether they are not better served by direct fiscal intervention (the usual liberal argument). Often the redistributive means and ends of social policies are implicit, poorly monitored and at variance with social objectives and the pure liberal might argue that redistribution via social policies would be inefficient inevitably.

PRIVATIZATION AND LOAN SCHEMES

The present market for higher education is dominated by state finance and state regulated provision. The dominance of the public sector has been maintained by licensing arrangements, such as the conservative creation of charters for new entrants, and financial controls which 'cap' public expenditure and only permit, with reluctance, the financing of students at radical new ventures such as the University College at Buckingham. Such barriers to entry give benefits to providers and the state.

This section reviews briefly the problems associated with liberalizing charter creation and refinancing higher education, either partly or completely, with student loans. One conclusion of this analysis will be that even if the costs of some particular loans scheme were thought to be less than existing arrangements and a loans scheme were introduced, then the effects on incentives and efficiency would be slow because of the imperfections and rigidities of the supply side of the market. Improved efficiency requires new incentive mechanisms and these, which could be introduced with or without a loans scheme, are discussed in the next section.

At present (1982) the advocates of systems of student loans seem primarily concerned with the privatization (= reducing public expenditure) of higher education. The Conservative government appears to regard the loans mechanism as a means by which part of the cost of higher education can be shifted off the Exchequer. By regulating the value of student grants, the real purchasing power of the student is being eroded with the possible effect in time that loans will appear to be an attractive alternative to the majority of students in financial difficulties. However, there are a variety of problems associated with the ad hoc evolution of partial financing of higher education by student loans.

The first problem is associated with the nature of the supply of loans: who will provide loans and on what basis? An extreme liberal position would be that the market should provide the loans. However the absence of collateral may make commercial banks and other financial institutions cautious: their investments might 'brain drain' and leave them with 'bad debts'. Even in the absence of collateral, existing financial institutions are lending money, although the nature and extent of this has not yet been researched thoroughly. However the flow may be inadequate and if the institutions are making an economic decision not to invest in human capital, such a decision can only be altered by subsidies in one form or another.

One such form of subsidy would be a government guarantee of collateral: ie the state meets bad debts. Another possible subsidy programme would be for the state to give a collateral guarantee and for it to subsidize the interest rate payable on the loan: ie the student could borrow at a rate below that in the market. Such variations as these in the pure market full cost loan mechanism bring us close to the Peacock-Prest-Wiseman proposals.

The important points to recognize are that the alternatives offer differing degrees of subsidization and that such schemes are unlikely to lead to net savings in expenditure in the short run. If a policy decision is taken that existing grants are the limit of the state subsidies, then students would be obliged to borrow at the market rate for the loan increments they need to supplement their grants. If such loans are subsidized, the inevitable question that will arise is would it not be more efficient to subsidize by supplementing the grant rather than subsidizing the loan? The liberal response would be to favour the loan because of the predicted beneficial efficiency effects on the behaviour of producers and consumers. Such effects must be identified and measured: theoretical assertions are no substitute for empirical evidence.

Loan schemes, whatever the level of subsidy, are unlikely to lead to significant reductions in public expenditure on higher education in the short run. The schemes are likely to be introduced slowly for political reasons and the loans will be paid back over the working life of the investor in human capital. A loans scheme may provide the state with a method of containing the rate of growth of public expenditure on higher education but the workings of the particular form of loan scheme that is adopted requires careful examination: do its benefits exceed its costs?

Loans schemes come in many varieties from the conservative to the radical. A conservative scheme could 'tie' loans to 'approved' public institutions and its impact on the behaviour of decision-makers might be limited. A radical scheme, as implied by most of the liberal writers on the subject, which permitted the borrower to spend his funds on any institution offering higher education, public or private, might, over time, induce more competition and produce differentiation. However, it is unlikely that change would be rapid as the vested interests are powerful and will be reluctant to yield their power and income. Again these possible outcomes, both conservative and radical, are theoretical and need to be substantiated with evidence: our predications from theory might well be confounded by actual behaviour in the market place.

Whatever student loan scheme is adopted, supplementary or full-cost, radical or conservative, the incentives to consume higher education are likely to be altered. The prediction of economic theory is that an upward movement change in the price (opportunity cost) of an activity is likely to reduce the quantity consumed. Who will reduce their consumption of higher education and by how much?

One group which may be affected adversely is the female students. Having and rearing children is a labour-intensive activity which leads usually to withdrawal, either partial or complete, from the labour force. Changing social mores are leading to increased labour force participation over the life cycle. However, withdrawal from the labour force leads to depreciation of human capital. Mincer and Ofek (1982) have indicated that such losses are usually replaced rapidly on return to work. They conclude that the decline of wages (re entry compared to exit) is higher the greater the period out of work, and that in some cases 'returnees' never fully restore their earnings potential. These effects have implications for the capacity of female students to repay their loan debt during the life cycle. In effect, the female student enters the child-rearing phase of her life with a 'negative dowry' whose burden may have effects on education decisions (and on the selection of a spouse!).

Female participation rates in higher education have been increasing: eg in medicine by the mid-1980s about one in two of the intake will be female. The introduction of a loans scheme which increased the opportunity cost of higher education to females might affect their participation. One market reaction to this outcome would be that it is efficient: why should you subsidize females who produce less during the life cycle due to their involvement in the child production process and early retirement? If social goals were such that the outcome would be regarded as inefficient then a variety of subsidy arrangements would be possible: eg Peacock and Wiseman (1964) proposed suspension or cancellation of repayment obligations during periods of child-rearing, ie as a society we are paying for the child-rearing of the female by subsidizing her education.

Another area of dispute is the effect of a loans scheme on the behaviour of potential students from the lower income groups: would a loans scheme dissuade able children from poor families from consuming higher education? This is an area of dispute where the theoretical argument is fierce but the empirical outcomes are not clear. The evidence is such that it cannot now be doubted that the education system as a whole 'filters' out children from working-class backgrounds at an early stage in their life. Halsey, Heath and Ridge (1980) show that over 55 per cent of the working-class children (defined as classes VI, VII and VIII on the Hope-Goldthorpe scale) has no post-secondary school education and only 1.8 per cent of the children in this class went to university. This compares with 29.6 and 20.1 per cent respectively for children from service-class households (Hope-Goldthorpe classes 1 and 2). The Rowntree follow-up study (Atkinson, Maynard and Trinder 1981) gives further insights into inter-generation patterns: eg on average 23.7 per cent of Rowntree children had academic qualifications, whereas in poor groups (parental income less than 120 per cent of National Assistance rates in 1950) only 9.7 per cent of children had such qualifications.

Thus children from working-class households are unlikely to consume higher education: a variety of factors 'weed' them out of the education process earlier in their life cycle. However, even though the percentage of children from working-class households in higher education seems to have altered little since the 1920s, the absolute number of such children has increased as the size of the student body has risen. Whether their participation would be adversely affected by a loans scheme depends on the nature of that scheme, in particular how it affects children from poorer backgrounds, and this is an empirical problem. If the effects are inconsistent with policy goals, there are a variety of ways in which a loan scheme could be adjusted.

The debate about the effects of loans schemes on migration is another area in which conclusions can be arrived at only by analysing the evidence, theoretical debates alone are inadequate for policy purposes. As Maureen Woodhall has shown (1970, 1980) mixed schemes of grants and loans are in use in France, Germany, the Netherlands, Sweden and the United States. The 'brain drain' problems of these schemes do not appear to be too costly.

Thus all the problems associated with loans schemes depend on the nature of the scheme adopted and are matters of debate about empirical outcomes rather than theoretical possibilities. The theoretical problems of loans schemes can be compared with the actual problems of the existing grant arrangements. However, the actual choice of schemes to be used, grant, loan or a mixture of the two, depends on the objectives of the policy-makers and the relative merits of the alternative policies. Such policy statements are rare because of the possible political costs of explicitness and the inherent inability of decision-makers to define clearly the purpose of their activities.

MARKET REALITIES
The advocacy contained in the previous sections contains behavioural propositions that can be tested by experiment and analysis of empirical evidence. Such experimentation has been advocated (Maynard 1975) but even without this experimentation some of the propositions can be explored more thoroughly at the a priori level. This section will explore first how the liberals believe the market works and then how it actually seems to work.

Liberal Nirvana
The basis of the market analysis is that private self-interest working in an environment of established private property rights and voluntary contracting between traders (buyers and sellers) will result in society's scarce resources being used in a fashion which maximizes benefits and minimizes costs. Free exchange and production will produce, via trade, the efficient allocation of resources. Questions about the justice of the initial distribution of property rights, be it unequal or equal, are separate issues which the liberal believes are separable from the debate about the merits of the market as a means of allocating resources: if the market is unjust, the liberal would put it right by transferring income rather than destroying the market mechanism.

The first characteristic of any functioning market is that education, or any other good or service, should not be provided free of charge. The resources used in the higher education sector are scarce and, given the well-established theorem that as the price of a good or service falls more will be demanded, a zero money price implies that more resources than are necessary will be drawn into the education system. Such over-utilization of resources in education will deprive other sectors of resources and these inputs could be used to produce other goods and services of greater value than those produced in education. Efficiency dictates that marginal costs and marginal values should be equalized. Education services which are free at the point of consumption generate outcomes which use resources inefficiently.

Clearly information in the competitive market (or indeed any market!) will not be perfect. However, information is valuable and its usefulness will often pay people to specialize in information production and exchange. This effect will mean that markets may provide more information than non-markets. Resources will be rationed by price and not by subjective concepts, usually of a self-interested élite, of 'need'.

This élite is created, so the liberals would assert, by regulation. Thus Smith (1776, 1976, volume 1, page 117):

'People in the same trade seldom meet together, even for merriment and diversion, but the conversation ends in a conspiracy against the public, or in some contrivances to raise prices.'

The collective action observed by Smith over two hundred years ago interferes with the price mechanism which may cease to reflect values and costs at the margin. Often this private collective action, by producer cartels or labour professions (unions), is supplemented by public regulation. All these acts create barriers to entry into the profession or market.

The liberals oppose regulation. Regulation gives monopoly power to individuals and institutions and this power generates higher incomes for the monopolists and the power for such people to assert their values and ensure that what they want is both viewed as 'best' and provided in markets: the consumer ceases to be the primary decision-maker. The liberals argue that those with superior skills and knowledge should not be permitted to assert their values and determine market allocation. Consumers are the best judges of their welfare and the liberals argue that the best resolution to the problem of inadequate knowledge is the provision of information not the regulation of the market place (see Friedman 1962, especially chapter 9).

Without consumer sovereignty the regulators can influence, if not determine, expenditure on higher education and a consumer's expenditure in education is a provider's income from his trade. Regulation usually creates barriers to entry (eg you need a Royal Charter to give degrees) and inflates the income of those thereby protected from competition. Without competition the fraudulent claims and inefficiencies of the regulators cannot be exposed because the relevant information markets are not created and sustained.

Not only does the liberal oppose regulation of the supply side of the market, he also rejects interference with the competitive workings of the demand side. In particular there is an opposition to compulsion of the consumer. Unlike some other markets such as health, the liberal's view about compulsion in the education market is constrained. Thus Hayek (1960, chapter 24) advocated compulsory education up to 'a minimum standard' but does not clearly define the minimum. Implicit in the advocacy of many liberals is the idea of a core curriculum and the compulsory provision of minimum skills. The acceptance of some minimum degree of compulsion does not vitiate the other aspects of the market model: diversity in finance and provision is, for the liberal, an essential part of the provision of the minimum and all other education.

The fourth characteristic of the liberal nirvana is the advocacy of profit seeking as an engine to generate efficient outcomes. The liberals see the pursuit of profit as the engine which generates information, competition and the efficient allocation of resources. Inevitably charities (non-profit-making firms) arise in education and the liberals welcome such institutions provided they are not subsidized directly or indirectly by the tax system or any other government interference. However, generally, the liberals argue, such institutions will carry out only a minor role if competition is permitted because charities do not provide adequate incentives for cost minimization.

The final characteristic of the liberal nirvana is that 'bad' distributions of income and wealth should be rectified by altering the distributions with direct fiscal action and not by interfering with the market mechanisms. The latter method of altering property rights usually makes redistribution inefficient and implicit and this may reduce the allocative efficiency of the market.

Thus the liberal favours private property rights, free exchange and voluntary contracting as the most likely way to acquire efficiency in resource allocation. He will oppose the absence of a cash nexus, reject private and public regulation of the market, oppose compulsion, prefer profit making, and solve unjust distributions of income and wealth with direct fiscal action not the 'social engineering' of expenditure programmes. These factors form the necessary conditions for the operation of a market. Unfortunately they are not always met.

Market Reality
The reality of the education market is that competition is very muted and it is difficult to create competition and incentives to minimize costs and maximize benefits.

Higher education is generally provided at zero price at the point of consumption. Most students have little idea of the magnitude or basis of the tuition fees paid for them on their behalf by local government. The tuition fees bear only an imprecise and partial relation to costs. The maintenance costs are provided from state grants, parental finance and student (own) resources. Again the cost borne by the student bears little relation to opportunity costs.

The consequence of the absence of a substantial burden of costs on consumers is that they have little incentive to search for the most efficient provider of higher education. There is little incentive for the student to demand and pay for information about the relative university performance of York and another market town like Oxford. The fact that Oxford probably provides an education in economics of a similar quality (measured in terms of process if not in terms of outcome) to York but at a higher cost is irrelevant to the consumer. There is no reason for him to choose the cheaper option when the gains from such a choice accrue to government in term of lower fees, rather than to him in terms of savings from lower expenditure. Similarly there is no incentive to York and Oxford to compete. Each institution knows that it will be able to fill its places with good students and that each place filled guarantees the university an assured income. The rewards for bidding for students are small as the state determines the fixed capacity of the university and any institution going 'over-quota' is not assured extra revenue.

Now firms cannot enter this market with ease because of the high degree of regulation, most of it designed to protect the quality of the service (usually inadequately defined) and the incomes of the participants. One man's expenditure is another man's income. The established universities are not keen on new entrants, particularly as the expenditure (= university income) pool is fixed and not growing: the new entrant's gains are the established producers' losses.

Entry can be inhibited by a variety of policy constraints. Thus initially the students of the University College at Buckingham could not get access to state grants and the Department of Education and Science has found many good reasons to delay the granting of a charter. If the state wished to limit its expenditure on education and feared the new places at Buckingham would have the converse effect, it could have limited the number of awards that were available and made them available for education in any institutions. If the state wished to control quality by controlling the granting of a charter, it could have made a policy decision to give any institution a charter and used the not inconsiderable bureaucratic resources of the Department of Education and Science to monitor the relative effectiveness of all alternative institutions which had a charter: ie to provide information to inform decisions by consumers.

The regulation of the labour market by the professions generates further possible limitations to competition. The process of acquiring tenure is minimal in time and in complexity for the average academic. Once acquired, tenure is given up rarely except by the foolhardy (such as the author!) and guarantees a lifetime earnings profile superior, even after taking account of recent redundancies, to that in most other activities.

This system of tenure (a meal ticket for life!) is unlikely to generate competition between academics. However good or bad a teacher, researcher or administrator, the academic is, subject to usually minimal constraints, unlikely to be removed from his job. Furthermore the incremental salary system provides little direct reward for initiative and success in any area of activity.

The provider can exert a considerable influence on his consumers: he arranges their life for them. The demand for higher education is like the demand for health care (Evans 1974, Newhouse 1981): because of his ignorance about the merits of alternative types of higher education, the consumer demands the services of professionals to advise them and to act as their agents in the decision-making process. The academic (and the teacher generally) is the consumer in that he assumes, by agreement, the student's role as the interpreter of educational needs and the arranger of how these needs will be met.

This agency relationship is more powerful where professional monopoly power is great and this power constrains both competition between these professionals and information about the qualities of the alternative suppliers of education. This relationship makes it difficult to distinguish between the supply and demand sides of the market in education. The academic, as the neutral assessor of his students' educational needs, can act in a disinterested and efficient way. But if he takes into account things such as his income and leisure, the size of his 'empire' and the merits of his life style, then the quality and quantity of the services he provides may be related more to producer preferences than to those of the consumer: an outcome clearly in the mind of Adam Smith!

Thus there can be a wide divergence between the myth of the market place in the minds of many liberals, and the reality of the market place as it is experienced by most consumers and producers. The reaction of the ultra-liberals (eg Friedman 1962, Hayek 1969) to this conclusion is that the market will function efficiently if the 'necessary' reforms, without which the market mechanism is unlikely to work efficiently, are carried out. This requires major changes in social institutions. The existing institutions give considerable benefits, in income and power, to those who work within them and these people are unlikely to agree to changes which disadvantage them. The answer to these people's question as to what's in it for them, is that there may be precious little benefit for them. Indeed they might have to bear considerable costs, with the benefits going to consumer groups. Such a scenario seems to have limited allure in most university senior common rooms!

Conclusion
It has been shown that there is a significant gap even at the a priori level between the myth and the reality of the liberal position. As can be seen quite clearly a considerable amount of this debate has mistaken empirical issues for theoretical ones and, as a consequence, has sought theoretical answers to empirical questions. Considering what is known and what we can make reasonable guesses about, we must conclude that market allocation is always and everywhere seriously defective. The perfect market could produce excellent results no doubt, but it seems that only a 'pale shadow' of a market can 'realistically' be expected to exist. If some liberals continue to emphasize the image of the market place as it exists in the mind or the textbook only, rather than in the reality of the market, the liberal analysis must be irrelevant. Theorizing and crystal-ball gazing are no substitute for experimentation and the testing of competing hypotheses (Maynard (1975)): markets must be shown to have the predicted outcomes and these outcomes must be seen to be consistent with policy goals.

INCENTIVES FOR SUPPLIERS
The choice of financial arrangements depends on policy objectives and it is likely that the combined influences of policies such as reducing the rate of growth of public expenditure and a desire, because of postulated efficiency effects, for privatization and a cash nexus, will lead to the use of a mixed loan-grant system in Britain in the near future. Whether this

forecast is proved true or false, there is a separate opportunity to introduce new incentive systems to affect the efficiency with which resources are used in higher education. The purpose of this section is to explore such possibilities: how can supply side inefficiencies be reduced by altering the incentive structures of existing institutions?

The first requisite for any policy whose aim is to change for the better the efficiency with which higher education resources are used is to improve the information about the characteristics of the system. Ideally we should get measures of the outcome of the system but, as happens in the health care field, an exact measure of the outcome is difficult to acquire. Faced by such problems in the health field, the response has been to advocate the measurement and analysis of process (Donabedian 1980).

The analysis of process is largely concerned with the organization and allocation of education inputs: eg

i   Who uses education (= instruction) services relative to 'need'?
ii Do the practitioners in the system adhere to professionally defined criteria and standards of instruction?
iii What differences are there in the use of education (instruction) services and how have these changed over time?
iv Is the size of facility relative to function the best?
v   Is the process of allocation of functions to classes of personnel appropriate?

The analysis of outcome would seek to answer different sorts of questions: eg

i   What are the indices of education outcome and what do they tell us about the performance of the system? How do these outcomes vary between institutions and sectors (public and private), and how have they changed through time?
ii Are the public satisfied with the system as measured by complaints, political pressure, social surveys, etc?
iii What are the education output effects (on lifetime income, intergenerational mobility and other measures) of differences in the use of education inputs (= instruction)?
iv Are there cheaper ways of achieving output targets (ie cost benefit analysis)? Or how much does it cost to improve outcomes by the most cost-effective policy?

The education system can be assessed or monitored using measures either of process or of outcome. The advantages of the process approach are that educators should have no great difficulty in specifying the criteria and standards of good education, at least for technical management of education. Even when these standards and criteria are not fully validated by empirical evidence, they can be used as interim measures of acceptable practice and modified in the light of experience. The use of such information makes it possible to identify from whence the standards arise (and who is responsible for them). Thus credit or blame can be easily apportioned and the necessary corrective action adopted.

The major limitation of the analysis of process for the assessment of the quality of care is the weak scientific basis of most accepted practices in higher education. The use of prevalent norms as the basis for judging the quality of the system may encourage dogmatism and the continued utilization of defective practices. Educators will prefer to adopt conservative practices, they may over-utilize inputs just to be on the safe side. This preference will arise naturally from the fact that the standards primarily represent educators' concerns and because such data sources usually have little bearing on the nature of the staff/student relationship.

The use of outcome measures to assess the quality of the service also has advantages and disadvantages. The emphasis of outcome obliges us to recognize that many inputs may affect the outcome and the measure of outcome must reflect the contributions of all these inputs, not the least important of which will be that of the student himself. A direct measure of staff/student relationships can be acquired in this quality assessment process by measuring client satisfaction with the service.

There are several disadvantages with output measures. Even the most expert of the alleged experts in higher education find it difficult to specify the magnitude, timing and duration of the outcomes of the services they provide. When an output of higher education is produced (eg a particular rate of return to undergraduate education) it is difficult to know how much is due to the formal education process and it is difficult to identify the relative contributions of the segments of that process. Also the measures of outcomes may emerge slowly and this delay may raise ethical issues because people may be disadvantaged.

The practice of measuring process and outcome in education is in its infancy. It is paradoxical that an industry with parallel problems, health and health care, should have progressed more rapidly with an acceptance that randomized controlled trials (RCTs) are expensive, difficult, possibly unethnical, but unavoidable. RCTs in higher education are noticeable by their rarity. Yet the scope for experimentation of a scientific, rather than of a casual ad hoc nature, is great and must be a priority if we are to separate facts from fiction and myths from reality. Indeed we could argue that the absence of such evaluation is unethical as it permits us to commit resources and have little knowledge of the impact of these inputs on human capital formation.

The analysis of process and the measurement of outcome, and adapting and developing the research tools used already in health care, could generate information relevant to the efficient management of the higher education system. This flow of information could enable institutions, public and private, to develop systems of peer review and audit.

Peer review consists of the establishment of standards of practice (process) by practitioners and the monitoring and enforcement of such standards by peer pressure. The problem associated with review in medicine is that the standards adopted tend to be conservative (the standard which generates least resistance!), and as the size of the peer groups rises the monitoring of deviance becomes less effective (the costs of control rise).

An alternative performance regulator is audit. With audit the standards of practice are set by an outsider (an external examiner?). Again the problems are the adoption of conservative standards and the problems associated with the policing of deviance as group size rises.

The prejudice of the economist (it can only be proved by experiment of an RCT nature) might be that information generation and review/audit alone are inadequate and that a cash incentive is essential to ensure efficient resource use. Why should academics monitor performance and seek to be efficient? Why should people adopt more efficient policies and make their human capital redundant? What is in it for them? The answer must be nothing except moral superiority unless a cash element is introduced in to the assessment structure!

A conservative way in which a cash nexus could be introduced would be to relate performance in review/audit to salary payments. The existing salary structure could be altered to give a basic salary (eg the national average wage) with an incremental and decremental system of payments related to the performance of the academic in relation to agreed criteria of performance. Thus an individual could go up and down the salary scale and his titles might also fluctuate with senior lectureships and professorships being awarded and lost in relation to performance.

A more radical measure would be for all students to carry their fees with them in the sense that their registration in a department determined that department's income. Thus an economics course would contract to provide to the student x courses of nature y in the next year for example. The ability of the department to attract students would determine its income.

The income of the department would finance its activities. If it did not attract custom it would be unable to pay its staff. One reaction to this would be to point out the existence of tenure. But tenure need not be affected: the individual in the unattractive department would still have a job but it would generate no income. A more conservative approach might be to guarantee a job and a small basic income only.

An arrangement by which a student bought courses directly with his money or indirectly with his grant, would make the department the budget holder. The manager of the department might have to allocate rewards and tasks in relation to performance on process and outcome measures if the clients' trade were to be assured. This process of developing the hierarchy of the department in relation to performance would, in the limit, be equivalent to the students voting for faculty and electing the chairman of the department. At the a priori level, there seems no reason to believe that this would necessarily be inefficient if performance and outcome measures were good.

The resource allocator in the department, if he kept any profits (surplus of revenues over costs) in the department for use in financing and rewarding innovation, would have the means for substituting, where profitable, capital (computer programme learning) for labour (academics), and an incentive (cost cutting) to seek the input mix which minimized costs but met student requirements. The drive to reduce costs, particularly if departments could compete on price (eg an elementary economics course at half the cost of an elementary politics course), would enable the department to compete for students: if prices were not flexible, the cost-effective department could offer more service and better outcome performances within the income-determined budget.

Many of the incentive mechanisms in the liberal proposals could be generated in institutions which are publicly financed and owned. Such reforms would face similar opposition as that generated by the student loans proposal: the losing groups, in particular labour, would oppose reforms which gave their members losses of income and status. Thus the problems faced by socialists and liberals are very similar: reforms which benefit a client group such as students who are numerous and have only transient interests in the system of higher education, and impose costs on relatively small groups (academics) working for 40 years in the same trade, are unlikely to succeed unless they are carefully designed, 'sold' to producer groups with care, and monitored rigorously. Privatization and the market mechanism offer few new solutions and many of the same old problems! The policies of the ideological debate consume scarce resources which might be better employed in resolving the problems associated with devising efficient evaluation methods, incentives and property right structures in public and private institutions.

CONCLUSION
The liberal nirvana in higher education consists of a set of hypotheses about the behaviour of producers and consumers under incentives systems different from those inherent in the present education system. The purpose of these liberal reforms is to achieve the ultimate liberal goal of freedom via diversification and decentralization of decision making in a competitive market. The validity of these hypotheses is an empirical matter: it is asserted by many liberals but it is not axiomatic that these assertions are valid.

Rather than debate the intrinsic worth (or worthlessness) of competing ideologies it would be a more efficient use of resources to concentrate on the problems of evaluation, incentives, and property rights in public and private institutions. Whatever your ideology, the obstacles to change and the more efficient use of scarce resources are very similar.

BIBLIOGRAPHY

Atkinson, A.B., Maynard, A.K. and Trinder, C.G. (1981) *From Parents to Children: Living Standards in Two Generations* University of York, two volumes, mimeograph

Becker, G.S. (1964, 1976) *Human Capital* New York: National Bureau of Economic Research, Columbia University Press

Corner, D. and Culyer, A. (1969) University teachers and the P I B *Social and Economic Administration* 3, 127

Culyer, A.J., Maynard, A., and Williams, A. (1982) Alternative systems of health care provision: an essay on motes and beams. In Olson, M. (Editor) *A New Approach to the Economics of Medical Care* Washington DC: American Enterprise Institute

Donabedian, A. (1971) Social responsibility for personal health services *Inquiry* VIII (2) 3-19

Donabedian, A. (1980) *The Definition of Quality and Approaches to its Assessment* Michigan: Health Administration Press, Ann Arbor

Evans, R.E. (1974) Supplier-induced demand: some empirical evidence and implications. In Perlman, M. (Editor) *Economics and Health and Medical Care* London: Macmillan

Ferns, H.S. (1969) *Towards an Independent University* London: Institute of Economic Affairs, Occasional Paper 25

Friedman, M. (1962) *Capitalism and Freedom* Chicago: University of Chicago Press

Gallie, W.B. (1965) Liberal morality and socialist morality. In Laslett, P. (Editor) *Philosophy, Politics and Society* Oxford: Blackwells

Glennester, H., Merrett, S. and Wilson, B. (1968) A graduate tax *Higher Education Review* 1

Halsey, A:H., Heath, A.F. and Ridge, J.M. (1980) *Origins and Destinations: family, class and education in modern Britain* Oxford: Clarendon Press

Hayek, F. (1969) *The Constitution of Liberty* London: Routledge and Kegan Paul

House of Commons Select Committee on Education, Science and Arts (1980) *The Funding and Organisation of Courses in Higher Education* H.C. 363 xii. London: HMSO

Hunter, L. (1981) Employers' perceptions of demand. In Lindley, R. (Editor) *Higher Education and the Labour Market* Guildford: Society for Research into Higher Education

Lindley, R. (1981) *Higher Education and the Labour Market* Guildford: Society for Research into Higher Education

Maynard, A.K. (1975) *Experiment with Choice in Education* London: Institute of Economic Affairs

Mincer, J. and Ofek, H. (1982) Interrupted work careers: depreciation and restoration of human capital *Journal of Human Resources* XVII (1) 3-24

Mishan, E.J. (1973) *Making the World Safe for Pornography* London: Alcove Press

Newhouse, J.P. (1981) The demand for medical care services: a retrospect and a prospect. In van der Gaag, J. and Perlman, M. (Editors) *Health, Economics and Health Economics* Amsterdam: North Holland

Peacock, A.T. and Culyer, A.J. (1970) *Economic Aspects of Student Unrest* London: Institute of Economic Affairs, Occasional Paper 26

Peacock, A.T. and Wiseman, J. (1964) *Education for Democrats* Institute of Economic Affairs

Prest, A.R. (1963) In the Robbins Committee Report (1963)

Prest, A.R. (1966) *Financing University Education* London: Institute of Economic Affairs, Occasional Paper 12

Robbins Committee Report (1963) *Higher Education* Evidence. Cmnd 2154-XII; London: HMSO

Smith, A. (1776, 1976) *An Inquiry into the Nature and Causes of the Wealth of Nations* R.H. Campbell and A.S. Skinner (Editors) Oxford and London: Oxford University Press

Woodhall, M. (1970) *Student Loans* London: Harrap

Woodhall, M. (1980) The use of student loans in the finance of higher education: a summary of international experience. In *House of Commons Select Committee on Education, Science and Arts* (1980)

FINANCIAL SUPPORT FOR STUDENTS

by Maureen Woodhall

INTRODUCTION

The present structure of financial support for students in Britain dates from 1962. There have been some modifications in the system of student awards, but the basic principle of providing means-tested mandatory awards for all British full-time students in higher education was recommended in 1960, by the Anderson Committee, and put into effect in 1962. The Education Act of 1944 gave local education authorities the power to grant scholarships or other allowances to any pupil or student over the minimum school leaving age 'for the purpose of enabling pupils to take advantage without hardship to themselves or their parents, of any educational facilities available to them.' However, it was the Anderson Committee which first formulated the principle that all British residents admitted for the first time to a first degree course at a university, and having two 'A' level passes, should receive as of right a grant from public funds (Dept. of Ed. 1960). This was adopted, and extended to other forms of higher education, such as teacher training, and it formed the basis for the system of student awards that still exists, twenty years later, with only minor changes.

When the system of mandatory student awards was introduced, in 1962, it represented a major innovation. The Robbins Committee noted that 'Apart from the Soviet Union, none of the countries visited makes provision from public funds for assisting as high a proportion of students as Great Britain' (HE 1963). In the USA the federal government did not begin to provide financial support for students until 1958, when a small loan scheme was introduced as part of the increased support for scientific and technical education which was a direct response to the launching of the Russian Sputnik. The main federal government programmes of student aid were not, however, introduced until 1965. In Canada the federal government introduced a student aid programme in 1964, and in Sweden the present system of student aid was also introduced in 1964.

The British system of student grants was the envy of students in many other countries in the early 1960s, and it laid the foundation for the post-Robbins expansion of higher education. However, a system of student support which was devised more than twenty years ago is not necessarily the most appropriate for higher education in the 1980s and 1990s. There have been various criticisms of the existing system of student grants and a number of proposals for change, including the introduction of student loans, a graduate tax, the abolition of the means test, or parental contribution to student awards, the introduction of a comprehensive system of educational maintenance allowances for sixteen to nineteen-year-olds, the removal of the distinction between mandatory and discretionary awards, relaxation of the rules determining when a student is regarded as financially independent, and various other major or minor modifications.

The purpose of this chapter is first to summarize the present system of student support, showing the level of aid provided for different categories of student, the conditions of eligibility and the relationships between financial support for students in higher education and other forms of support for young people, including training allowances and supplementary benefit. Secondly, it will discuss the effects of this system on access to higher education, on the participation of working class students and mature students and on the structure of higher education. Finally, it looks at proposals for change and at some future options for student aid policy.

THE STUDENT GRANT SYSTEM

There are two types of grants for students in higher education, mandatory awards, which all LEAs are required to pay to eligible students attending 'designated courses', and discretionary awards, which may be given, at the discretion of individual LEAs, to students who are not eligible for mandatory awards or who are taking non-designated courses. In addition, there are separate grants for postgraduate studies, offered by the DES or the research councils on a competitive basis.

Students are eligible for mandatory awards provided they have been ordinarily resident in the UK throughout the three years preceding the first year of their course of higher education, and provided they have not previously attended a course of advanced further education for more than two years (except students wishing to take the Postgraduate Certificate in Education (PGCE) or an Art Teacher's Certificate or Diploma, who may be eligible for a further mandatory award). This means that LEAs are not obliged to give grants to students who change their minds about the course they wish to follow, or who wish to change their careers, after completing some higher education. Normally, students who abandon a course before completion forfeit their right to a future mandatory award if they wish to resume the course, or start another. Thus, the system of grants is designed for students who follow the traditional paths of entry and completion, and it tends to penalize those who change courses or drop out, for any reason. The Department's guide to the regulations states quite clearly that 'a mandatory award is normally given to enable the student to attend one designated course, however long or short it may be. There is no general entitlement to an award for any particular number of years' (DES 1981, p.6).

If a student is not eligible for a mandatory award, on residence or other grounds, but is following a designated course, he or she may be given an award at the discretion of the LEA. Students who are entitled to mandatory awards have their fees paid in full by the LEA, regardless of income, and in addition receive means-tested maintenance grants.

The designated courses, for which students receive a mandatory or full-value award include: full-time or sandwich courses leading to a first degree, a DipHE or HND or a TEC or BEC higher diploma, full-time teacher training courses, and some part-time courses of teacher training.

Courses which are not designated for grant purposes include non-degree courses, for example for occupational therapists, physiotherapists, radiographers and other para-medical professions, non-advanced FE, adult education and other part-time courses. In some cases, special grants are available: for example the DES provides adult education bursaries and the DHSS provides grants for some para-medical training. In the case of other non-designated courses discretionary grants may be available, but both the value and conditions of these grants are determined by the LEA and the local authorities are under no obligation to provide grants for non-designated courses.

The latest year for which full information on student grants is available is 1979-80. In that year mandatory awards accounted for seventy-one per cent of all awards made to students, discretionary awards accounted for twenty-five per cent and the remaining four per cent were postgraduate awards. Eighty-five per cent of all awards were granted for advanced courses (including postgraduate study) and only fifteen per cent for non-advanced FE. Table 4.1 shows the total number of student awards in 1979-80 and the distribution between different types of higher and further education.

In the case of mandatory awards, ninety per cent of LEA expenditure is reimbursed by means of a DES specific grant, and the local authorities finance the remaining ten per cent. In the case of discretionary awards local authorities finance forty to fifty per cent of the expenditure, and the remaining fifty to sixty per cent comes from central government via a block grant. The DES and research councils finance postgraduate awards.

Table 4.2 shows expenditure on all forms of student support in England and Wales in 1979-80. The total expenditure on maintenance in 1979-80 was £436 million in England and Wales, of which about eighty-eight per cent was for undergraduate and comparable courses of advanced FE, nine per cent was for postgraduate students and only about three per cent was allocated to discretionary awards for non-advanced FE. In addition, payment of students' fees cost £255 million. Detailed figures are not yet available for later years, but the most recent estimates suggest that in 1981-82 the total cost of maintenance is £517 million in England and Wales, whilst payment of fees cost £395 million.

MANDATORY AWARDS
All students receive a minimum grant (currently £410 a year) with the exception of a few students, who receive free board and lodging. Any

TABLE 4.1
Number of student awards 1979-80

		(000s)
MANDATORY AWARDS		
First Degrees	– Universities	183
	– FE establishments	78
Teacher Training	– Universities	6
	– FE establishments	35
Other Advanced FE		21
Total Mandatory Awards		323
DISCRETIONARY AWARDS (FULL VALUE)		
First Degrees	– Universities	2
	– FE establishments	2
Teacher Training	– FE establishments	1
Other Advanced FE		40
Total Full-Value Discretionary Awards		45
LESSER-VALUE DISCRETIONARY AWARDS		
Non-Advanced FE		69
Postgraduate Awards		19
TOTAL STUDENT AWARDS		456

Source DES *Statistical Bulletin* No 16/81, November 1981.

additional grant for maintenance is means-tested. Students under twenty-five are considered financially dependent on their parents, even if married, unless they have supported themselves out of their earnings for three years before starting a course of higher education. In 1979-80 eighty-seven per cent of all students receiving full-value awards were considered financially dependent on their parents. This means that their parents are expected to contribute to their maintenance costs, unless their residual income (after allowing for deductions such as mortgage interest, number of dependants, etc.) is below the minimum, which was £4,700 in 1979-80, £5,800 in 1980-1 and is £6,600 in 1981-2 and 1982-3. The contribution, calculated on the basis of a sliding scale, is subtracted from the main rate of grant, to determine how much each student actually receives. The DES tells students, in its brief guide to student grants: 'There is no statutory obligation on your parents to make their contributions, but if they do not do so your resources will fall short of your assessed needs' (DES 1981). Nor is there any statutory obligation on parents to provide details of income, but if they do not, a student will receive only the minimum grant. Up to 1976-77 this minimum was only £50, but it was raised to £80 in 1977, £200 in 1978, £335 in 1979 and in 1981 and 1982 the minimum grant is £410.

TABLE 4.2
Public expenditure on student support in England and Wales 1979-80

	(£ million)
MANDATORY AWARDS AND FULL-VALUE DISCRETIONARY AWARDS	
Fees	235.0
Maintenance	381.7
Total	616.7
LESSER-VALUE DISCRETIONARY AWARDS	
Fees	3.6
Maintenance	14.2
Total	17.8
POSTGRADUATE AWARDS	
Fees	16.6
Maintenance	40.2
Total	56.8
TOTAL EXPENDITURE ON STUDENT SUPPORT	
Fees	255.2
Maintenance	436.1
Total	691.3

Source Department of Education and Science

In addition to the main rate of grant, which determines the maximum most students can receive in normal circumstances, there are a number of supplementary allowances. Students over twenty-six who have been in full-time employment for a total of three years during the six years preceding the start of their course receive an older students' allowance as a compensation for loss of earnings; disabled students may receive a supplement; those with dependants receive additional amounts; and there are a number of allowances for travel expenses, for necessary equipment for students of medicine, architecture or other courses with special requirements, or in other special cases.

The maintenance grant is intended to provide sufficient funds for students to maintain themselves 'without undue hardship' during term-time and the Christmas and Easter vactions, but it is not intended to cover the long summer vacation, when students are eligible for supplementary benefit if they cannot find a job or support themselves.

The main rates of grant for mandatory and postgraduate awards in 1981-2 and 1982-3 are shown in Table 4.3, together with the additional grants and supplements paid in special cases. Table 4.4 shows the scale of parental contributions in 1981-82. This refers to 'residual income',

TABLE 4.3
Rates of grant for mandatory awards and postgraduate awards 1981-2 and 1982-3

				1981-82	1982-83
1	MANDATORY AWARDS (for undergraduates and other students taking designated courses)				
	i	Fees (paid direct)		900	480
	ii	Main Rate of Maintenance Grant			
		a	Students living away from home, in London	1825	1900
		b	Students living away from home, elsewhere	1535	1595
		c	Students living in parental home	1180	1225
	iii	Minimum Grant		410	410
	iv	Mature Students Grant			
		a	Students aged 26	150	155
		b	Students aged 27	295	305
		c	Students aged 28	445	465
		d	Students aged 29 and over	590	615
	v	Disabled Student Grant		250	260
	vi	Dependants' Allowance			
		a	Adult	965	1070
		b	Child (according to age)	140 – 580	220 – 835
	vii	Supplements			
		a	Special travel (expenses in excess of £50 are reimbursed by LEA)		
		b	Special equipment	70	75
	viii	'Two homes' Allowance for independent students		355	370
2	POSTGRADUATE AWARDS				
	i	Fees (paid direct for all award holders)		1320	1413
	ii	Main Rate of Maintenance Grant			
		a	Students living away from home, in London	2770	2880
		b	Students living away from home, elsewhere	2245	2335
		c	Students living in parental home	1640	1705

Source Department of Education and Science

which takes into account the number of dependants, payment of interest (including mortgage interest), contributions to pension schemes, and certain special conditions (eg disability). These tables show, for example, that in 1981-82 an undergraduate studying outside London and living away from home would be entitled to a maximum of £1,535 for maintenance, in addition to the payment of fees of £900, but if the parents' residual income was £10,000, then they would be expected to contribute £474 and the student would actually receive a grant of £1,061.

In the case of married students over the age of twenty-five, the contribution expected from a spouse is actually greater than the parental contribution at the same level of income. Thus a parent with a residual income of £12,000 is expected to contribute £724, but a spouse is expected to contribute £1,020. If a student is married but under twenty-five, he or she would still be assessed in terms of parental income, and parents would be expected to contribute, regardless of the marriage.

Figures are not yet available to show the average level of grant in 1980 or 1981, but in 1979-80 mandatory award holders received, on average, £1,033 for maintenance. This figure includes students who received the minimum award (£335 in 1979-80) who accounted for eight per cent of all students. The maximum maintenance grant in 1979-80 (excluding additions for mature students, dependants or other supplements) ranged from £985 for students living at home to £1,485 for students living away from home in London.

PAYMENT OF FEES

Since 1977-78 all mandatory award holders have had their fees paid in full, and in 1979-80 this amounted to an average subsidy of £636; if this is added to the average maintenance grant of £1,033, it means that the average value of a mandatory award is £1,669. This, of course, is not the whole subsidy for students in higher education. The average cost per student in universities in 1979-80 was £3,336, so that the average fee of £636 represented just under twenty per cent of this and the bulk of the subsidy came in the form of grants to institutions rather than grants to students.

The question whether subsidies should be given to institutions or to students raises many issues which cannot be covered here, but it is worth drawing attention to the changes in government policy on fees that have taken place in the last decade. The Robbins recommendation that fees should be increased so that they provided at least twenty per cent of university income, instead of about ten per cent as in 1962, was based on the arguments that 'it is a source of strength that public finance should come through more than one channel,' and that 'up to a point it is better to subsidize students than institutions' (HE 1963). The recommendation was not adopted, however, and by 1974-5 fees accounted for only about five per cent of university income, but fees were substantially increased in 1977. However, since that time the fees of all students who are eligible for a mandatory award are paid directly by the LEA. Since 1977, therefore, fees have provided between fifteen and twenty

TABLE 4.4
Scale of parental contribution for mandatory awards

Residual Income	Assumed Parental Contribution in 1981-82 and 1982-83
£	£
5,800	-
6,000	-
6,500	-
6,600	20
6,700	34
6,800	48
6,900	62
7,000	77
7,500	148
8,000	220
8,100	234
8,200	248
8,300*	262
8,400	274
8,500	287
9,000	349
10,000	474
11,000	599
12,000	724
13,000	849
13,100	862
13,200*	874
13,300	881
13,400	889
13,500	897
14,000	935
15,000	1,012
16,000	1,089
17,000	1,166
18,000	1,243
19,000	1,320
20,000	1,397

Scale continues at £1 for every complete £13 of additional income

* Indicates the points at which the rate of contributions change. Below £8,300 the parental contribution increases by £1 for every additional £7 of residual income. Between £8,300 and £13,200 the contribution increases by £1 for every £8 and above £13,200 it increases by £1 for every additional £13.

Source Department of Education and Science

per cent of university income, but from 1982-3 fees for undergraduates will be halved, and the proportion of income derived from fees will again decline.

For the future, there are a number of options. One possibility, occasionally advocated by those who disapprove of the fee differential between home and overseas students, would be to charge full-cost fees to all students, but continue to pay the fees of mandatory award holders. This would make the size of the subsidy clearly visible to all, which it is not, at present; but it would sharpen the distinction between students eligible for mandatory awards and those who do not qualify. An alternative would be to abolish fees for home students altogether, and provide all subsidies by means of institutional grants, as is done in most European countries. This would have the disadvantage of making institutions totally dependent on a single source of finance. For the present, however, payment of fees must be treated as one element of financial support for students, which is the reason for including fee payments as well as maintenance grants in Tables 4.2 and 4.5, even though logic might suggest that they be regarded as financial support for institutions rather than students.

PARENTAL CONTRIBUTIONS

If student grants had not been means-tested in 1979-80 it would have cost an additional £94 million to pay all students following designated courses the full-value maintenance award. The figure of £94 million represents the total value of assessed contributions by parents or spouses (in the case of married students over twenty-five), including estimated contributions for 27,000 minimum award holders. The total value of parental contributions was twenty per cent of the estimated total cost of maintenance for the 369,000 award holders, and the LEAs and DES together met eighty per cent of the cost. This meant that, on average, parents contributed £256 per student, compared with the cost to public funds of £1,033. However, this average figure does not give a true picture, since parents with incomes below £4,700 were not expected to make any contribution. If these are excluded, the average parental contribution from parents liable to make contributions was £419, which was approximately one-third of the total cost of maintenance.

If all parents actually paid their assessed contributions, therefore, this would mean that the costs of maintainance for students whose family income was above the limit of £4,700 were shared between parents and the taxpayer in the ratio of 1:2. However, it is well known that many parents are unwilling or unable to make their assessed contributions, which means that the burden falls on the student, in the form of lower living standards. A survey of student income in 1974-5 (OPCS 1979) showed that seventy-three per cent of the students whose grants were reduced because of assessed parental contributions received less than the full amount of the assessment.

The share of the parental contribution relative to maintenance costs has increased since means-tested grants were first introduced because the parental income levels used as a basis for the means test have not been fully adjusted to keep pace with inflation. The National Union of Students estimates that the decision not to raise the lower income threshold and the scale for parental contributions in 1982-83 means that the parents of an additional 20,000 students will become liable for contributions, and that parents will be expected to contribute up to £150 more in 1982-83 than in 1981-82 (NUS 1982b).

However, if payment of fees is taken into account, as well as maintenance, the parental contribution relative to the total cost of student support has declined since 1977. The National Union of Students (NUS 1975) estimated that the average parental contribution rose from sixteen per cent of the total costs of student support in 1965 to about twenty-seven per cent in 1972 (including parents of students who received only the minimum grant). In 1979-80, however, total assessed parental contributions represented only thirteen per cent of the total costs of support if all students are included, and if the parents who were not liable for any contribution, because of low income, are excluded, the average parental contribution represented twenty-two per cent of the total costs of support as shown in Table 4.5.

The figures in Table 4.5 show the average contribution by parents, spouses and students, on the assumption that assessed contributions are paid in full. Table 4.6 shows the range of parental assessments, on the basis of a sliding scale of residual income. This table includes only students who are financially dependent on their parents, which was 323,000 in 1979-80. Parents of one-third of these students were not expected to make any contribution, and these students therefore received the maximum grant. In only nine per cent of the cases were parents expected to contribute more than £1,000, including those where the minimum grant of £335 was received. Since the fees of all mandatory award holders were also paid, this means that even minimum award holders received a subsidy of £971 (£335 + £636) which was just over half the estimated average cost of student support of £1,925. Thus the parental contribution to the costs of student support ranged from zero to fifty per cent, but the majority of students taking designated courses received at least eighty per cent of the combined costs of fees and maintenance from public funds. Table 4.6 shows that twenty-eight per cent of dependent students at university received the full grant, compared with thirty-eight per cent in advanced FE, and in general the parents of university students were expected to make a bigger contribution than those of FE students. Less than a quarter of the parents of FE students were assessed for contributions of more than £400, compared with more than a third of the parents of university students.

Unfortunately there are no similar data for students taking non-designated courses, but since discretionary awards are not necessarily intended to cover the full costs of fees and maintenance, it is

TABLE 4.5
The value of assessed parental and spouses' contributions to the costs of student support 1979-80

		Total Value (£ million)	Average Value per Student (£)
1	Estimated cost (before deductions for parental contributions) (maintenance)	476	1289
2	Assessed contributions from parents, students and spouses (maintenance)	94	256
3	Assessed contributions from parents, etc. liable for contributions (maintenance)		419
4	Mandatory and full-value awards – LEA expenditure (maintenance)	382	1033
5	LEA expenditure (fees)	235	636
6	Total LEA expenditure	617	1669
7	Total student support (assuming full payment of parental, etc. contributions)	711	1925
	Public contribution (6 as % of 7)		87%
	Parental contribution (2 as % of 7)		13%
	(3 as % of 7)		22%

Source Department of Education and Science

clear that these students, or their parents, are expected to make a greater contribution than students with mandatory or full-value discretionary awards, and, indeed, many of them must pay the full cost with no assistance.

DISCRETIONARY AWARDS
Much less information is available about discretionary awards than mandatory awards. The most recent comprehensive information is contained in a report of a DES survey of LEAs in 1977 (DES 1978) which collected information about discretionary awards for 1975-76 and 1977-78. This survey showed that about 55,000 students held full-value discretionary awards, but between 1975 and 1977 the number of new awards declined by 2,000 although the number of eighteen and nineteen-year-olds had increased. If the number of discretionary awards had kept pace with this increase, a further 5,000 (or roughly ten per cent of the total) would have been needed, so there was clear evidence that it was becoming more difficult for students to get a discretionary award. The survey also showed

TABLE 4.6
Parental assessments towards full-value awards 1979-80

Parents' Residual income in Financial Year 1978-79	Percentage of Students[1]		
£	University	Advanced FE	Total
Under 4,700	28	38	33
4,700 to 6,507	24	26	25
6,508 to 7,707	14	12	13
7,708 to 8,507	7	5	6
8,508 to 14,262	17	12	14
14,263 or over[2]	10	7	9

[1] Excluding students who were financially independent
[2] Including all minimum award holders

Source Department of Education and Science *Statistical Bulletin* 16/81, November 1981.

that the average value of discretionary awards rose by less than the value of mandatory awards.

The picture was worse for students taking non-advanced FE than for those taking degree-level courses. The survey concluded that forty-five per cent of LEAs make grants to under nineteens which are more restricted than those recommended by the local authority associations, and eighty per cent make grants to students over nineteen which are less generous than those recommended. The proportion of LEAs making grants at rates lower than the rate for mandatory awards increased from 1975 to 1977, and the survey showed that in 1977 students with discretionary awards paid at lower rates received, on average, about seventy-five per cent of the value of mandatory awards. Some LEAs simply deduct a fixed amount, or take a proportion of the mandatory award, when determining discretionary grants; others simply use the previous year's rates of mandatory grant.

It is clear from this survey that most authorities are more restrictive in giving discretionary awards than mandatory awards. In the case of designated courses any student who is offered a place and meets the eligibility requirements automatically becomes entitled to a grant, but in the case of discretionary awards seventy-nine per cent of the LEAs did not regard acceptance for a course as sufficient proof of suitability for an award, but required additional information, and seventy-one per cent of LEAs stipulated age limits.

In the case of part-time students, some LEAs gave no discretionary awards, the majority gave discretionary awards to Open University students, and some gave awards to other part-time students, but the proportions of LEAs giving awards for some part-time courses in very low, as Table 4.7 shows. The general conclusion of the survey was that 'there are substantial differences between the practices of individual authorities and also in the demand for awards and the availability of courses' (DES 1978).

Since 1978 the number of discretionary awards has continued to fall, although not much information is available. The number of full-value discretionary awards, which was 55,000 in 1977-78, was only 47,000 in 1979-80. The National Union of Students has conducted its own survey of LEAs, which showed that between 1978 and 1981 forty-one per cent of all LEAs had cut the number of awards by up to twenty-five per cent (NUS 1981).

TABLE 4.7
Percentage of LEAs giving discretionary awards to part-time students 1977-78

Assistance given for:	
1 Open university students	
a Full fees, irrespective of income	3
b A proportion of fees, irrespective of income	76
c Full fees (means-tested)	16
d A proportion of fees (means-tested)	7
2 Day release courses	16
3 Block release courses	28
4 Correspondence courses	35
5 Specific subject areas: eg law, accountancy	32
6 Students under 18 – all courses	26
7 No part-time courses	18

The table does not add to 100 per cent, as some LEAs give assistance of more than one type

Source DES *Discretionary Awards* op.cit., p.19.

OTHER SUPPORT FOR YOUNG PEOPLE

Grants for students in full-time higher education are only one of the ways in which the government provides financial support for young people. Pupils in secondary schools may, in some cases, receive educational maintenance allowances and their parents may continue to receive child benefit while they are in full-time education. School-leavers who are unemployed may receive an allowance while undergoing training under the Youth Opportunities Programme (YOP) or may claim supplementary benefit. Older unemployed workers may receive training and an allowance under the Training Opportunities Scheme (TOPS) or may claim unemployment benefit. There are different rates of pay for all these different allowances, and Table 4.8 compares the weekly rate of pay for recipients in 1981-82 of mandatory awards, YOP and TOPS training allowances and supplementary benefit.

There are also differences in the rules governing eligibility for different types of assistance. Mandatory awards are means tested, although all students receive a minimum grant for maintenance, as well as fees. Supplementary benefit is means tested, but the training allowances provided under TOPS and YOP are not. Table 4.8 shows that students receiving the maximum mandatory award receive considerably more, per week, than unemployed young people on YOP or receiving supplementary benefit. They receive slightly less than those who have a training allowance under TOPS. However, most TOPS courses are relatively short, and in normal circumstances no one can receive TOPS training for more than a year. This rule is specifically designed to exclude most higher level or professional training, to ensure that TOPS training does not compete with advanced FE (MSC 1978).

A comparison of the various allowances and grants available to young people shows that the group receiving least support are those who are in full-time non-advanced education, or post-compulsory schooling. Pupils over the minimum school leaving age may receive educational maintenance allowances (EMAs) at the discretion of their LEAs, but there are considerable differences in both the level of EMAs and the proportion of pupils receiving them. A survey by the DES in 1971 showed that the average amount paid per pupil varied from £31 to £123 and the proportion of pupils above the school leaving age receiving EMAs varied from 0.5 per cent to 16.6 per cent (Expenditure Committee 1974). There is very little up-to-date information about the extent of financial support for school pupils, but there are four LEAs (ILEA, Sheffield, Newcastle and Wakefield) which provide means-tested EMAs up to a maximum of £7 a week (Labour Party 1982). In 1980-81 total expenditure on EMAs amounted to £4 million.

Students aged sixteen to nineteen taking non-advanced FE may receive discretionary awards and these are included in the number of lesser-value discretionary awards shown in Table 4.1. Once again, however, the number is relatively small and there are considerable differences between LEAs. Thus, sixteen to nineteen-year-olds taking non-advanced courses are likely to receive very little towards their maintenance (apart from the child benefit of £4.75 a week) and may even be charged fees:

> 'Most sixteen to nineteen year olds on non-advanced courses such as GCEs, TEC and BEC national certificates and diplomas, and certain professional courses, receive no financial support whatsoever. ... It has until recently been the widespread practice of LEAs not to levy fees for sixteen to nineteen year olds in FE who were following courses broadly similar to those provided in schools, in order to avoid disparities between the two sectors. Even though this remains the advice of the

local authority associations and is the practice of many authorities, some are departing from it at the present time of severe financial constraint.' (Labour Party 1982, pp. 90 and 93)

At present, sixteen to nineteen-year-olds who are unemployed may study part time, for less than twenty-one hours a week, and still claim supplementary benefit, but when the new Youth Training Scheme (which will replace YOP) is introduced in 1983, sixteen-year-olds will no longer be able to claim supplementary benefit; they will instead be eligible for a training allowance of £15 a week.

When sixteen to nineteen-year-old students who are taking non-advanced FE on a full-time or part-time basis are compared with students taking advanced courses who receive a minimum mandatory award of £10.50 a week, as well as having their fees paid in full, the favourable position of the latter is striking.

So far, no mention has been made of other sources of support for students, apart from parents and spouses. Some mature students receive financial support from employers while they undergo full-time or part-time education. A recent survey by the NIAE estimated that approximately one million people receive some form of paid educational leave (PEL) in 1976-77 (Killeen and Bird 1981) but it proved very difficult to estimate the extent of assisted educational leave, for example where an employee is given extra pay for attending an evening class in his own time, or financial assistance towards fees.

There is little up-to-date information available on the sources of income of students apart from that contained in a survey of undergraduates in 1974-75 and of postgraduates in 1975-76 (OPCS 1979a and b). The undergraduate survey showed that ninety-seven per cent of students received a grant from an LEA or SED, two per cent received no assistance, one per cent were sponsored by the armed services and one per cent received other support, including industrial scholarships. In the case of postgraduates, seventy-eight per cent of university students and sixty-nine per cent of polytechnic students received an award from the DES or from research councils, twelve per cent of university students and nine per cent of polytechnic students were supported by their employer, twelve per cent of polytechnic students received a TOPS allowance and nine per cent of both university and polytechnic students were self-supporting.

CRITICISMS OF THE PRESENT SYSTEM
There is no shortage of criticism of the present system of financial support for students. Apart from criticisms of the level of student grants — 'We have been singled out for worse treatment than almost any other section of society' (David Aaronovitch, NUS President, in NUS 1982a) — the main criticisms of the NUS are centred on the means test, the unfairness of the distinction between mandatory and discretionary awards, the

TABLE 4.8
Student grants compared with other forms of financial support

	Maximum Mandatory Award 1981-82 per week in term-time London	Maximum Mandatory Award 1981-82 per week in term-time Elsewhere	TOPS Allowance per week (from 1.2.82)	YOP Allowance per week (from 11.1.82)	Supplementary Benefit per week (from 1.11.81)
16 to 17-year-old living in parental home	N/A	N/A	N/A	£25	£14.30 + 2.55 £16.85 Rent Allowance
16 to 17-year-old living away from home, not in someone else's household	N/A	N/A	N/A	£25	£23.25 + Rent
18-year-old living in parental home	£33.70	£33.70	N/A	£25	£18.60 + 2.55 £21.15 Rent Allowance
18-year-old living away from home, not in someone else's household	£55.20	£45.53	N/A	£25	£23.25 + Rent
19+ year-old living in parental home (no dependants)	£33.70	£33.70	£36.70	Not normally applicable	£18.60 + 2.55 £21.15 Rent Allowance
19+ year-old living away from home, not in someone else's household (no dependants)	£55.20	£45.53	£36.70 +40 (if has to live away from normal residence)	Not normally applicable	£23.25 + Rent
25-year-old living with spouse in matrimonial home (no children)	£55.20 +18.56 £73.76	£45.53 +18.56 £64.09	£36.70 +22.80* £59.50 *Provided wife's take home pay not more than £36.00 pw	Not normally applicable	£37.75 + Rent
25-year-old living with spouse away from matrimonial home (no children) (two homes)	£55.20 +18.56 + 6.83 £80.59	£45.53 +18.56 + 6.83 £70.92	£36.70 +22.80* +40.00 £99.50	Not normally applicable	£37.75 + Rent
Student on minimum grant	£10.50	£10.50	N/A	N/A	N/A

absence of a comprehensive system of support for 16 to 19-year-olds and the complexity of the grant regulations.

Dr Rhodes Boyson, parliamentary under-secretary of state, voiced his own disquiet about the distinction between mandatory and discretionary awards, when he referred to 'the number of people, including Open University students, who at present got nothing. There are people training for chiropody, speech therapists, those going into law after their degree and those going into social work. However much certain people who are getting full grants may like it, hundreds of thousands of others are getting nothing' (Hansard, 10 February 1981, Col. 729).

There have been many criticisms of the absence of comprehensive support for sixteen to nineteen-year-olds. In the SRHE Leverhulme seminar on access to higher education Alan Gordon surveyed the evidence and concluded:

'While financial support, albeit subject to parental means-test, is widely available for the over-eighteens in higher education, there is little monetary help for young people (and their families) when they first choose to stay on beyond the minimum school leaving age. Research evidence indicates that the introduction of educational maintenance allowances on a national basis would help to raise demand for post-compulsory education. Any government concerned with equalizing educational opportunities, and with the provision of highly skilled personnel for the future development of the economy, would do well to place the introduction of educational maintenance allowances very high indeed on an agenda of educational reforms.' (Fulton 1981, p.141)

On grounds of equity, Blaug also argues that generous aid should be provided for sixteen to nineteen-year-olds, and makes clear how it should be financed: 'In an ideal world, we would give grants in inverse proportion to parental income, or even better to students' income, to all those who stayed on in full-time education beyond the (school leaving age) right up to the Ph.D. level; in that world, we would never have to make difficult policy choices. ... In the real world, however, education must compete with the other social services in face of budgetary restraints. ... If we are going to make use of student aid to equalize educational opportunities ... we ought to reduce public subsidies in higher education and apply the funds released thereby to subsidize upper-secondary education' (Blaug 1972, pp. 296-7). On the present system he is forthright: 'Judged in terms of effectiveness per unit of costs, the present grants system is perhaps the least efficient method conceivable of increasing working-class participation in higher education' (Blaug 1972, p. 296).

To summarize the various criticisms of the existing system of student aid serves to emphasize that since, like other systems of financial support, the present grant system tries to satisfy a number of different (sometimes conflicting) objectives at the same time, it is difficult to evaluate its effectiveness. Any evaluation of student aid policy must look at the effects on equality of opportunity and also equity, on the structure of higher education and on participation by different social groups and age groups, on women, and finally, but inevitably, on the level of public expenditure.

The effect of student grants on educational opportunity has been less than was hoped. In the SRHE Leverhulme seminar on access, John Farrant showed that 'The social composition of the university intake has scarcely changed over twenty-five years' (Fulton 1981, p.60) despite availability of grants, and despite the fact that a third of all mandatory award holders receive a full maintenance grant, designed to cover all living costs as well as free tuition. On grounds of equity, many people would agree with Blaug that 'Almost half of the grants system simply gives to those who already have. ... To defend grants in higher education on grounds of social equality is a monstrous perversion of the truth' (Blaug, 1972, p.296).

The effects of the distinction between mandatory and discretionary awards on the structure of higher education is certainly to reduce flexibility and innovation. If students on advanced courses are treated much more generously than those in non-advanced FE, then there will always be pressure to upgrade non-advanced courses, to raise entry qualifications or lengthen courses in order to make them comparable with degree-level courses, and so allow students to qualify for superior grant status. If part-time students are treated less generously than full-time students, there will be less incentive to develop new, more flexible courses. If a system of grants is designed primarily for school-leavers, it will provide insufficient incentive for mature students. The present system of grants has been criticized on all these grounds.

It is widely recognized that the system of discretionary awards discriminates against part-time students and those taking non-advanced courses. The rules governing the mature student allowance make it difficult for married women to qualify, since a 'mature student' must have been in full-time employment for three out of the six years immediately before the start of a course, and no exceptions are made for looking after children or for unemployment. The level of the mature student allowance and the dependants' allowance mean that it is particularly difficult for adult students with family responsibilities to finance higher education. The rules about grants for those who change their minds about courses or careers are not designed to encourage flexibility, and reflect the fact that the system of student grants was designed before the idea of continuing education had any real influence on policy.

Recent trends in student grants show clearly the conflict between the pressure to rectify many of these anomalies and the pressure to reduce public expenditure. Various politicians have expressed the desire to extend discretionary awards or to abolish the distinction between mandatory and discretionary awards, to reduce or to abolish the parental means test, to relax the rules determining the independence of students, and to extend aid to the sixteen to nineteen-year age group. However, the cost of such proposals has always proved prohibitive, and, instead, the real value of student grants has fallen in recent years, as the maximum grant has risen by less than the rate of inflation. The maximum grant for students living away from home, outside London, is £1,535 in 1981-82 and will be £1,595 in 1982-83. To maintain the purchasing power of the 1962 student grant, students would have to receive £1,820 in 1981-82 and £2,000 in 1982-83. The increase in 1982-83 will be four per cent, considerably below the expected rate of inflation and well below the increase in students' accommodation costs (NUS 1982b) but the government announced that this was 'to take account of the policy of restraining public expenditure and is in line with Government guidelines for pay awards in the public sector'. John Farrant showed clearly the declining real value of student grants, in his paper for the SRHE Leverhulme seminar on access. Whereas an index of juvenile wages rose from 100 to 750 between 1965 to 1980, and an index of male manual earnings rose from 100 to nearly 600, the student maintenance grant rose to only 421 (Fulton 1981, p. 78). This reflects government policy on public expenditure, but it also reveals clearly one cause of student dissatisfaction: the widening gap between student grants and the earnings of their contemporaries in employment. In April 1980 the average earnings of young male manual workers aged eighteen to twenty were £78 per week, which was seventy per cent of the earnings of adult male manual workers.

It is becoming increasingly obvious, not only in Britain but in other countries, that expansion of student support, to satisfy at the same time the demands of students for higher living standards and greater independence, to increase the participation of low income groups and older students, and to treat different categories of students with greater equality, would impose unacceptable burdens on public expenditure. Thus, in Britain, proposals for student loans are being re-examined, and various ways of limiting the availability of mandatory awards have been discussed, although there are no immediate plans to introduce such changes. At the same time there have been proposals for a comprehensive system of 'educational entitlement' or educational and training allowances covering every type of post-compulsory schooling, but in many cases this would be linked with loans. For example, in an earlier SRHE Leverhulme seminar, Oliver Fulton proposed that every citizen should be entitled to support for education, regardless of its level, by means of an age-related maintenance grant plus free tuition for a maximum of four years full-time or its part-time equivalent after the compulsory school-leaving age of sixteen. The entitlement would be supplemented with a system of state-supported loans for further periods of education or training (Fulton 1981, p. 37).

There are, of course, many proposals for expanding the existing system without fundamental changes such as loans. The Labour Party has proposed a comprehensive system of 'student traineeships' for all sixteen to nineteen-year-olds (Labour Party 1982), but is opposed to student loans. The last Labour government in fact proposed a pilot system of educational maintenance allowances in 1978 and estimated that mandatory EMAs would have cost about £100 million. However, student awards already account for ten per cent of total educational expenditure and more than twenty-five per cent of expenditure on higher education, and the present government is therefore seeking ways to limit future spending rather than increase it. This is why proposals such as the imposition of a cash limit on LEA expenditure on awards have been discussed, and why student loans are again being examined as an option.

The Robbins Committee did not, as many people now think, reject the idea of loans, but concluded 'on balance we do not recommend immediate recourse to a system of financing students by loans. At a time when many parents are only just beginning to acquire the habit of contemplating higher education ... for their children ... we think it probable that it would have undesirable disincentive effects. But if, as time goes on, the habit is more firmly established, the arguments of justice in distribution and of the advantage of increasing individual responsibilty may come to weigh more heavily and lead to some experiment in this direction' (HE 1963, p. 212). Lord Robbins himself certainly believes that time has now come (Robbins 1980). There is evidence that public opinion may also be changing, in favour of a mixture of loans and grants (Lewis, Sandford and Thomson 1980).

Advocates of loans, for example Maynard (1975), point to the experience of other countries, which successfully operate loan schemes, as proof of their feasibility. Opponents, such as the NUS (1980), point to the difficulties that have arisen in other countries (for example high default rates in the USA) to prove they would be unworkable here. While international experience can never prove conclusively whether student loans could be successfully introduced here, the experience of other countries does provide some valuable lessons. The next section of this chapter therefore summarizes the lessons from recent experience in other countries, particularly Canada, Sweden and the US, and the final section considers some of the options available for student aid policy in the 1980s and 1990s.

STUDENT AID OVERSEAS
Apart from Britain, there are few Western countries without some form of student loan scheme, but few countries, except for Japan, which rely exclusively on loans. In many European countries, in the whole of Scandinavia, in Canada and in the US students receive both loans and grants, supplemented in the US and parts of Canada by a work-study programme, which provides subsidized job opportunities for students, often on the university or college campus (Woodhall 1970, 1978 and 1982).

During the last year both the Australian and Irish governments have considered introducing student loans, and loans are the predominant form of student aid in Latin America.

Loans for students may be provided by a state loan bank, as in Sweden and Norway, or by commercial banks, as in Canada, US and Finland, but in either case the government guarantees the loan, and meets the costs of repayment for those who are ill, are unemployed or who die before repayment is complete. In the majority of schemes loans are subsidized, often to a considerable extent. The government normally pays the full cost of interest while a student is in higher education, and the rate of interest paid by graduates is, in most countries, well below the market rate of interest.

The proportion of students receiving financial aid varies considerably, but is generally considerably lower than in Britain. The only country which approaches the British proportions of ninety per cent of all home students and ninety-seven per cent of undergraduates receiving awards is Sweden, where about ninety per cent of students in higher education receive financial support, but only ten per cent of this is a grant. The remaining ninety per cent is a long-term low-interest loan. In most other countries the proportion of students receiving aid is much lower; in Canada, for instance, the proportion has fallen during the 1970s from about half to forty-four per cent in 1980.

In most countries student grants and loans are means-tested, although in Sweden and Norway parental income is not taken into account; it is only the student's own income which determines eligibility. In the US there are highly subsidized loans and grants for low-income students but the main source of student support is the Guaranteed Student Loan Program (GSLP), which provides loans at a higher, but still significantly subsidized rate of interest. This was a means-tested programme when it was first introduced in 1965, but the Middle Income Student Assistance Act of 1978 (MISAA) made GSLP loans available to everyone, regardless of income. The result was a explosion of demand for loans, and President Reagan therefore reintroduced a means test in the summer of 1981 so that those students who no longer qualify for GSLP loans may now borrow auxiliary loans at fourteen per cent interest compared with the nine per cent GSLP loans and five per cent National Direct Loans for low-income students.

In the US and Canada student grants and loans help students to pay tuition fees, but in Europe, where tuition is free, student aid is needed only towards maintenance costs. There is a trend in many countries now towards greater equality of treatment for students in different types of higher education. Few countries distinguish between advanced and non-advanced HE in the way that Britain does, and in Scandinavia, particularly Sweden, financial support is available for part-time as well as full-time students, and special assistance is available for adults taking short courses.

There is a growing tendency to provide more generous support for secondary school pupils above the statutory leaving age. In Sweden, for instance, all pupils and students below twenty receive a basic grant of £22 a month (in 1981-82) and means- and needs-tested supplements of £13 or £20 a month, plus loans of up to £50 a month for sixteen and seventeen-year-olds and £100 a month for eighteen and nineteen-year-olds. One reason for this is the growing awareness that student aid at the college or univesity level is not, by itself, sufficient to ensure equality of opportunity. For example, in Sweden the State Study Assistance Committee recently proposed increasing the amount of aid for secondary school pupils, on the grounds that it was at this stage that pupils faced crucial choices determining their future careers (SOU 1980). in Canada, a Federal-Provincial Task Force on student assistance concluded 'while economic factors are important barriers to accessibility, these barriers operate less at the point of entrance to post-secondary education than at earlier stages. ... This means that student aid, which operates mainly at, or above, the point of entrance, is a relatively weak tool in encouraging participation' (Council of Ministers, Canada 1980).

In the US also, evaluations of student aid are pessimistic about the effectiveness of student aid in equalizing opportunities: 'While a great amount of effort has been expended to enhance equality of educational opportunity, the disadvantaged and poor are only slightly more likely to be in college than they were ten years ago' (Congressional Budget Office 1979). The reason for the pessimism is that many studies have shown that student aid will not, by itself, ensure an increase in participation of low-income students. The Canadian Task Force concluded that 'student aid programs were necessary but not sufficient in society's overall efforts to increase the participation of students from lower income families' (Council of Ministers, Canada 1980, p. 106).

In that case, does it matter whether aid is given in the form of a loan or a grant? The Canadian Task Force concluded that 'There is growing, but not conclusive evidence that the form which aid takes may not be especially important to increasing participation (Council of Ministers, Canada 1980, p. 99). Certainly there is no evidence that loans necessarily deter low-income students, or women. In all the countries where loans are available, women and low-income students are willing to borrow. What matters are the terms of the loan, especially the degree of subsidy and the repayment terms. It is perfectly possible to devise a loan scheme, such as the Swedish system, which provides a long repayment period and automatic protection for those who cannot repay the loan because of low incomes, sickness or unemployment. This does not act as a disincentive to students, and need not lead to administrative problems and high default rates, as the opponents of loans have suggested. The American loan programmes have experienced very high default rates, partly because lenders had few incentives to minimize default rates because of the terms of the federal government guarantee, partly because there are no automatic provisions for postponement such as exist in Sweden. However, the last few years have seen vigorous attempts to reduce default rates in the US and these have been quite successful.

LESSONS FROM ABROAD

International experience suggests, therefore, that loan schemes can and do work, but that they seem most successful when combined with grants. In other words, it is a mistake to view student loans and grants as alternatives. A combination of grants and subsidized loans offers a more flexible means of supporting students than a system which relies exclusively on either.

There are no dramatic savings to be made from introducing loans. All the evidence from other countries suggests that unless a loan scheme imposes considerable repayment burdens on graduates, it will not be fully self financing. In the US the cost of interest subsidies amounts to about half the total size of the average student loan, over its ten-year life. On the other hand, in the long run the savings can be significant. In Sweden, for example, loan repayments in 1981-82 amounted to twenty-five per cent of total expenditure on loans, and were roughly equal to the expenditure on grants for adults taking short courses of retraining. The fact that past generations of students are repaying loans does, therefore, free public funds for alternative uses and makes it possible to reallocate the student aid budget in favour of secondary school pupils and adults. For this reason the majority of Swedish students accept that loans are an equitable form of financial support and the president of the Swedish NUS is on record as saying: 'The great majority of Swedish students want to maintain the loan system, we think it works very well ... we see education as an investment in our own future, and it's only natural that we should pay for that investment ourselves' (Wessberg 1980).

In addition, if loans are provided by commercial banks, as in Canada or the US, rather than by a state agency, as in Sweden, this would reduce public expenditure by limiting the government's role to guaranteeing loans and paying interest subsidies, rather than providing the full cost of student support. Given the present government's determination to reduce the public sector borrowing requirement this has obvious appeal. However, the US experience shows that it is all too easy to underestimate the costs of interest subsidies at a time of high market rates of interest. One American economist, criticizing the high costs of interest subsidies said: 'At its inception in the late 1960s the privately capitalized GSL program appeared remarkably low cost. ... The appearance of frugality, however, was achieved primarily by deferring very substantial costs of interest subsidies and default coverage to the future. Now, more than a decade later, that future has become the present' (Dresch 1980). In fact, the costs of interest subsidies and default rose from $100 million in 1970 to

$2,425 million in 1981, which is why eligibility for subsidized loans has been drastically reduced in 1982.

Certainly it would cost the government less to subsidize banks to lend to students than to lend directly. On the other hand, if banks are required to lend to students, other potential customers may be squeezed out, in times of credit restrictions, and American experience shows that banks may have to be given considerable incentives to participate, although there is now no shortage of banks willing to lend to students in the US.

However, the cost of these incentives, which includes a 'special allowance' to banks, and the creation of a secondary market in student loans (the Student Loan Marketing Association, known as Sallie Mae) is considerable.

There have been a number of problems with student loan schemes, including high default rates, which has already been mentioned, and the problem of the escalating cost of interest subsidies. When the present systems of student loans were first introduced in the 1960s interest rates were low and to charge graduates interest of three per cent was perfectly reasonable. Now that interest rates are so much higher, governments have a choice between charging a realistic rate of interest (the latest student loans introduced last year in the US charged fourteen per cent) or paying substantial subsidies (Swedish graduates pay four per cent). Inflation has brought further problems, and several countries have discovered the dangers of an open-ended commitment to student support such as exists in the case of 'entitlement' programmes, such as the GSLP in the US, which until last year gave a general entitlement to subsidized loans, or the Swedish study support system which is still built on the principle of entitlement, in the same way as the system of mandatory awards in Britain. There have been problems with loans, just as there can be problems with a system of grants, but the experience of many countries shows that these problems are not insuperable. Student loans can and do work.

What the experience of other countries does show, very clearly, is that it is possible to design student aid systems to satisfy a number of different objectives, but that the costs of student support will be largely determined by the degree of selectivity. For example, the abolition of the means test in the US after MISAA in 1978 has an enormous impact on the demand for student loans: it probably stimulated overall demand for higher education, and it certainly allowed students greater freedom of choice by permitting them to pay high tuition fees by means of highly subsidized loans, but it led to a very rapid escalation of federal government expenditure on interest subsidies. The re-imposition of an income ceiling in 1982 will certainly cut public expenditure but it will also deprive many students of financial support. The crucial question is the effectiveness of a more selective system. Many Americans have argued that it will be more effective because it will ensure that public funds are concentrated on the most needy. The abolition of the means test was in fact criticized as creating 'the real danger that federal benefits will drift increasingly towards the relatively well-off at the expense of the poor and neediest' (Gladieux 1980, p. 2).

FUTURE OPTIONS
In 1981-82 the cost of all forms of student support in England and Wales is estimated to be £912 million. Fees accounted for forty-three per cent of this, and maintenance costs were fifty-seven per cent or just over £500 million. The bulk of this expenditure goes to full-time students in universities and advanced FE. Part-time students and those taking non-advanced courses receive very little support, and secondary school pupils who stay at school after sixteen receive very little. In 1980-81 total expenditure on EMAs was only £4.4 million. If these priorities are to change, and more generous support is provided for sixteen to nineteen-year-olds, for students taking non-designated courses and part-time students, including mature students, the additional costs will be considerable. If, in addition, the means test were to be abolished, and the real value of student grants allowed to keep pace with prices, this would further increase the burden on public funds. Few estimates have been made of the costs of extending the present system of student support, but some very rough calculations will give some idea of possible orders of magnitude.

The cheapest reform would be simply to provide full-value mandatory grants for all those taking non-designated courses of advanced higher education. It has been estimated that this would cost about £16 million. If part-time students, including those taking Open University courses, were to have their fees paid in full about £40 million would be added to the student support bill. If the 70,000 students receiving lesser-value discretionary awards in 1979-80 had received full-value maintenance awards, averaging £1,000, instead of the lesser-value awards, the additional cost would have been £60 million. The value of parental contributions for mandatory award holders in 1979-80 was £95 million. If the means test had been abolished for all students holding both full-value and lesser-value awards, the cost would have been at least £120 million in 1979. In 1978 the cost of providing means-tested EMAs for all pupils over the compulsory school leaving age was estimated at £110 million for England and Wales (Maclure 1979). To have extended student support to all young people over the age of sixteen and to have abolished the means test would, therefore, have increased the cost of student maintenance by at least fifty per cent.

By 1982-83 it is estimated that the real value of student grants will be approximately twenty per cent below the value in 1962-63 because the level of grant has not kept pace with inflation. If this were to be rectified, and students in 1982 given the same purchasing power as their counterparts twenty years ago, the cost of student support would increase by about £125 million.

None of these calculations takes into account the additional demand for higher education that could be generated by more generous student support. The DES has estimated the effect of various economic variables on the demand for higher education using data for 1966-78, and concluded that an increase of ten per cent in the real value of the average maintenance award would increase demand in the university sector by three per cent and in the public sector (teacher training and advanced FE) by nearly five per cent (Dolphin 1981). There is no evidence to suggest what would be the cumulative effect of all the changes proposed. In any case, the experience between 1966 and 1978 suggests that demand for higher education is more responsive to changes in graduate starting salaries than changes in the real value of student maintenance awards or earnings foregone (Dolphin 1981; Pissarides 1982). The effect of an increase in the level of student support would, therefore, depend on other variables, particularly the labour market for graduates and school-leavers.

Even though it is impossible to be precise about the likely costs of extending student support these rough estimates show, all too clearly, the enormous costs of attempting to satisfy all the various demands for improvement simultaneously. It would be possible to restore the real purchasing power of student grants, to extend support to those taking part-time or non-advanced courses, to provide EMAs for all pupils beyond the compulsory leaving age and to abolish the means test. However, the combined effects of all these changes would probably be to double the student support bill.

On the other hand, there have been various proposals to reduce expenditure on student support, for example by the introduction of cash limits on LEA expenditure on awards or limiting mandatory awards to two, rather than three years, both of which were discussed in the educational press last year, when the Public Accounts Committee drew attention to the dangers of an open-ended commitment on student aid expenditure.

Clearly, all these proposals, whether for increases or reductions in expenditure, raise the question of priorities. For example, if a limited amount of money were available, should it be used to encourage participation by mature students as Squires suggested in the SRHE Leverhulme seminar on access, or should it be used for EMAs for working-class pupils as Gordon suggested (Fulton 1981)? Conversely, if eligibility were to be reduced, where should the cuts fall? The logic of the argument also points very clearly in the direction of student loans. The Swedish system of student support does, in fact, automatically link the amount of student aid with the cost-of-living index, it provides basic grants for all sixteen to nineteen-year-olds in schools and it provides aid for part-time as well as full-time students in all forms of higher education, including short courses for adults; students over the age of twenty are regarded as financially independent and there are no upper age limits for eligibility. However, more than half of all student support is in the form of loans, and in the case of university students the proportion is ninety per cent. The fact that Swedish graduates can repay their loans up to their fiftieth birthday in normal cases (up to their sixtieth in the case of older students), and the fact that those whose income falls below a fixed minimum are automatically allowed to postpone repayment means that the burden of debt is not regarded as a problem by most graduates and the idea of a 'negative dowry' does not deter female students.

Such a system could not be introduced immediately in Britain without drastically changing both the private costs of education and demand. However it would be possible to move gradually in that direction by introducing a small loan element for mandatory award holders, and then increasing the loan in relation to the grant in subsequent years, at the same time making loans available to additional groups of students. In Sweden loans have increased as a proportion of total student aid from seventy-five per cent in 1965 to ninety per cent in 1981, but this has been accompanied by an increase in grants for sixteen to nineteen-year-olds and for adults (which are partly financed by a special payroll tax).

In Britain the introduction of loans might begin at a more modest level, with perhaps twenty-five per cent of the mandatory award being given as a loan, which would mean about £400 a year for students outside London in 1982-83 and £475 for students in London. This would mean that about £125 million of the £500 million currently spent on maintenance grants would be converted to loans, and if the proportion of loan to grant were to rise, then as much as £200 to £250 million (in constant prices) would eventually be lent to students each year.

The advantage of a mixed system of grants and loans is that it provides a much more flexible form of student support than one based on grants alone, since the proportions of grant and loan can be varied, together with the rate of interest on loans and repayment terms. In the US for example, low-income students pay a lower rate of interest than those with a higher level of family income. However, the American experience also underlines the dangers of an open-ended commitment to subsidized loans. The extension of loan subsidies in 1978 to all students regardless of income, together with rising interest rates, meant that the costs of GSLP loans to the federal government rose from $670 million in 1978 to $2,425 million in 1981 and would have been $3,400 by 1983 if drastic cuts in eligibility had not been imposed. In other words, the cost of subsidizing student loans can, unless controlled, impose considerable burdens on public funds.

Unfortunately, it is not practicable to present estimates here of the costs and potential savings of various types of loan programme, because there are so many variables, including the rate of interest, the length of repayment, likely rates of default or postponement. It is possible to devise a model to calculate the costs of different loan proposals, with different assumptions about interest rates, repayment terms and administrative costs. An American model calculated the cost per $1,000 borrowed of six different loan proposals, including an income-contingent loan scheme, where graduates would pay a fixed proportion of their income each year, and a graduated payment loan, where repayments would increase over time. When these loan proposals were compared with the two existing loan programmes the model showed that the cost to the federal government per $1,000 loan could vary from $191 to $861, according to the assumptions and terms of repayment, while the two existing programmes involve subsidies of $456 and $596 per $1,000 loan. This shows clearly why subsidized loans have been described as 'hidden grants', and it also shows that rough estimates of the potential savings of loans which underestimate interest subsidies may be seriously misleading. If banks were to lend £200 million a year to students, as suggested above, then we cannot simply assume that loan repayments would eventually equal £200 million a year. At least half of this, or more, might be needed to pay interest subsidies; what we need to know is the present value of future loan repayments and interest.

Although it is not possible to make accurate estimates of the costs or savings that would result from the introduction of loans, it is clear that student support based on a combination of loans and grants could be more flexible than a system of grants alone, and it could also be more equitable than the present system in Britain, which favours mandatory award holders at the expense of those taking other forms of education or training.

The last few years have seen a dramatic shift of emphasis and resources towards training for the unemployed, through the growth of TOPS and YOP, and now the Youth Training Scheme, to be introduced in 1983, extends this further, by offering all unemployed school-leavers a full year's preparation for work, in the form of training plus work experience. However, this underlines the need for a comprehensive system of support for students and young people in full-time or part-time education, in order to ensure that young people are not tempted away from school by the prospect of a training allowance.

If students were given £400 a year in the form of a loan, rather than a grant, then loan repayments could be used to help finance grants for younger students, although it would take some years before the repayment of past loans could provide a significant proportion of the costs of such a scheme, and, as already emphasized, interest subsidies would reduce the value of loan repayments.

Alternatively, the repayment of student loans could be used to finance a relaxation of the means test, for example by bringing forward the age of independence from twenty-five to twenty-one. A loan scheme could increase student independence in other ways too, by allowing students who change their minds about courses or careers to finance a second course of study by means of a loan. There are many different options which would have to be carefully costed and compared. One thing is clear from recent experience in Britain and abroad: governments are no longer willing to enter into open-ended commitments.

What is really important is to break away from the strait-jacket of thinking of student support in terms of loans or grants. A combination of loans and grants would recognize that higher education brings benefits both to society and to individual students, by ensuring that both the taxpayer and the student share the costs of student support. The NUS implicitly accepted this in its Grants Memorandum for 1978-79, even though it was explicit in its opposition to loans: 'Unlike other forms of indirect taxation where the person paying the tax benefits from goods and services received, the parent paying the parental contribution is not doing so on the assumption of personal benefit or gain. It is society as a whole and the student in particular who benefits from the "purchase" of education. Society benefits through the provision of skilled and educated individuals who apply their learning directly or indirectly to the benefit of the community. Students benefit personally by increasing their earnings potential through the acquisition of qualifications' (NUS 1979, p. 8). After this faultless statement of the facts, NUS followed with an amazing non sequitur: 'Thus it is central to NUS's policy that full non-means tested grants must be paid for out of direct taxation.'

If, instead, the NUS were to follow the logic of its own argument, it would be arguing for a mixture of grants and loans that would be sufficiently flexible and adaptable to cope with changing patterns of demand, changing labour market and economic conditions and changing patterns of provision and institutional structure in higher education. It is time to abandon sterile arguments about loans or grants, and concentrate the future debate on questions such as:

i The desirable level of subsidy for different courses and different groups of students.
ii The most appropriate mechanisms for student support: ie what combination of grant, subsidized loan, or even work-study opportunities would be most suitable for different students, including part-time as well as full-time and mature as well as nineteen to twenty-one year-old students.
iii The terms and conditions of loans: ie who should provide the capital, a government agency or commercial banks; what should be the rate of interest; what kind of 'insurance' element is necessary to protect the low-paid, or those without a job; what should be the repayment period; should repayment be variable with respect to income level (ie income-contingent loans or traditional mortgage-type loans)?

If such questions are tackled now, our student support system, which was designed in the 1950s and 1960s, can grow and develop in response to the needs of the 1980s and 1990s.

REFERENCES

Blaug, M. (1972) *An Introduction to the Economics of Education* Harmondsworth: Penguin Books

Congressional Budget Office (1979) *Federal Assistance for Post Secondary Education: Options for Fiscal Year 1979 Budget Issue Paper for Fiscal Year 1979* Washington: Congress of the US

Council of Ministers of Education, Canada and Secretary of State (1980) *Report of the Federal-Provincial Task Force on Student Assistance* Toronto: Council of Ministers of Education and Secretary of State

Department of Education (1960) *Grants to Students* Cmnd 1051. London: HMSO

Department of Education and Science (DES) (1978) *Discretionary Awards 1975/76 to 1977/78: A Report of a DES Survey* London: DES

Department of Education and Science (DES) (1981) *Grants to Students: A Brief Guide* London: DES

Dolphin, A.M. (1981) The demand for higher education *Employment Gazette* July 302-5

Dresch, S. (1980) Financial and behavioural implications of federal student loan programs and proposals. In Tuckman, H.P. and Whalen, E. (Editors) *Subsidies to Higher Education: The Issues* New York: Praeger

Expenditure Committee (1974) Third Report (Session 1974) *Educational Maintenance Allowances in the 16-18 Years Age Group* London: HMSO

Fulton, O. (1981) (Editor) *Access to Higher Education* Guildford: SRHE

Gladieux, L. (1980) What has Congress wrought? *Change* 12 (7)

Hansard (10 Feb. 1981) *House of Commons Official Report* London: HMSO

HE (1963) Committee on Higher Education (Chairman, Lord Robbins) *Higher Education Report* Cmnd 2154. London: HMSO

Killeen, J. and Bird, M. (1981) *Education and Work: A Study of Paid Educational Leave in England and Wales 1976/77* London: National Institute for Adult Education

Labour Party(1982) *16-19: Learning for Life* A Labour Party Discussion Document. London: The Labour Party

Lewis, A., Sandford, C. and Thomson, N. (1980) *Grants or Loans?* London: Institute of Economic Affairs

Maclure, S. (1979) Financial support for the 16-18s *Education Policy Bulletin* 7 (1) 99-124

Manpower Services Commission (1978) *TOPS Review* London: MSC

Maynard, A. (1975) *Experiment with Choice in Education* London: Institute of Economic Affairs

National Union of Students (NUS) (1975) *The 1975 Annual Review: Grants Memorandum* London: NUS

National Union of Students (NUS) (1979) *The 1978-9 Annual Review: Grants Memorandum* London: NUS

National Union of Students (NUS) (1980) *The Case Against Student Loans* London: NUS

National Union of Students (NUS) (1981) *Submission from the Executive Committee of the NUS to the DES concerning the Review of the Education (Mandatory Awards) Regulations* London: NUS

National Union of Students (NUS) (1982a) *NUS Grants Special* London: NUS

National Union of Students (NUS) (1982b) *NUS Student Accommodation Costs Survey* London: NUS

Office of Population Censuses and Surveys (OPCS) (1979a) *Undergraduate Income and Expenditure* London: HMSO

Office of Population Censuses and Surveys (OPCS) (1979b) *Postgraduate Income and Ependiture* London: HMSO

Pissarides, C.A. (1982) From School to University: The Demand for Post-Compulsory Education in Britain *Economic Journal* September

Robbins, L. (1980) *Higher Education Revisited* London: Macmillan

Wessberg, H.G. (1980) Text of a speech by Hans Gustav Wessberg, President, Swedish National Union of Students, mimeo.

Woodhall, M. (1970 *Student Loans: A Review of Experience in Scandinavia and Elsewhere* London: G. Harrap

Woodhall, M. (1978) *Review of Student Support Schemes in Selected OECD Countries* Paris: OECD

Woodhall, M. (1982) *Student Loans: Lessons from Recent International Experience* London: Policy Studies Institute

5

NEW MODELS FOR FUNDING UNIVERSITIES

by Peter Moore

INTRODUCTION

Over the past sixty years since the University Grants Committee (UGC) was established in 1919 universities in the UK have grown in student numbers by a factor of about eight (see Table 5.1) and the number of institutions involved has roughly doubled. Universities are nowadays big business, with a total turnover of about £1½ billion per annum, employing nearly 100,000 people, a third of them highly skilled academic staff.

This chapter concerns possible scenarios for the future financing of universities and I must, for brevity, leave to others the case for university level education, not just in science, technology and medicine, but also in the arts and social sciences. Universities are not merely the repositories of knowledge, they are the progenitors of new knowledge and the last decade has demonstrated well the difficulty of predicting precisely future national needs for skilled and knowledgable manpower. The views expressed here are personal only, and in no way commit or bind any institution.

EXISTING PRACTICE

Before the Second World War fees, donations and endowments formed the basis of university financing but the enormous expansion since 1945, particularly since 1958 or thereabouts, has dramatically changed the picture so that direct (or one remove) government finance has dominated the scene. The strategic importance of the UGC's buffer role in the relationship between the universities and government has correspondingly increased. The basis of the system used (until 1977) was the quinquennial approach by which the total UGC grant was fixed for a five-year period (broken down into the separate years). This sum was in turn allocated to individual universities in line with plans jointly agreed with universities both as to overall student numbers and broad subject breakdowns (traditionally arts, sciences and medicine). A further condition imposed on universities was that the budget expenditure for the final year of the quinquennium should not exceed the sum actually allocated for that year.

This system took the universities through the big expansion of the sixties and early seventies, reaching 235,000 students by 1972 and with confident expectations of being asked to reach 350,000 by 1982. Indeed long-term planning targets for the various universities had this total as background and, although large amounts of additional capital expenditure would have been required to meet them, the planning groundwork existed for a total system of that size. The expansion was, by any standards, an immense achievement by both the universities and the UGC, and received wide acclaim at home and abroad. In terms of manpower planning as between subjects the pace of expansion itself enabled changes in subject balance to be readily achieved — increases in one subject did not require off-setting reductions elsewhere.

By 1972, however, signs of financial stress were starting to emerge; rising costs were not always fully compensated, and the first year of the new quinquennium was given a provisional allocation only, with no firm base for further planning. The white paper of February 1973 was less harsh than expected, although it involved a modest reduction in unit of resource per student by 1977. But the energy crisis of late 1973 led to further squeezes in revenue, and a cut of about half in the existing rate of capital expenditure. The quinquennial form of settlement was effectively abandoned with universities being put on a basis of annual allocations with strict cash limits on their expenditure.

Student numbers rose slowly but steadily until 1979, when in August of that year the so-called level funding policy was introduced, combined with economic fees for all future overseas students. It was clear that the target population for universities (which had been put at 312,500 in early 1979) would now be unattainable and a figure of around 300,000 seemed to be the likely limit on the financing expected. Allocations were being made on a year-by-year basis. In late 1980 and early 1981 the government announced plans to reduce the expenditure on universities in real terms by 8½ per cent over a three-year period. This reduction had to be coupled with the withdrawal of the overseas students proportion of total recurrent income plus fees, a sum that was virtually impossible to replace in its entirety due to world competition from subsidized institutions in other countries. Combined, the two changes implied a cut in the system as a whole of about 15 per cent of total income.

This situation proved a watershed, in that the UGC was forced to cut allocations (and hence staff, which form about 70 per cent of costs) and, to preserve standards and research opportunities for staff, to limit home student numbers to some 5 per cent below the 1979-80 level. In reaching its decisions the UGC's thinking was primarily directed by consideration of the availability of subjects within the system, using this to determine the size and shape of individual universities. Inevitably the decisions pleased few and infuriated many, but the change from a student number-led system to a finance-led system, albeit at a lower level than hitherto, could not be other than painful. Undergraduate intakes are still in the process of being cut and, whilst some priority has been given to science, engineering and medicine, the total number of home graduates produced by universities will start to fall in 1984 and plateau (on present reckoning) some 8 per cent below the 1981 level in about five years time.

DETERMINING NEEDS

Higher education is expensive and, since the government currently foots virtually all the bill, it is inevitable that the role of manpower planning in the financing of universities is a matter of public concern. Some countries, such as Singapore, have rigid manpower planning targets set by government for the university sector on a subject by subject basis. Others, such as France or the United States, have a more relaxed student-led approach, except possibly in expensive subjects like medicine. The UK is in the middle of the spectrum in that, whilst its approach has been primarily student-led, governments have been firm in some areas like medicine and have tried to exhort universities to work against student inclinations (or possibly in advance of them) in subjects like science or engineering, whilst the UGC has discouraged overreaction, eg in the case of new law schools following the Ormerod report.

There are three major interrelated problems in manpower planning for universities. First, to plan and mount a new degree level course and to obtain graduates from it requires a minimum of five years, and can require as much as seven or eight years. Secondly, to forecast manpower demands five to eight years ahead is not easy, particularly for highly specialized fields. Moreover, there is a clear need to distinguish between stock and flow. Thus if a total shortage of 400 in a stock of 1,000 scientists in zootanology is met by an increased flow of, say, 100 new scientists per annum the situation rapidly leads to a gross over-supply, a situation that occurred with chemists in the sixties. Thirdly, the input of feedstock in terms of students with appropriate entry qualifications has to be there to undertake the courses planned. This imposes limitations on, for example, the students who can enter numerately based degree courses.

If industry, commerce and indeed government clamour for new specialized skills, the need for which has only just been appreciated, there will be cases in which the need cannot be met quickly from new graduates, but must be met more by conversion of existing graduates with related skills.

Forecasts currently made are of two kinds. For the first, the number of qualified 'A' level students who are likely to present themselves year by year for higher education at universities is estimated. The second type of forecast relates to the expected supply of places in different subject areas. The former is attempted regularly by the DES and others and the results have not been conspicuously successful. In the sixties actual demand exceeded forecasts, whilst in the seventies the position was reversed. Currently demand clearly exceeds supply and it is the mix of demand that is more important than the total numbers.

In the long run it is not clear whether the intention is to limit university places according to estimates of qualified manpower needs, or to allow student demand to fix the total size, combined with a 'broad steer' concept to decide upon proportions of different subjects. The USSR and Singapore both use (!) the former approach and, by restricting total entry, accept intense competition for entry across the board; France rations Grandes Ecoles places, but allows virtually unlimited supply in universities. The United States effectively has a hierarchy of institutions and this allows all potential students to find some appropriate level of higher education. Dangers in following qualified manpower demand forecasts too closely are clear, and British experience with doctors in the late fifties, with chemists in the sixties, and teacher training colleges in the seventies all illustrate these dangers.

A conceptual problem does indeed arise concerning the meaning to be attached to national needs. A first meaning is measurable from employers' past demands for manpower of different skills combined with attempts to project these figures into the future. A second meaning assumes there are certain needs that go beyond employer bids for labour; that if only employers would employ more Russian speakers or historians, or whatever the individual conceives of as important, the country would be more prosperous or happier, or benefit in some other way. In this sense manpower planning is a subjective concept and therefore unmeasurable on a global basis.

There is already some mismatching in the compromise position in which universities find themselves with the current shortage of university places in terms of those who desire, and are able to cope with, a university first degree course. Because of various pressures on the UGC (not just from government) and the universities there are national expectations in certain broad bands of subjects that do not precisely match student desires. The consequence is that average 'A' level scores (admittedly not the only or best indicator of suitability for admission) vary greatly from subject to subject and, ironically, some of the subjects that government and employers are keenest on encouraging are those for which potential students have 'A' levels at the lower end of the range of scores. Moreover, employment figures show that substantial numbers of those who graduate in the favoured areas, eg scientists and engineers, do not enter employments that use directly these specific subject skills. Hence even the translation of manpower planning into universities must necessarily be of a broad-based nature. A good degree course should, by making a student look at a subject in depth and understand its theories, teach him to think, to be knowledgable and to be adaptable. If, say, a student of gas technology has learnt solely the facts about gas, he may be unemployable if the industry for which he has trained does not subsequently want him. A scientifically trained mind can, however, be used in a variety of different ways.

The conclusions that I draw from this analysis are twofold. First, that whilst universities cannot plan to meet precise national needs on a year-by-year basis, they should not and cannot depart for long from what student demand suggests. Secondly we should be cautious in making first degrees too specialized in a technological as opposed to an educational sense.

BACKGROUND

Universities are autonomous institutions, having their own charters and degree-giving powers, and able to take their own decisions over a wide spectrum. In these respects they differ from institutions on the other side of the binary line. They carry out many activities for which they do not receive direct goverment funding: eg the teaching of overseas students, carrying out much research with the aid of various research grants, conducting post-experience courses, etc. Such activities account for as little as 10 per cent of income in some univeristies but up to nearly 50 per cent in some specialized universities. Hence the overwhelming bulk of university income comes from the government through recurrent grants via the UGC and from tuition fees, the majority of home undergraduate fees being effectively paid through public sources. Conversely, there are many conditions that are common to all universities: for example, the salary scales paid to academic staff, the three-term year with the summer vacation (with a few exceptions), and the basic three-year Honours degree (except in Scotland). Because of the commonality of funding mechanisms universities are possibly not as innovative as they might be, eg in considering seriously the possibility of a four-term/two-year degree option.

In considering alternative financial scenarios, it is important to distinguish between four distinct meanings of increased private support of universities, since the term is used somewhat indiscriminately. The first meaning is where more work is done outside the normal degree-type work and is paid for by non-public money of one kind or another. This gears up the possible level of university activity, enabling it to have a wider range of academic skills and research work. The second is where a company or other donor gives money to found a chair, say, in some subject which enables the university to start work in a new area and enrich its overall teaching and research activities. Generally these gifts are for a limited period. After that period the university would, if it wished to retain that activity, have to include it in its normal budget and hence, on present procedures, would look to public funds to support its continuation.

The third way in which extra funds could be generated is through alumni contributions on a continuing basis, along the lines common in US private universities. Whilst achievement of any significant sums in this way would undoubtedly need further changes in taxation rules, it would also require a fundamental shift in attitudes since universities are seen as public, not private institutions. Moreover, older established universities would have marked advantages over newer universities.

The fourth and final way in which less dependence upon public funds could occur would be for individual students (or their parents) to pay directly a greater proportion of the total cost than occurs at present. To have any reasonable chance of achieving such a change wold require two changes in Treasury attitudes. First, interest (and possibly capital) borrowed for educational purposes would have to rank as eligible for tax relief.

Secondly, money raised directly through graduate taxes or similar schemes would have to be credited to the university system and not taken into the general Treasury income acount.

When university students were few in number, the costs involved were not too important in relation to the economy as a whole and not a contentious issue. As demand (and need) for university level education has risen, it is perhaps only natural that availability of finance has been more closely linked to availability of public finance generally and squeezes have occurred which are likely to continue into the foreseeable future. Hence any scenario for the future has to bear in mind the vulnerability of funding systems depending heavily on public financing. If it were possible to introduce further private money into the system, this should ideally be supplementary, not substitutive. To be supplementary would imply giving universities an undertaking that any such additional sums raised would not be taken into account in deciding upon the level of public support for its basic teaching and research work. If this were not done, the alternative would be for some formula-based common level of support to be fixed, and to allow institutions to supplement this as best they could. Teaching facilities for students under such an arrangement could vary amongst universities, and between subjects.

Two further points are important. First, the current system leads to understandable frustration both inside and outside universities in that good quality home students have to be turned away who could come if they were from overseas (admittedly at a higher fee). This seems to many to be illogical. Secondly, the current student grant system with its mandatory grants virtually puts an automatic bar on any alleviation of the present position, unless outside funds are introduced, since the cash limit includes both the recurrent grant and the student grant. Any extra flexibility for one university could only be at the expense of another.

ALTERNATIVE MODELS
The possible financial models given below are in outline form only in order to concentrate discussion on the principles involved in each. The earlier models are close to existing practice whilst the later models assume a greater degree of financial autonomy of the individual institution and involve correspondingly increasing dependence upon non-government forms of finance. The models would not necessarily have to operate in isolation, and combinations could be considered.

Model A
Model A assumes basic maintenance of the system in operation in the 1970s and earlier, whereby quinquennial block grant from the government enabled both the UGC and the universities to plan over a five-year period. Recent events have underlined the desirability of such a planning period if the optimum use in national terms is to be made of resources available to

TABLE 5.1
Students in full-time higher education: Great Britain 1900-1980

	Universities (k)	All higher education (k)
1900-01	20	25
1924-25	42	61
1938-39	50	69
1954-55	82	122
1962-63	118	216
1967-68	206	387
1972-73	247	482
1979-80	301	525

Approximately 10 per cent of the students came from overseas, the majority from Commonwealth countries

universities. Such a time-scale enables universities to put forward well thought-out plans to the UGC for co-ordination although, if the future is to continue to be finance-led, there would necessarily have to be some iterative procedure to match individual university plans with the national limitation on funds. The advantage of this approach is the degree of protection and certainty it gives to the universities; the disadvantage is that in times of shortage of funds it would leave little room for manoeuvre between the quinquennial settlements.

Since the war universities have basically been expanding about as quickly as they each realistically could do, and hence relatively few instances occurred of cut-backs of aspirations. The main cause of concern was the steady lowering of the unit of resource by an average 1 per cent per annum through the seventies decade. The position now is rather different with a tight cash limit approach — linked to existing rather than potential national prosperity — and the prospect soon of some years of diminishing cohorts of 18-year-olds. In these circumstances a form of rolling quinquennial, or triennial, planning might be more acceptable to all concerned as allowing greater flexibility.

Model B

Model B supposes a form of formula financing as used in a number of countries (eg Canada) for national universities. Indeed it has been argued (Cook 1976) that the UGC already does it by formula. Professor G.A. Barnard, a then member of the UGC, refuted this assertion (Barnard 1977) but it is likely that there is some marked association between student numbers and recurrent grants. Under this arrangement a set of figures would be decided upon centrally for the grant (plus fee) to be made available for each undergraduate and postgraduate student, possible broken down by broad subject areas. Each institution would then be given a set of target student numbers and the associated total grant. The formula grant would have to include some element of immediate or foreseeable capital expenditure on behalf of the student place — a not negligible amount. Presumably the grant would be docked if numbers were below the target, and might possibly be also docked if numbers of undergraduates were above the target, unless the student grant problem had been resolved. Some form of oversight would still be required to ensure that the education offered in each university was up to the desired standard.

The principal advantage of this approach is its simplicity and apparent equity; disadvantages are that it is rather inflexible and takes little account of the different physical needs of universities (eg the age and condition of their estate) and of the very different resource bases required in the different universities under the so-called dual funding approach for basic research. Salaries scales, for example, could also differ from university to university. The danger would be that the formula rates fixed would be more appropriate to the current less expensive universities, thus levelling down the resource base, rather than the converse. In any event a gradual move to such a system would have to be carried out to avoid creation of some disorder in the system.

There is little room under this scheme, as was also the case in Model A, for universities to act in a market mechanism way and demonstrate their competitive advantages. If universities were to take extra students the fees charged could be a contentious issue. Presumably the fees would be at least at marginal cost but if they continued to be below average cost over a period, the Government might feel that this indicated the formula fees had been fixed at too high a level.

Model C

In Model C the normal recurrent grant (plus fees) allocations to universities include a substantial element providing what is commonly referred to as the research floor. There is no defined fraction specified for this purpose, but it is a common rule of thumb that university teachers are expected to devote between a quarter and a third of their time to the pursuit of original investigations and the publication of their results. The consequence of the current approach is that the allocation of this form of research money is effectively linked primarily to undergraduate student numbers at each university. It could be argued that it would be healthy to allocate, say, 85 per cent of current grant primarily on undergraduate student numbers, with the balance allocated against research plans put up by individual universities and linked rather more closely to postgraduate activity generally. Such plans would aim to identify research centres of excellence within the universities together with the promotion of new initiatives. These funds would necessarily have to be earmarked or indicated, and the model would thus imply some loss of sovereignty by individual universities, although all would be free to bid for these resources.

Model D

The three previous models have all envisaged an allocation to universities of a fixed number of home student places to fit the maximum financial commitment which the government is prepared to make. They all suffer from two basic dilemmas. First, the total number of places in the system is effectively fixed and, secondly, the allocation of places to individual universities has perforce to be made centrally. To relax the former restriction requires the injection of further money and is discussed in later models; the latter restriction could be overcome by a system whereby a student obtains a voucher to cover his fees and associated recurrent grant (and his student grant) and then takes his voucher to a university of his choice that is willing to take him. The number of vouchers would be the same as the total student numbers planned for centrally, and there would likewise have to be a central system for awarding the vouchers to individuals. Since the numbers involved would be extremely large it would be difficult to do it other than by competitive examination performance (as effectively occurs now in some other countries).

Such a scheme would introduce greater flexibility as between universities, but it would require them to cope with changes in numbers or subject mix on a routine basis. It would be possible to increase the number of vouchers by restricting their value to a level below the full programme cost: eg by making them cover a maximum of three years of university study only, leaving students to find the balance from other sources. Subjects considered to be in the national interest could, if felt desirable, be encouraged by extra grants or vouchers to increase their popularity.

Model E

The University of Buckingham receives no government grants (although UK undergraduate students normally receive student maintenance awards). In principle more universities could be founded to operate in this way, or alternatively some existing universities could opt out of the government system and become private institutions in this sense. This would be a drastic step for them to take voluntarily, and would seem only practicable if some sweetener were offered to such universities in the form of a large endowment for scholarship funds, combined with a lengthy changeover period from the existing form of funding to the new form of funding.

Such a change would not of itself guarantee more places overall in the system, unless the money saved by the government were used to provide greater availability elsewhere. One drawback would be that the more able students could aim for the 'free' places, particularly in the expensive subjects, leaving the private institutions to take the remainder. In the United States private universities are, however, sufficiently prestigious to attract able students in preference to the state universities even though they effectively have to pay the full cost. A further drawback is that, with falling cohorts of 18-year-olds in the middle and late eighties, the financial risks attendant on such a switch could be high for the universities concerned.

Model F
In strict economic terms the current cash shortfall in universities, as between the level of activity they are currently carrying out in terms of student numbers and what they collectively feel is desirable under the original Robbins concept (bearing in mind the other side of the binary line), is equivalent to about £500 per current student place per year. Model F would suggest that sums of this order of magnitude could be found by adjustments to either the fee structure or the student grant system or both, whereby individual students had to contribute slightly more than now (borrowing if necessary) and the block recurrent grant effectively increased by that amount.

One major disadvantage of this model would be the difficulty of determining where the line should be drawn between the funds to be made available by the government and the contribution to be expected from the student, once the current principles for student grant determination had been breached. (They have been marginally breached already by making the full maintenance award lower than the estimated costs of attendance.) Moreover, the model is likely to put more financial onus on students in times of high demand than in times of low demand.

Model G
The final model is again based on the voucher system, but would aim this time to provide greater flexibility on total numbers. Under this model universities would be offered, say, a target of 80 per cent of current numbers, with the current rate of grant per student, but would only receive for up to 40 per cent extra students half the rate of normal recurrent grant (and fees). There would be a further undertaking that no penalty would be incurred if outside funds up to some high percentage of the original base grant level were obtained. Students could still get personal grants from the government at normal rates, possibly combined with loan finance. Universities which wished to go further down the scale as a base point, eg to 70 per cent, could do so, but they would not be allowed to go above 120 per cent of original numbers or to obtain more than 50 per cent extra funds in relation to the original recurrent grant position. (The percentages used are only illustrative, not definitive.)

The disadvantage of such a system is that it could in theory reduce the total number of places available. This is unlikely to occur in that the scheme provides an irresistible invitation to all universities to have a range of activity up to some 20 per cent above the basic norm, but only provided that they take some extra students. Thus some expansion of overall numbers is likely at little, or even negative, cost to the Exchequer provided that the original base is set out on a realistic level. The university would be given flexibility in outside fund raising. There would be a problem relating to the provision of capital where the government would presumably only provide initial capital that was consistent with the 80 per cent level and not with the higher levels, but would give within recurrent grant a capital replacement element.

For students, such a system could provide a wider range of choice and free up some of the current problems, but it still has some serious disadvantages in relation to expensive subjects such as medicine and the staffing of universities if demand shifts as between subjects and universities.

COMMENTS AND ISSUES

Universities are extremely complex organizations with a multiplicity of objectives and a strong natural desire to shape their own destiny as far as is practicable. Reconsideration of the financing mechanism has primarily arisen because of the unprecedented financial crisis into which universities have been plunged. This has naturally led many to feel somewhat inhibited in seeking their own salvation. The drawbacks to the present system are broadly seen as threefold. First, it does not appear to give the university sufficient autonomy in deciding its own future. Secondly, many universities do not feel they are currently able to compete sufficiently freely in the market place. Thirdly, there is a widespread view that students who are acceptable and want to come to university are unable to do so, and that this situation should be remedied.

If changes are made to the current financial structures these factors should be borne in mind and it is important that the contemporary situation should not lead to hastily considered alternatives that will not stand the test of time. Greater freedom does, however, imply a need for greater flexibility and it is clear that to be more market oriented inevitably means that new forms of contractual arrangements for staff would necessarily have to be devised to safeguard universities.

The models that have been outlined above are possible instruments to put into effect rather different philosophical approaches to the principles of the financing of universities. To pick one's way through them, five policy issues need to be faced:

i   Should the grant allocation continue, as now, to allocate research money primarily on the basis of undergraduate numbers, or should money for undergraduate teaching be separated from that for postgraduate and research activities?
ii On what basis or bases ought the government to determine its contribution to the activities of universities? How far is the so-called Robbins principle still valid and how does this translate into cash terms?

iii How is the split between universities and other institutions of higher education to be managed? Universities currently produce about 75 per cent of the Bachelors degrees (excluding the Open University) but proportionately more in science based subjects. Is the split to be on input ability or on subject, or on the type of educational experience to be offered?
iv Within universities, how far should provision as between subjects be linked to student demand as opposed to perceived national needs?
v How far within the university system do universities wish to have (or ought they to have) greater autonomy and freedom to compete between each other for students and associated recurrent grant?

If stances on these various issues could be agreed, it would be possible to determine which model, or combination of models, ought to be the most appropriate for the system in the long run. Universities are fundamentally places of inquiry and innovation. They are concerned both with teaching and with research and development. Any financing structure must recognize the dual nature of a university and its need to retain the greatest possible measure of autonomy, but the method or methods by which it is financed play a large role in determining the esteem in which a university is held by the community.

REFERENCES

Barnard, G.A. (1977) How the University Grants Committee determines allocation of recurrent grants — a curious correlation *Journal of the Royal Statistical Society* Series A. 140, 202-9

Cook, R.W. (1976) How the UGC determines allocations of recurrent grants — a curious correlation *Journal of the Royal Statistical Society* Series A. 139, 374-84

6

RESOURCE ALLOCATION WITHIN THE PUBLIC SECTOR

by John Pratt

SUMMARY

The creation of a national body to oversee public sector higher education (PSHE) does not a priori solve the problems of financing the sector: it merely transposes them.

The 1982-83 apportionment of pooled funds incorporates a formula-based system of common and further funding. The former based on unit costs and the latter on past spending levels with a potential for making educational judgements.

Criticism may be levelled at the 1982-3 allocation on the grounds of the data base, technical problems, and judgements and assumptions.

Unit costs are an unsatisfactory measure of cost-effectiveness as they take no account of educational outputs and only relate input to input.

Clarification of the nature of the problem leads us to consider that the basic problem is to meet the educational needs of individuals and the nation as a whole.

The specific problem of how to allocate resources to PSHE can be tackled at a number of levels. The more fundamental the level, the more radical the solution is likely to be.

The specific problem cannot be isolated from the more general problems of providing an education service.

The specific problem of resource allocation is a judgemental one, involving political decisions on competing interests.

The solution has to meet many potentially conflicting criteria such as accountability, fairness, cost-effectiveness, political acceptability, cheapness and the assignment of responsible decision making.

A large number of solution options result from the varied combinations of solution variables of central/local funding, buffer/pooling and varied fee levels.

The allocation of responsibility is a matter of deciding who is best able to formulate problems and who to propose solutions.

A market system of PSHE funding with possibly full cost fees is congruent with government policy.

There is a similarity between student fees and common funding in that both involve per capita payments.

Funds could be allocated by the principles that underpin private sector investment, with a local authority or institution making a reasoned case for funds and a central body assessing its merits and likelihood of success.

Problem-budgeting is a means of relating allocations to problems external to education in accordance with the importance of the problems.

The concept of 'educational value added' can be used to evaluate courses in terms of the most educational change that can be achieved for least cost. Measures of educational change need to be established.

The task of the National Advisory Board for Local Authority Higher Education (NAB) is one of formulating the national problems to which individual institutions will propose educational solutions.

NAB should allocate funds to those institutions which seem best able to solve the problems.

There is no way of ensuring that colleges are educationally effective and efficient. NAB must seek to create an environment in which it is more likely that institutions will help to solve society's problems because it is in their interest.

THE PRESENT SITUATION

The education system established by the 1944 Education Act was 'a national system locally administered' in which, in particular, local education authorities (LEAs) were given the duty (S 41) to 'secure the provision for their area of adequate facilities for further education....'

In the immediate postwar period FE institutions served largely their local areas and LEA institutions were wholly financed by their maintaining authorities. Students from outside the local authority's area were paid for through 'recoupment' from their home authorities. As FE provision expanded recoupment became cumbersome, and a national 'pool' was created in 1958 for all advanced FE (AFE) provided by LEAs. LEAs contributed money to the pool theoretically in relation to the demand they made upon it, estimated from school population figures and non-domestic rateable values. Providing LEAs recouped funds according to their AFE provision estimated on the basis of teaching time devoted to advanced work. A separate pool operated for maintained teacher training institutions. Voluntary colleges of education received direct grant funding from the Department of Education and Science (DES) and from time to time certain institutions (eg the colleges of advanced technology) also became direct grant.

These arrangements operated unchanged in principle for twenty years, surviving even substantial institutional reforms such as the elimination of a separate teacher training sector and the subsequent amalgamation of the AFE and teacher training pools. It is important to note that there was no central government control of the pooling process except for technical work by the Pooling Committee. It was a mechanistic process with all spending decisions being taken at the LEA level, with the aggregate of spending forming the pool total.

The pool was widely criticized; its open-ended nature was said to allow providing LEAs to build up prestigious institutions at little or no cost to themselves; some (Lewis and Allemano 1972, Pratt 1976) criticized it as 'unfair' on both contributing and providing LEAs. Concern was expressed in the report of the Working Group on the Management of Public Sector Higher Education (the Oakes Report of 1978) that although the arrangements for controlling and financing higher education in the maintained sector 'have served well in a period of rapid growth they did not constitute an entirely satisfactory system of management and control and ... their deficiencies and the need for improved mechanisms for planning and controlling expenditure have become increasingly clear' (Oakes 1978).

In 1979 a major change transformed the pool overnight: the decision to impose a cash limit upon the larger part of it from 1980-81. This 'capping' of the pool had major implications for the AFE sector. Decisions on spending taken in the past at LEA level now became effectively the subject of central control. Government sought a decision framework or yardstick with which to compare institutional spending. It was initially decided to use a 'technical' method for allocating the funds and the allocations for the two financial years 1980-81 and 1981-82 involved formulae largely based on past expenditure levels which were widely regarded as unsatisfactory (Knight 1981, CIS 1980). In 1982-83 a unit cost method was used and the principles of this method seem likely to be used for resource allocation for some time into the future.

For the voluntary colleges, similar controls on total spending have been introduced. A new system which fixes the cash total payable to colleges in advance was introduced for 1982-83, and will be continued with modifications to allow in 1983-84 onwards for some competitive bidding between colleges for funds.

At the same time, government has been seeking institutional as well as financial changes. In 1981 discussion was initiated on long-term arrangements for a 'central focus' to 'oversee the financing and management of higher education outside the universities' (DES 1982a). In the meantime, as an 'interim' measure, arrangements were made to establish the National Advisory Body for Local Authority Higher Education (NAB) which started work at the beginning of 1982. From now on, the AFE Pool will be allocated on the advice of the NAB.

IMMEDIATE PROBLEMS

Pooling
The allocation system established in 1982-83 was based on the work of a Study Group on the Management of the AFE Pool (GMP) set up at the DES. It was found that student staff ratios (SSRs) accounted for by far the largest share of observed variations in lecturer costs per student. Other costs such as support services and overheads seemed to be a fairly constant proportion of lecturer costs.

Funds were allocated to LEAs in two stages — 'common funding' was based on a notional SSR and 'further funding' reflected past expenditure levels in institutions. Common funding was calculated by determining notional lecturer numbers for an LEA by applying standard SSRs to November 1980 student numbers expressed as full-time equivalents (FTEs) and multiplying these by standard unit costs. Different SSRs and unit costs were used for different kinds of institution (polytechnics and others) and for different subject categories (eg laboratory based). The SSRs were set so that common funding accounted for 85 per cent of the pool quantum, allowing 15 per cent to be allocated as further funding and to prevent LEAs with low unit costs being allocated more than they spent in 1980-81. Further funding was allocated by reference to the difference between common funding allocations and estimated expenditure, to ease the transition of institutions with high unit costs to a lower cost level.

TECHNICALITIES

Data Base
The 1982-83 allocation was based on the latest student number data then available, that for November 1980, in preference to LEAs' estimates. The enrolment figures were derived from the Further Education Statistical Record (FESR) returns made by LEAs to the DES. This individualized data system was designed for other purposes, and its use for allocation purposes raises a number of problems. First, because the return is based on enrolments as at 1 November it excludes a significant number of enrolments made after that date (about 9 per cent on average in polytechnics in 1980-81). Similarly, enrolments on short special courses are usually omitted. Institutions which enrol students late (often a problem with overseas students) or those with high proportions of courses starting after 1 November will be penalized in such an allocation system.

The system also penalized the scrupulous. Not all FESR forms are submitted to DES by the 30 November deadline, and it is not unknown for institutions to add in enrolments made after 1 November. Those who delayed longest had the highest FTE count and allocation.

'Lagging'
In order to avoid the danger that institutions would 'bid-up' student numbers as a means of attracting extra revenue (DES 1982a), the 1982-83 pool distribution was based on 1980 student numbers, with the likelihood that in the longer term funding would be based on agreed student number targets. The major problem with the 1982-83 expedient is that it only works fairly if all institutions' student numbers remained constant between 1980 and 1982-83 or all increased or decreased at similar rates.

The method penalizes institutions which have expanded on the basis of earlier course approvals and favours those who have declined or expanded least.

The method of lagging cannot serve in future allocations if 'educational judgement' is to be employed, as it will be directly counter productive. Educational judgements imply that some institutions are to develop at different rates from others, but lagged data will not reflect the changes.

FTE Weightings

The common funding component of the allocations relies on the calculation of the FTE student enrolment figures. FTEs are calculated by representing part-time students as a fraction of full-timers. It is obvious that the answer depends entirely on the weighting used. The conversion factors used for advanced students were:

Full-time (including short full-time)	1.00
Sandwich	0.90
Part-time day (including day and block release)	0.35
Evening only	0.15

These weightings were established from an analysis of the 1977 AFE Pool Spring Survey which compared average weekly contact hours of sandwich and part-time courses with those for comparable full-time courses.

It is difficult to calculate the precise effects of different FTE conversion factors, but a rough and ready calculation suggests that allocations to institutions with high proportions of part-time students would be substantially increased by relatively small changes in the weightings.

The weightings were greeted with dismay in many AFE institutions as under-estimating part-time students. They penalize institutions offering high proportions of part-time and particularly evening-only courses, and those offering substantial numbers of special short courses.

Institutional Cost Accounting

The level of 'further funding' for individual institutions in 1982-83 was determined in large part by the levels of expenditure in 1980-81. This system will only work if expenditure figures accurately reflect spending. There is reason to doubt this. Within days of the announcement of the 1982-83 allocation it was reported that some LEAs had under-estimated the cost of AFE, whilst others had received 'more money than they need' (*Education* 1982). It is technically difficult to separate genuine expenditure on AFE from other FE spending, and indeed sometimes difficult to separate expenditure on FE from other parts of a local authority's expenditure. Again, those institutions whose costs are most clearly accounted for will be those most penalized by the new system.

PROBLEMS OF PRINCIPLE

Hidden Judgements and Assumptions
The system requires judgements about the allocation mechanism to be taken at several stages: the balance between common and further funding, which determines the extent to which 'high spenders' will be penalized; the range of the penalty; and the distribution (uniform or non-uniform) across institutions; the classification into three subject groups; whether or not to set different notional SSRs for these subject groups; the differential between kinds of institutions, eg polytechnics and OMEs. Furthermore as we saw, the system is extremely sensitive to a variety of other assumptions. These include the weightings used for FTE calculations and the date selected for enrolment figures.

Assumptions and judgements of some sort are, of course, inevitable with any system of resource allocation even by formula (Wagner 1981). The problem with these particular assumptions is that they are all arbitrary; no principle — and certainly no educational principle — underlies them. They were taken, as the GMP records, either because no other practical basis exists (as in the case of FESR enrolment figures) or simply to make the final distribution of resources broadly acceptable to a range of conflicting interests.

Accountability
The GMP recognizes the problem of hidden judgements saying, 'any system for distributing resources in AFE will inevitably imply judgement... it is in principle preferable that such judgements as there are should be explicit and thereby open both to discussion and to refinement'. Wagner (1981) went further, arguing that institutions 'should have a say in deciding the principles on which resource allocation decisions' are made.

The problem is that the system is effectively closed. Allocations are based on data about individual institutions' enrolments that are not publicly available. Any attempt, for example, to examine the sensitivity of the allocations to different factors involves recalculation of all stages of all institutions' allocations — a task that can only be done by the allocators, not the receivers! Although the principles of allocation have been published by the Minister to the Education, Science and Arts Committee, the doors to 'discussion' and 'refinement' still need a computer programme to open them.

Unit Costing and Funding
The major assumption within the method of allocating the AFE pool in 1982-83 is that the bulk of institutions' funds should be allocated on a unit cost basis. There are a number of problems of principle with the ideas of unit costing and unit funding which have been noted elsewhere (eg Sizer 1981). The problems go some way to explaining the variety of

average unit cost figures for institutions. In 1979-80, the highest average unit cost in polytechnics was 75 per cent higher than the lowest (Pooling Committee 1981). The statistic alone is meaningless, and the convergence of unit costs which the allocation system implies and which the GMP anticipated is purposeless. The GMP recognized the problem, saying:

> 'It has to be stressed at the outset that any unit of funding derived from this system must not be seen or used as any kind of standard or target; far less should it be taken at this stage to represent a measure of what institutions "ought" to spend. To the extent that there will be any convergence of unit costs among institutions in future years, this may eventually be a proper construction to put on the unit of funding. But for the moment it should be seen as nothing more than a unit of calculation, pure and simple.'

But they used the method, just the same.

The Evaluation/Allocation Confusion

Even if unit costs were a measure of efficiency or cost-effectiveness, it does not follow — as the study group noted — that they should be used as a basis for funding. Indeed, their use for funding eliminates their value as a measure of efficiency because everyone reaches the average in due course. Unit funding does not take account of aims and the extent to which they are being achieved. It precludes improved efficiency in individual institutions, because they all get the same money for similar students. The problem is a confusion between an evaluative measure and an allocation system.

The Moving Target

The years since 1979-80 have seen four different kinds of allocation system used for AFE funds; fee levels have been halved; the 'open pool' has been variously re-defined; colleges have been subjected to at least three revisions of the system of course approval. This may not matter in the sense that it is all now history. But further developments of the allocation system are inevitable and promised: the government is still considering permanent central machinery for the management of all public sector higher education. For institutions the changes are bewildering. It is hard to see how they add up to a coherent policy, and it means that educational purpose becomes subordinate to attempts to anticipate administrative change.

Subversion of Educational Policy

Many of the problems listed above contribute to a further problem: the arrangements subvert rather than support educational policy. The most obvious example of this is the conversion factors for student FTEs, which penalize institutions emphasizing part-time education of the kind encouraged by government, but the other hidden judgements and assumptions have educational effects, many of them inconsistent with educational policy.

Subversion of Institutional Control
It is easy when looking at the arrangements for allocating AFE resources and for central control of PSHE to forget what the AFE pool is for. The pool allocates *local authorities'* money to providing authorities for the AFE *courses* that they offer. It does not award central government funds, nor does it finance institutions. But the effect of recent changes is to subvert the basis of PSHE. The tendency is now for local authorities to regard pool allocations as funding for institutions — particularly as far as polytechnics are concerned — and any difference between the pool allocation and estimated expenditure on the institution as a 'deficit' for which the authority has to bail out the institution by increasing rates. The statutory position is that the LEA maintains (or aids) its institutions and is reimbursed for certain kinds of provision (AFE) by other authorities through the pool. But the capping of the AFE pool, and its consequent centralization of decision, the use of formulae and once-and-for-all allocations undermine the LEAs' responsibility for what their colleges do and for funding it.

Financing Voluntary Colleges
The funding of voluntary colleges comprises two sources: a deficit grant from the DES and fee income. In recent years general fee income covered about 25 per cent of total expenditure. In the case of the deficit grants there has always been a limit on the total of funds to be allocated, although it was determined by agreements with the colleges.

The deficit grant was calculated by a process of negotiation between DES officers and representatives of colleges. Estimates of enrolments and staffing were agreed and total estimated costs divided by applying an agreed unit cost to these figures, keeping the total within the resources available and an SSR band of 1:10 to 1:11. Once all the student targets and the gross expenditure estimates had been approved by the DES, deficit grants were calculated on the basis of gross expenditure minus fee income.

The old system seems to have operated well enough for both the DES and the colleges. The relatively small number of colleges made the scrutiny and knowledge of each quite easy. A memorandum from the Association of Voluntary Colleges (AVC) stated: 'The voluntary colleges prefer a continuation of the present system of financing, which constitutes, in their opinion, a responsible partnership in financial allocation and control' (House of Commons 1980c).

A new system is partially in operation for 1982-83. The major change is that there is a fixed cash limit on the amount of money available to the colleges, which is set prior to the colleges submitting estimates. The DES retains a small central reserve of funds for emergencies and unexpected contingencies to be allocated to colleges for specific claims (DES 1982b).

For 1983-84 the same process is to take place but with the inclusion of margins of flexibility. In a situation of declining resources in real terms, the only means of incorporating flexibility is through competition between colleges for resources. The refined system will have two components, with some similarities to the common and further funding elements of the AFE pool. Two per cent of the cash total will be held back to provide the margin for flexibility, for which colleges will make supplementary bids. The system is to be operated as a two-year rolling programme with first-year firm allocations and second-year provisional allocations.

The finance of voluntary colleges suffers from some, but not all, of the problems associated with the finance of maintained colleges. It is not dependent, for example, on past enrolment figures. Student targets are agreed, but actual enrolments are left to each college. FTE weightings are not of crucial significance for voluntary colleges as they have fewer part-time students. The accounts of the colleges, as autonomous institutions, present fewer problems in attributing common costs.

The system is vulnerable to all the problems associated with unit funding, and to the hidden assumptions within it. Again, however, the relative homogeneity of the sector mitigates some of these. Ironically, the new system will, unlike that for maintained institutions, be moving away from uniformity to a variation in overall unit costs between colleges.

Problems of a National Body

The creation of the NAB in 1982, although intended to resolve some of the problems of the existing system, also adds to them. Michael Locke and I have argued (Locke and Pratt 1981; see also Fowler 1981) that the creation of the national body merely transposes rather than solves the problems facing higher education in the public sector. It faces difficulties in three respects.

First, the national body faces all the problems of resource allocation that the present arrangements face and which were discussed above. To these are now added the difficulties of allocating some or all resources on the basis of 'educational judgement'. Second is the problem of control. There is little evidence to suggest that central bodies are effective. There are what seemed to us to be insuperable technical and practical problems for a central body in assembling and using information to do the kind of job envisaged for it, and of ensuring that its policies or decisions are carried out.

Research by my colleagues and I (Pratt and Burgess 1974; Burgess and Pratt 1970; Locke 1978; Locke 1982) suggests that the major determinants of development in the FE system are the administrative constraints and opportunities within which institutions operate, and which the NAB does not directly control.

Third is the problem of policy. A central body for AFE separates it from non-advanced FE, and the rest of the higher education system, and threatens to divorce the country's manpower needs from the advance of knowledge.

PRINCIPLES FOR REFORM

This section turns to principles on which a system of resource allocation in PSHE might or ought to be based. It does this by considering public institutions as an attempt to solve some problem or problems. One immediate implication is that resource allocation in the public sector of higher education is only part of the solution of a wider problem. Resource allocation mechanisms are enabling devices: to enable, in this case, educational institutions to undertake their tasks, which are, in turn, means to other ends. It is important to avoid what Roger James has called 'solutioneering' — the tendency to propose solutions without being clear what the problem is (James 1980).

A second implication of this approach is the need to distinguish between basic problems and what my colleagues and I have come to call the 'problems of the solution'. In PSHE, the latter have come to dominate the former, and much energy is devoted to solving them, building even more complex solutions each with their own problems.

The Basic Problem

Formulating the basic problem in an education service, at least in broad terms, presents relatively few difficulties, although it is nonetheless rarely done, and its importance is by no means diminished by its relative simplicity. Indeed, neglect of problem formulation is in my view one of the causes of the problems the system faces.

In this context, the education system can be regarded as an attempt to solve a number of problems. These include primarily the problems of individuals — to free them for example from ignorance and dependence. Education is first and foremost a personal service; but it also offers solutions to other problems, such as those of the national economy — its need for skilled manpower, for example. These kinds of problems can be readily discerned in the formulation of the aims of higher education set out by the Robbins Committee in 1963: first was 'instruction in skills to play a part in the general division of labour'; second was the promotion of 'the general powers of the mind'; third was 'the advancement of learning'; and fourth was 'the transmission of a common culture and common standards of citizenship'.

The system attempts to solve these problems or achieve these aims by a variety of means: for example by educating individuals, by undertaking research and consultancy for firms, government, etc., by continuing scholarship and so on. There is, thus, no one single activity, nor a single output of the education service. It is worth noting that education is only one solution to these ends. Others are possible, and are in use.

The Specific Problem

This discussion has a number of implications for the solution to the specific problem of resource allocation. It cannot be isolated from the more general problems of providing an education service. In particular:

i   It should be judged ultimately in terms of achieving changes to them or on their behalves. This means that systems of resource allocation have to be judged in terms of the educational changes they permit, encourage, or frustrate, and that the cost of a system should be related to the educational changes achieved. This leads me to the idea of 'educational value added' which is developed below.

ii The ability and attainment of individuals on entrance to higher education varies considerably, and their attainment on exit also varies, both within a course and between kinds of course. Thus, any measure of change achieved has to accommodate this range of 'input' and 'output' variables.

iii Because a variety of educational activities are undertaken by institutions it may be appropriate for financing to be by kind of activity rather than by kind of institution, an idea which is considered below.

iv If the purpose of education is, inter alia, to meet the needs of individuals, firms, etc., then one way of monitoring the success of institutions in so doing is by use of market mechanisms. The implications of this are discussed below.

v   If education is regarded as part of a solution to national problems, then resources should be allocated in relation to the importance of the problems, rather than the cost of the solutions. This leads to the idea of 'problem budgeting' outlined below.

vi Educational change is qualitative. It may be possible to allocate marks to attainment in limited areas, but it would be a bold man who would value quantitatively the level of attainment in a degree compared with an 'A' level; or who could compare quantitatively the attainment of an HNC against a degree (unless it was attempted in terms of time spent achieving this, which is of course a measure of input, not attainment). This implies that, if resource inputs are related to education outputs, the most that can be done is to assess the quantitative costs of qualitative changes. Simple quantitative measures of cost effectiveness (such as costs per student) are misleading, even as proxies.

vii These considerations mean that the specific problem of resource allocation is a *judgemental one*. It cannot be isolated from such educational issues as the ways and extent to which educational aims are achieved, or from the educational problem of making judgements between different kinds of educational changes. This is a point of some significance, as the developments of the last few years in AFE funding have been towards technical, formulae-based methods of resource allocation. There is a danger of confusing facts and decisions. Popper has argued convincingly for the independence of facts and decisions: that it is impossible to reduce decisions to facts. Decisions cannot derive from facts, though they must be compatible with them, and the facts are useful in examining the consequences of alternatives between which choice has to be made (Popper 1945). Similarly, from a quite different philosophical and political position Gramsci has observed the danger of applying statistics to politics: 'in the service and art of politics it (the use of statistics) can have literally catastrophic results which do irreparable harm' (Joll 1977). Formulae-based funding methods basically ignore this distinction and its dangers.

viii The problem of resource allocation is also a *political* one, in the sense that it raises questions of deciding between competing interests. Issues such as these, though couched in terms of resource allocation, are precisely the kind of problem that Crick describes in *In Defence of Politics* as being the subject matter, indeed raison d'etre of politics (Crick 1964). Solutions, then, have to be sought in political terms, and the task becomes one of determining the nature of the institutional arrangements rather than the technical details of allocation formulae to settle them.

Requirements of the Solution

These considerations condition the nature of the problem, but the range of possible solutions is constrained by a number of further requirements. Some of these have been made explicit by government. Others are implicit, and sometimes overlooked.

What follows is a brief discussion of the main requirements of any solution to the problem of resource allocation in the public sector of higher education. Many of these requirements are, in effect, the converse or a positive restatement of problems of the present arrangements and are summarized only briefly here.

Supportive of Educational Purpose

The major requirement of any system of resource allocation in PSHE must be that it should support rather than hinder the educational purposes of the institutions. This would seem unexceptionable, but for the fact that many of the administrative arrangements in PSHE actually prevent the attainment of educational aims. (The phenomenon of 'academic drift' is an obvious example of the disfunctional effect of administration upon institutions (see Pratt and Burgess 1974.) An allocation system should promote, amongst other things, the achievement of educational changes to individuals.

Supportive of Statutory Arrangements
It is similarly a truism that resource allocation arrangements for PSHE should support rather than subvert the statutory distribution of responsibilities for the service. This means that at present they should support the local authorities' responsibilities for securing the provision of adequate facilities, the secretary of state's responsibility for determining the national policy, and governing bodies' responsibilities following the Education (No. 2) Act 1968. The present arrangements undermine this distribution of responsibilities, and many of the possible alternatives would require a change in the statutory basis of PSHE.

Apt Distribution of Responsibility
A related requirement is that financial arrangements should allocate responsibilities to those best able to take decisions in those topics. In particular, they should recognize distinctions between different kinds of responsibility or decision, for example between financial and educational decisions, between decisions about the importance of problems and the likely success of solutions to them. Similarly, they should allow decisions about the pattern of institutions, courses to be run, how to teach, etc. to be taken by those best able to do so. The present arrangements are being undermined by, on the one hand, centralization of many educational decisions, and on the other the requirement for educationalists to take decisions about the nature and importance of national economic problems.

Accountability
PSHE is by definition 'public'. Public money is being spent on public institutions by statutory bodies operating within the law. A basic requirement in a democratic society is that in such a system the bodies should be accountable to an electorate for their actions. The present arrangements for resource allocation preclude monitoring by practically anyone outside the Pooling Committee, and conceal important decision-points. Decisions at the moment are taken on 'technical' grounds by officers serving the Pooling Committee not directly accountable to any electorate. Similarly, NAB, which will be advising on future allocations, is not directly accountable to anyone. At the very least there should be an obligation on the NAB to make public the grounds on which they will act, to explain their decisions, and to make available for public scrutiny data upon which any allocation systems are based.

Cost Control

Any allocation system for PSHE must enable the total spent to be controlled. Cost-effectiveness and 'value for money' are watchwords in government these days, but their relation to the basic problem becomes important here: 'effectiveness' or 'value' have to be educational terms if they are to be useful. The difficulty in PSHE and the education service in general is to determine what they mean. A related problem is to devise systems which encourage institutions to be what Michael Locke and I have called 'cost responsible' (Locke and Pratt 1981). Current administrative and resource allocation mechanisms often discourage economy, and fail to provide incentives.

Fairness

The pursuit of 'fairness' in allocating funds can be chimerical — for it all depends on what fairness is taken to mean. The problem has been evident in the field of public finance for some time. A green paper on local government finance in 1977 identified three different concepts — equity, equality and equalization and was able to operationalize none of them (DoE 1977). In general, it is better to seek to avoid obvious unfairness. In PSHE resource allocation this suggests the following:

— LEAs providing AFE should not bear an unduly high share of the cost; in particular, if the system is changed for 'national' reasons, LEAs providing AFE should not bear an undue share of the cost of change.
— LEAs should contribute to the cost of AFE provision roughly in proportion to their 'demands' for it.
— Providing LEAs should not be able to expand AFE for their local benefit at the cost of others.

Technical Competence

The recent consultative document on PSHE (DES 1981b) spoke of relating the 'technical competence of resource allocation' to educational judgement, although there is little evidence that such technical competence exists (Locke and Pratt 1981). As already noted, a host of issues has to be resolved at the conceptual and operational level.

Cheapness

Put simply, any system to allocate resources must not be itself disproportionately expensive. It would be salutary for example to assess the hidden cost of the time given by all the academic staff and officials to the UGC and NAB and their committees and subcommittees. I have shown elsewhere that the level of activity of the UGC is comparable to that of a government department (Pratt 1975).

Political Acceptability
To be acceptable, a system of PSHE funding has to satisfy a variety of political masters — local and central. This is an area where pre-eminently the problems of the solution come to dominate the basic (educational) problems. This is not to argue that education is too important to be left to politicians, or that political acceptability should not be a requirement of any system of public sector finance. The challenge is to ensure that political decision is informed by educational argument.

The requirement of political acceptability makes some possible solutions less likely to be implemented than others, and for this reason a series of proposals for discussion is presented here, some radical and some less so. It is to the components of possible solutions that we now turn.

COMPONENTS OF A SOLUTION

Allocation of Responsibility
The choice of solution depends primarily on decisions about allocation of responsibility — who should be responsible for deciding what. There is little denying the function of central government, reflected in legislation, in formulating the overall national problems to which higher education is seen as a solution, what Kogan and Boys (1981) call 'framework decisions'. But it is important to recognize the limitations on this function: of formulating problems rather than prescribing solutions, and the practical difficulties even of doing the former. Similarly, it would be unrealistic to deny the responsibility of central government for determining the total to be spent on higher education and for ensuring that this expenditure is controlled. Again, it is important to note the limitations of this: for determining the *total* of spending and for *ensuring* that it is under control as distinct from controlling it itself.

Direct Government Finance
There are several ways in which PSHE could be funded directly from central government. All would require legislative change. They include:

Direct Grant In this system, institutions would become legally independent and receive grants directly from the DES. Direct grant institutions have existed in the past (eg the CATs), and a limited number (eg Cranfield) exist at present, whilst the voluntary colleges and the Scottish institutions are all direct grant. The system has obvious difficulties of central control. In the past, direct grant status has been regarded as beneficial (Burgess and Pratt 1970) but that was in expansionary times and with a small number of such colleges. Direct grant status for all PSHE colleges would present substantial problems, first of selecting which colleges should be included, second of accommodating the funding of advanced and non-advanced work, third of encouraging 'academic drift', fourth of the extreme administrative burden on the DES itself.

Central Funding via a Buffer Arrangements could be established similar to those for the universities, in which a parliamentary vote for PSHE would be distributed by a grants committee. This raises similar problems of selection of institutions and the split between levels of work, but has the advantage of relieving the DES of detailed administrative responsibility, protecting the institutions from direct government interference and permitting academic and financial responsibility to be combined. But the experience of the UGC suggests that its size has become a problem (Pratt 1975; Crowther-Hunt 1976); it exercises excessive central control; it appears to act arbitrarily; and it becomes in effect an arm of the state anyway. It does not of itself contain a mechanism for meeting 'national needs'.

Local Authority Funding Local authority funding can be considered in conjuction with several other mechanisms, particularly recoupment and pooling. But it can also be operated without these, on the basis of the present legislative arrangements. The case for this has been argued elsewhere (Pratt, Travers and Burgess 1978; Burgess 1981) on the grounds of accessibility, self-government, responsiveness, practicality and the 'seamless robe' principle. Local authorities would simply 'secure the provision' for all further education for their area. They could if necessary combine in consortia to do so as Fowler (1981) has suggested. Difficulties arise over the treatment of out-of-LEA students and hence with fee and grant arrangements. There is the problem that providing LEAs would be paying for other LEAs' student education. Some of these problems could be tackled by recoupment.

LEA Funding with Recoupment LEAs providing AFE (or any FE) could recoup the costs from students' home LEAs — or could arrange 'free trade'. This was the system which operated for AFE until 1959. The system would retain the present clear statement of statutory responsibilities and match financial responsibility with legal responsibility. Difficulties arise over the cost of administration and of setting fee levels — full or marginal costs? How would an LEA cope if faced with different prices in different institutions? Would providing LEAs be subsidizing some students from other LEAs? These difficulties led to the creation of the AFE pool.

LEA Funding with Pooling Under this arrangement, local authorities remain responsible for securing FE provision under the 1944 Act, but spread the burden of expenditure between all LEAs. In the past, pooling was 'open ended', it separated allocation of finance from practical management, cost-control and political accountability. A 'capped' pool — the present system — was introduced to deal with the problem of open-endedness but still leaves the other difficulties unresolved and creates a series of new problems.

A National Body To tackle some of the unresolved problems of the existing pooled, LEA and fee-funded system, NAB was created, to advise the secretary of state on funding and structure for AFE. NAB's existence transposes rather than solves the basic problems of how to allocate resources. In addition, it poses problems of centralization, and faces serious practical and technical difficulties in undertaking the tasks proposed for it.

Fees — a Market System?
The consultative paper on PSHE (DES 1981b) placed great emphasis on the sector's 'key contribution' to the 'provision of courses specifically designed to reflect the opportunities and requirements of the country's employment market'. The paper went on to note the impracticability of central determination of the required output from the system and placed 'chief responsibility' on institutions and those in them to respond to demands and opportunities. Similarly, the Education, Science and Arts Committee dismissed manpower planning and commended the idea of the 'student market' (House of Commons 1980a).

The most obvious way of implementing a market system is by a system of full-cost fees, or educational vouchers. The system could be introduced as an extension of existing arrangements. Students could receive their fees or vouchers as part of their grant, and the present statutory requirements of LEAs would remain unaltered.

There are disadvantages to market mechanisms. The consultative paper referred to 'wasteful duplication of resources' which could result from 'unfettered and uncoordinated offerings of institutions'. A perfect market, economists would tell us, eliminates wasteful duplication. The problem is more the inability of the system to respond quickly enough to change, because of administrative constraints. But there are more serious problems. One characteristic of a market is that it responds to immediate demands, but not necessarily to longer-term needs. Unless new ideas about the nature of public investment (see below) are developed, a market system can never be satisfactorily 'proactive'.

There are technical problems, on such matters as determining fee levels (whether and how to use marginal or average cost) and how to finance fixed institutional costs. It would reduce the security of institutions and their staff, and it could have an adverse effect on students who pay their own fees, notably part-time, mature and postgraduate students. One further consequence of the system could be that if present arrangements for student grants were retained, 90 per cent of the cost would be met by central government, a substantial shift in the balance of spending on higher education.

Nevertheless, given the present government's commitment to market mechanisms it seems surprising that the system has not received more consideration, and particularly odd that the government should have reduced fee levels in the last year.

It is important, too, to note the relationship between fees and the present system of common funding. Both are sums of money associated with students, and at present, in most cases, the student does not himself have to find the money, it is paid on his behalf by local authorities. So although the present secretary of state has reduced the tuition fee to below marginal cost, the effective fee (in common funding) is close to average cost. There seems little benefit in such duplicate arrangements, and future developments should involve further thinking about the nature of the whole system and level of fees. At present the common funding arrangements seem to have many of the disadvantages of central control with few of the advantages of the market system that high fee levels offer.

No Fees
At the other extreme to the full fee system is a no-fee system. Some have argued for the abolition of fees on the grounds that they are merely a paper transaction for most students with local authority awards but tax those who for one reason or another are without, and penalize part-time students. Abolition has the advantage of administrative simplicity, and potentially greater security for institutions, but has the disadvantages of losing diversity of funding and the incentives of the market mechanism.

Differential Funding for Different Activities
If we start our consideration from the most basic formulation of the problem, not just of funding PSHE, but of providing an education service, it is clear that the education system attempts to meet the various needs of the nation and the people and organizations within it by different activities. Two main ones are the education of students and the pursuit of research. One possible way of financing higher education in general would be to finance the different kinds of activity by different methods.

There is more than just expediency to this argument. The strongest case for differential funding rests on a considered view of the nature of knowledge, which has been developed by Tyrrell Burgess (1977), while a scheme along these lines was proposed in the minority report of the Education, Science and Arts Committee (House of Commons 1980) and is on the agenda for debate by at least one political party.

Put briefly, the argument is that there are two distinct traditions in British higher education. Education in the 'service' tradition might be funded by a method which reflects the demands of individuals and the needs of the nation. Arguably, these are best met by funding via public authorities, such as local authorities, though with a substantial fee element brought by students. All undergraduate education could be funded in this way, including that in universities. The statutory framework already exists for such a scheme particularly in S 84 of the 1944 Act. 'Autonomous' activities, such as research and postgraduate education, would be financed by some arrangement akin to that of the research councils and the UGC (see also Burgess 1981). Individual institutions could seek funds as appropriate from either (or additional) sources.

Techniques for Allocation
The question of allocation of responsibility raises also the question of initiative. If determination of educational solutions is best left to educational institutions, then the initiative for proposing them and for seeking financial support should rest with institutions. It is not possible for example for central government to run all institutions in PSHE. This has been recognized in the present 'national system locally administered'. Similarly, the Weaver reforms of college government (DES 1966) recognized the need to limit local government intervention in college affairs. The role of any funding agency — central or local — becomes that of deciding between competing bids for resources. So on what basis are funding bodies to allocate funds between competing claims? There is a model of how this might be done, and it is that of institutional investment.

The Investment Model
Raven has argued (Raven 1982) that since some 75 per cent of GNP is under some form of government control, public spending is a major component of wealth generation and its supervision needs to employ many of the techniques and concepts normally associated with the private sector. One approach of this kind is that of institutional investors — pension funds and the like. In lending to private industry, the investors work on the assumption that they are not competent to tell a company how to run its business. Companies approach investors with proposals, and the investor makes an assessment of the risk involved. In effect, the investor asks the company to explain why it should invest: the onus is on the company to satisfy the investor's concerns about its past record, likely sales, profits, market share, etc. The investor's expertise is confined to investment appraisal, and it does not as a rule propose changes in, for example, manufacturing technique: that is that company's business. An important aspect of the investment is that it takes account of the business cycle; long-term projects attract different investment terms from short-term ones — and the investor will apply a set of monitoring criteria appropriate to the project. The investor will monitor developments against these criteria and act if they show unfavourable signs, but basically the market is the arbiter of success or failure.

The parallels for PSHE are interesting. Funding would be a *negotiation* between authorities or institutions and the funding ('investing') body. The body would allocate funds to what seemed sound proposals. Applications for funds would be on criteria published by the body. Clearly, the system could be run at a variety of levels, by course, institutional programme, or LEA as a whole. The model is particularly suited to a problem-budgeting approach (see below) where the funding body assesses proposals in terms of the likelihood of their solving the problems identified in national policy. The body would negotiate with applicants the criteria and methods for monitoring progress.

Programme Budgeting
It has become popular in government in the last decade or so to attempt to decide on problems of resource allocation by some form of programme budgeting (DES 1970). In this, budgets are set out in relation to the purposes for which they are to be spent, rather than the type of resource employed. The basic idea is to relate expenditure to objectives. It is attractive in principle, but has raised a number of problems in practice. In education, it has run up against substantial difficulties because objectives are multiple and intangible, and the outputs often impossible to quantify: it is not always clear which activities contribute to which objectives. Often programme budgets have been reduced to using inputs (eg number of students) as proxies for outputs, thus negating the purpose of the exercise — educational change (Pratt 1970).

Although programme budgeting has not so far been an appropriate method for education, the ideas behind it are of some importance. In particular, the principles — that expenditure should be related to purpose, that cost of alternatives should be compared, and that achievement should be evaluated — are all of value. These principles could be developed along the following lines.

Problem Budgeting
One of the weaknesses of programme budgeting is the identification of 'objectives', because as usually formulated they confuse ends and means, problems and solutions. What is needed is a 'problem budget' rather than a programme budget, in which activites and expenditure are related to the problems the system attempts to tackle. This has several implications. First, problems — not 'objectives' — should be identified and expressed in terms external to the education system. Second, funds should be allocated in relation to the importance of the problems (the problem budget). Third, choice between alternative solutions (activities) could be based on the comparative cost-effectiveness of those activities, using such concepts as educational value added. Fourth, the evaluation of the system should relate its overall effectiveness in solving the problems to the costs of doing so.

Unit Funding
Unit funding is a tempting way to allocate funds to institutions or activities. It is seemingly 'objective': funds are related to the cost of the activity. In the 1982-83 AFE pool allocation, the costs are based on an analysis of their 'determinants', the statistical relationship between costs and lecturer numbers. But the attractiveness of the method is largely illusory. Its

objectivity is spurious; unit funding relies on judgements and assumptions that are concealed; and it is fundamentally methodologically flawed both in terms of determining the unit and the cost. In so far as it has a use, it is as a monitoring or evaluation technique, of which more below.

Evaluation
One of the consequences of the failure to regard public policy as an attempt to solve problems is a tendency to regard activity as success. The solution becomes an end in itself: increased opportunity in higher education (though desirable) has become more important than what is learned — to the eventual detriment of increased involvement (Burgess 1981); enrolment numbers are taken as the basis for calculation of costs, rather than the educational change achieved; and so on.

Evaluation must involve an attempt to relate what happens to what was intended. In terms of resource allocation, this means relating costs to the problems tackled.

Rate of Return
If education is seen as contributing to meeting the needs of the national economy, then decisions as to its funding should be conditioned by two factors: first, evidence of the demand for the output of the system, and secondly, the costs of producing these outputs. One way of doing this is through rate of return studies. These bring problems in calculating costs and more seriously in assessing the return which accrues over the working lifetime of the individual, but one important advantage: they relate the cost of educational activity to 'external' benefits. Rate of return studies take, as a proxy for benefit, the increased output measured by increased earnings of the educated over the uneducated person. They also enable comparison to be made between different kinds of courses as they reduce qualitative differences to quantitative economic resources. Rate of return studies thus show much more favourable cost: benefit ratios for part-time rather than full-time courses. Similarly, they allow comparison between the costs and benefits to individuals and to society as a whole (the private and social rates of return) and differences between them, which may invite corrective action.

Educational Value Added
One of the main tasks of education is to transform uneducated entrants into educated leavers. In assessing which course or institution justifies an injection of funds, a funding body would wish to know which of them can achieve most change for least cost. Most important it will want to know the 'educational value added' — the change in student characteristics from input to output, and to assess the relative costs of different educational values added. Educational value added offers a basis for recognizing differences in inputs as well as outputs. Institutions

which take less 'qualified' applicants — like many polytechnics — and get them to degree level can legitimately argue that they are more efficient or need more resources than those which take the best qualified and also get them to degree level — like say Oxford or Cambridge Universities.

There is thus no single measure of cost-effectiveness or cost-efficiency. What is possible is a series of measures of the financial costs of different educational changes. Decision is not avoided: it has to be taken according to judgements of the value of different educational change and the cost associated with it.

Using educational value added is not easy. One of the problems is the evaluation of the educational change. The education service has not evolved many ways in which the quality of its output can be measured: existing examinations and assessment rarely measure the difference education makes: there is some doubt if they measure anything at all (Beard 1970). Assessment is often tautologous: the examination is set and prepared for and the success of the preparation judged.

Even external validating bodies like the CNAA have failed so far in this respect. CNAA is responsible for ensuring that its courses are comparable with university degrees, but has validated not output but input — the entry qualifications of students, the time taken on the course, the qualifications and experience of staff — the colleges' facilities and so on. But the failure does not invalidate the need. It is a necessary task for those in education to begin to assert what they actually attempt to achieve.

Choosing a Solution — the Case for Simplicity
This discussion has illustrated the range of possible solutions. The choice between them depends ultimately on the level at which the problem is formulated. The more radical the formulation and the fewer constraints upon the solution, the more radical the preferred solution. In this choice it is worth recognizing that the way in which any solution operates is much dependent on its complexity or simplicity. The more complex, the less reliable, comprehensible, operable, and (usually) less publicly acceptable the solution. A useful basis for choice is the concept of elegance, which is:

<u>What a solution accomplishes</u>
Its complexity

The present arrangements for PSHE resource allocation do not score well in this respect. A system of different funding for different activities would most clearly reflect the formulation of the basic educational problems; and it could accommodate the advantages of the market reflected in informed student preference, perhaps embodied in high cost fees. A national body, such as NAB, would not be a necessary component of this system. In allocating their own funds to undergraduate education, local authorities could use the concepts of problem budgeting and educational value added, perhaps in the light of a statement of national problems from the secretary of state.

Consideration of possible solutions also has to recognize that there is a current solution, and that, unfortunately, change has to proceed from the present situation. The last section here looks at how the present arrangements could be reformed and operated to become most consistent with educational purpose.

A NATIONAL BODY IN A SYSTEM LOCALLY ADMINISTERED
Put briefly, the case for a central body in PSHE relies on the belief that such a body can formulate, in a way that individual institutions cannot, the needs of the nation: the DES consultative paper on PSHE argued, for example, that 'the ultimate range of needs must be assessed nationally and strategic decisions taken on a basis wider than is possible local authority by local authority' (DES 1981a). The task of NAB should be that of formulating the national problems to which individual institutions propose educational solutions, and to judge and fund which of the proposed solutions are most likely to help solve these problems — and no more than that. A body such as NAB cannot, of its nature, prescribe educational solutions.

How might this be done? It would require a process with three main stages. The first stage would be the public statement by NAB of the problems to be tackled and the criteria to be used in allocating resources. Second would be the scrutiny of proposals by institutions and authorities to tackle these problems and the allocation of funds. A third continuing component would be the monitoring and evaluation of institutions', authorities' and NAB's performance.

The formulation of national problems is no mean task, and one wonders whether those who favoured a central body realized the magnitude of the difficulty involved. What would be required is first a statement of the kinds of overall problems that PSHE might tackle. This could be along the lines of Robbins' four aims of higher education. (This might be thought obvious, but the obvious, as Talleyrand said, is none the worse for being stated.) Second would be an elaborated statement of particular problems. If PSHE were to contribute to the development of the economy, for example, what would be needed would be a kind of 'national scenario' like that suggested by Sizer (1981) — a statement of where we are now, nationally, and where we wish to be — a statement of the general problems of the nation to which the education service might be expected to make a contribution. This might include:

— present and anticipated economic development, national, regional, sectoral
— employment, national, regional and sectoral
— investment, national, regional, sectoral

— developments in public services
— known and anticipated labour and skill shortages etc.

This statement should outline problems — in the sense of stating where we are now and where we wish to be. It is not a forecast of where we will be, nor will it prescribe solutions to the problems, for that is the colleges' job.

Sources upon which such a statement could be based include government documents, parliamentary reports, publications from national agencies, such as NEDO or MSC, though none of this is wholly adequate. It is alarming how difficult it is to find an overall view of the state of the nation and the direction in which it is desired to go. But nothing less will suffice if a central body for PSHE resource allocation is to make sense.

A major component of any statement by NAB would be its priorities, which would be reflected in its broad allocation of funds by problem budgeting. NAB would indicate which problems it regarded as most important, and indicate the levels of resources it anticipated devoting to their solution. The important point here is that resources would be allocated in relation to the importance of the problem.

Included in the statement would be the criteria to be employed in considering proposals from institutions or authorities. They may include such criteria as 'cost-effectiveness' and should recognize the importance of concepts such as 'educational value added'.

NAB would have to recognize that not all activities in an institution are teaching; learning requires research. Some research could be funded on the basis of problem budgeting. The national body could indicate the problems which it wished to have tackled by research. Some research may need an 'autonomous' style of funding, allocated perhaps through a subcommittee or separate unit, for spending at the absolute discretion of the institution on the problems it wishes to tackle.

The second main stage of the resource allocation process would be the scrutiny of proposals from institutions or authorities, and the allocation of funds to them. An annual allocation in the light of a three to five-year rolling plan might be appropriate. Some of the ideas for programme financing in the Oakes Report (1978) would be appropriate here. There is no reason in principle (and some possible advantages) why NAB should not simply agree student number targets for institutions and allow the allocation of resources between institutions to be settled by a fee system (rather like the situation in voluntary colleges).

The proposals from authorities or institutions would take the form of a costed academic development plan. They would set out the institution's or authority's response to the 'national scenario'. The character of an institution and the problem of education it offered would be seen as an attempt to tackle problems identified in the scenario statement and would be justified in these terms, amplified where appropriate by more local information. The proposals would be judged by NAB in the light of its published criteria; it would be up to NAB to ensure that the overall distribution of funds to different kinds of activity reflected its problem budget. The proposals would cover all kinds of educational activity — research as well as teaching — in so far as they were attempts to tackle the formulated problems. They would set out the balance between full-time and part-time work, and between kinds of courses, and identify costs per unit of educational value added. They would relate AFE to non-advanced provision, and the provision in one institution to that in others. It would be a matter for institutions' and authorities' judgement as to what kind of detail would be necesary to convince NAB of its case. Authorities or institutions might combine into consortia in the submission of plans and bids for funds.

The important points about this second stage of the process are not matters of technical financial detail but of principle. First the process will and must be judgemental. Because of this, the second important point is accountability. NAB must be accountable for its decisions, in what is essentially a political process. It is therefore no accident that the process proposed here resembles the procedures set out in S42 of the 1944 Education Act. The partnership between LEAs and their institutions and the secretary of state was reflected in the Act in the provisions of S42 for local authorities to submit development plans to the secretary of state for approval. The provision was used after the war and has since been neglected. Despite what the authors of *The Legal Basis of Further Education* suggest (DES 1981c) it remains on the statute book. Its neglect is shameful, since the method of approval is one of the most creative devices in education — its principles are embodied in the operations, for example, of the CNAA — and it embodies the requirements of visible judgement and accountability required of a system of resource allocation in PSHE — of publicly available proposals submitted by publicly accountable bodies to a secretary of state accountable to parliament.

The third stage of the resource allocation process is in some respects the most important. The history of further education in England suggests that colleges will respond not in a spirit of obedience or 'common interest' but in an effort to maximize benefits to themselves. For the most part they will seek resources (money, staff, buildings, equipment), prestige or status, and students, and they will endeavour to exploit the administrative measures, methods of allocating funds, etc. to their own advantage. They will respond to the constraints and opportunities of their environments, environments which NAB can affect to a considerable extent. The entrepreneurial instinct in FE has been the inspiration on which it has responded to needs, demands and markets: it is, arguably, its glory. There is no way of ensuring that colleges are cost-effective or meet national needs, and attempts to do so by instruction will fail.

What NAB can do is to help create the environment in which it is more likely that institutions will help solve society's problems — and will do so because it is in their self-interest. NAB should consider how the constraints and opportunities of the administrative framework can encourage a 'cost responsible' approach among institutions and provide a framework in which staff have incentives to make themselves more cost-effective. It should assess and then influence how the various aspects of the colleges' environments are publicly created and controlled: eg, the 'market' in students is modifiable through the grants system and FTE and level of work calculations; even intangibles such as status are controllable.

What all this means is that the national body must cope with the fact that the outcomes of its actions are not predictable. It must be open to scrutiny and to argument about its aims, policies and perception. It will have to accept that it is engaged in a process of trial and error. It will have, as a matter of urgency, to establish mechanisms of monitoring the effects of its own actions, and of finding ways of assessing how far what happens in colleges is consistent with its aims, that is solving the problems of individuals and the nation as a whole through education.

REFERENCES

Beard, Ruth (1970) *Teaching and Learning in Higher Education* Penguin

Bevan, John S. (1980) The advanced further education pool: post 1981 *Capping The Pool* Coombe Lodge Report 13 (4) 146-152

Burgess, T. and Pratt, J. (1970) *Policy and Practice: The Colleges of Advanced Technology* London: Penguin

Burgess, T. (1977) *Education After School* London: Gollancz and Penguin

Burgess, T. (1981) *Changes Required in the Next Decade within Higher Education* Paper for the SRHE Leverhulme Seminar on Institutional Adaptation and Change, mimeo

Centre for Institutional Studies (1980) *The Funding and Control of Advanced Further Education. Notes on the Likely Consequences of Government Actions* Commentary No.11

Crick, B. (1964) *In Defence of Politics* London: Penguin

Crowther-Hunt, Lord (1976) The UGC and the university *Times Higher Education Supplement* 28 May 1976

Department of Education and Science (1966) Report of the Study Group on *The Government of Colleges of Education* London: HMSO

Department of Education and Science (1970) *Output Budgeting for the DES: Report of a feasibility study* London: HMSO

Department of Education and Science (1972) *Education: A Framework for Expansion* Cmnd 5174. London: HMSO

Department of Education and Science (1981a) *Arrangements for the Management of Local Authority Higher Education in England* Press Notice, 20 November 1981

Department of Education and Science (1981b) *Higher Education in England outside the Universities: Policy, Funding and Management* A consultative document, July 1981

Department of Education and Science et al. (1981c) *The Legal Basis for Further Education* June 1981, mimeo

Department of Education and Science (1982a) *Advanced Further Education Pool Allocations 1982-83* Press Notice, 19 January 1982

Department of Education and Science (1982b) *A New Approach to the funding of Voluntary Colleges: Estimates 1982-83 and 1983-84* Voluntary College letter 1/82 January 25th

Department of the Environment (1977) *Local Government Finance* Cmnd 6813. London: HMSO

Education (1982) AFE Pool: Will DES dare ask for the money back? 29th January 1982, p.80

Fowler, G.T. (1981) *The Evolution of the Higher Education System and of Institutions Within It* Paper for the SRHE Leverhulme Seminar on Institutional Adaptation and Change, mimeo

House of Commons Committee on Education, Science and Arts (1980a) *The Funding and Organisation of Courses in Higher Education* Fifth Report 1979/80. Vol. 1 — Report. London: HMSO

House of Commons Committee on Education, Science and Arts (1980b) *The Funding and Organisation of Courses in Higher Education* Fifth Report 1979/80. Vol. II — Minutes of Evidence. London: HMSO

House of Commons Committee on Education, Science and Arts (1980c) *The Funding and Organisation of Courses in Higher Education* Fifth Report 1979/80. Vol. III — Appendices. London: HMSO

James, R. (1980) *Return to Reason: Popper's thought in public life* Open Books

Joll, J. (1977) *Gramsci* Fontana

Knight, Peter (1981) The 1980-81 AFE Pool: the end of an era *Higher Education Review* Autumn 1981, pp. 17-32

Kogan, Maurice and Boys, Christopher (1981) *The Politics of Sectoral Change in Higher Education* Paper for the SRHE Leverhulme Seminar on Institutional Adaptation and Change, mimeo

Lewis, P. and Allemano, R. (1972) Fact and fiction about the pool *Higher Education Review* Spring 1972, pp. 20-32

Locke, M. and Pratt, J. (1981) *Agenda for a Central body: A response to the DES' consultative document on public sector higher education* CIS Commentary No. 21. London: NELPCO

Locke, M. and Russel, M. (1982) *Colleges of Higher Education: The Emergence* CIS Commentary No. 17. London: NELPCO

Locke, M. (1982) *Colleges of Higher Education: Constraints and Opportunities* CIS Commentary No. 19. London: NELPCO

Oakes, G. (1978) *Report of the Working Group on the Management of Higher Education in the Maintained Sector* Cmnd 7130. HMSO

Pooling Committee (1981) *Study Group on the Management of the AFE Pool: Apportioning the 1982/3 Capped Pool* September 1981

Polytechnic Finance Officers Group (1980) *Polytechnic Expenditure Statements* November 1980

Popper, K.R. (1945) *The Open Society and its Enemies* Vol I and II. London: Routledge

Pratt, J. and Burgess, T. (1974) *Polytechnics: A Report* Pitman

Pratt, John (1970) The DES, budgeting, planning and objectives *Education and Training* July

Pratt, J. (1975) The UGC department *Higher Education Review* Spring 1975, pp. 19-32

Pratt, J. (1976) Pooling: some revised conclusions *Higher Education Review* Spring 1976, pp. 23-37

Pratt, J., Travers, T. and Burgess, T. (1978) *Costs and Control in Further Education* Oxford: NFER

Pratt, J., Russel, M. and Locke, M. (1982) *Colleges of Higher Education: The Students* CIS Commentary No. 18. London: NELPCO

Raven, John (1982) Public policy in a changed society *Higher Education Review* Spring 1982

Robbins, L. (1963) *Higher Education* Report of the Committee under the Chairmanship of Lord Robbins. Cmnd 2154. HMSO

Sizer, John (1981) *Institutional Performance Assessment, Adaptation and Change* Paper for the SRHE Leverhulme Seminar on Institutional Adaptation and Change, mimeo

Wagner, Leslie (1981) *Institutional Change — the Policy Agenda* Draft paper for SRHE Leverhulme on Institutional Adaptation and Change, December 1981, mimeo

FUNDING VERSUS VALIDATING

by Richard Lewis

The purpose of this chapter is, first, to explore the implications of the different types of relationship between 'funding' and 'validating' bodies and, second, to make policy recommendations as to the most appropriate form of the relationship. In this context a funding body will be regarded as an organization which either itself distributes funds to institutions — the UGC — or advises others on its distribution of funds — new National Advisory Body for Local Authority Higher Education (NAB).

VALIDATING BODIES
In a sense the phrase 'validating body' is misleading; in the UK the validating bodies do more than validate the work of institutions in that the qualifications themselves are awarded to successful students by the validating bodies. However, the awards are granted on completion of courses organized by the 'client institutions' over which the validating bodies exercise varying degrees of control. The principal validating bodies operating nationally are the Council for National Academic Awards (CNAA), the Technician Education Council (TEC) and the Business Education Council (BEC). In addition a number of universities validate courses offered by colleges, largely former colleges of education situated in the same region as the validating university.

Other bodies, notably the professional institutions, recognize awards for the purposes of membership of their institutions or for the purpose of exemption from part of the examinations leading to membership. While the two activities — 'award making' and 'award recognizing' are conceptually quite different some professional bodies assess courses in a manner which is very similar to that adopted by the award-making validating bodies and they can therefore be seen as an alternative source of information for funding decisions for some courses. It is also relevant to observe that the activities of the professional bodies are trans-binary and thus, within their own areas, the professional bodies are potentially a valuable source of information regarding trans-binary comparisons. In the postgraduate field the research councils discriminate between courses in the way in which studentships are awarded.

THE VALIDATION PROCESS
Validation is essentially a course-based activity. The major validating body in the UK operating at both undergraduate and postgraduate levels is the

Council for National Academic Awards and under the terms of the Council is required to approve courses leading to its awards. This follows from the fact that the awards remain those of the Council and it is the running of the courses which is delegated to the associated institutions. The other validating bodies in the UK also operate at the level of the course.

In its early days the CNAA's approach to the approval of new courses and the reapproval of existing courses was to adopt the attitude of external inspectors. The broad general criterion for validation was, and remains, the notion of comparability of standards with those prevailing in universities. The applicant institution was required to submit details of syllabi, reading lists, course structure, methods of assessment, staff likely to be involved in the course, and so on. The course team then had to defend their submission before a team of CNAA members mostly drawn from academics involved in similar courses at other CNAA institutions or universities. Approval was only given for a limited period, to a maximum of five years, after which courses had to be reapproved using similar procedures to those applied the first time.

Since 1979 the Council has been modifying its approach, along the lines indicated in *Developments in Partnership in Validation*. The main thrust of the new approach is a movement towards a partnership between the Council and its client institutions although the Council guards its ultimate right to approve courses leading to its awards. The partnership approach is particularly evident in the procedures which are applied to the reapproval of existing courses, in that institutions are strongly encouraged to make their own critical appraisal of the operation of the courses and this forms the central focus for the discussions between Council members and course team. While seeking to maintain a rigorous approach but at the same time wishing to encourage a more open and co-operative approach to the identification of strength and weaknesses the Council has experimented with a number of different models whereby the staff of the institutions can become more closely associated with the decisions of the CNAA. For example, institutional staff have been invited to serve as full members of the CNAA visiting party or, in a less extreme form of the model, staff from the institution have been invited to be present at what would otherwise be private meetings of the visiting parties during which the visitors' findings are formulated. Following the publication of *Developments in Partnership in Validation* courses are normally given 'indefinite approval', but such approvals are given subject to a progress review visit which will normally take place after five years. From an institution's point of view there is probably little which distinguishes a fixed-term approval for five years from an indefinite approval subject to a review after five years. However, the use of the latter formulation does serve to reinforce the concept of confidence and partnership as it moves the main focus of the five-yearly visit from the question of whether or not the course should be reapproved to a joint review of the way in which the course has operated and developed.

The course validation work of the Council is the responsibility of five subject committees, for art and design, arts and social studies, business and management studies, education, and science and technology, each of which is supported by a number of subject boards, panels and working groups. While in practice the decision is made by the visiting party as to whether a course should be approved or reapproved or what conditions, if any, should be imposed, the decisions are formally the prerogative of the subject committees (who may, and in practice do delegate the right to the appropriate subject board). The meetings of the boards and committees at which individual submissions are discussed do in some way help to ensure consistency in the validation process within but not across the whole range of subjects.

In addition to its course-based activity, the Council also carries out review visits, generally at five-yearly intervals, to its client institutions. Originally the prime purpose of these visits was to determine whether the institution provided a suitable environment for the operation of courses leading to Council awards but latterly the emphasis has changed. The visits are now largely concerned with establishing whether the institution has a structure and procedures to ensure that the standards of the courses will be maintained and to examine the extent to which the procedures are effective. The Council's statutes also require that a course should only be approved 'after having regard to ... the facilities available ... for that course' (Statute 8(5) (b)(i)). While some types of facilities can be assessed on a course basis others, such as the library, are central services which can more readily be assessed in the context of an institutional visit. Thus, the validation process also applies to the academic environment in which the courses are located.

Like the CNAA, TEC and BEC operate at the level of the course. The approval of TEC and BEC differs from that of the CNAA in that they allow institutions far less freedom in the way in which the courses are designed. Their approach to the validation of courses is also very different from that of the CNAA. The two education councils normally do not meet the teachers responsible for the course but instead consider the submissions on the basis of the papers only.

Validation requires a criterion or set of criteria against which judgements can be made. In the case of the CNAA the prime criterion is that the standard of the awards and thus the courses leading to the awards should be comparable with those of the universities. This begs a number of questions, including whether the standards in the universities are uniform and, if not, whether it is sufficient for the purposes of approval for a CNAA course to be of the same standard as the worst university course, which in turn implies that such standards can be, and have been, identified and measured. In practice it is probably fair to suggest that CNAA members responsible for course validation are expected to have in their mind some intuitive measure of minimum acceptable standards. It is also likely that, as the CNAA has developed, the yardsticks originally derived from university experience have to a considerable extent been complemented by measures based on experience of approving, teaching and examining CNAA courses.

The process of validation is essentially concerned with the determination that a course's aims and objectives and related content are academically legitimate, coherent and achievable in the light of the resources (including staffing) available. The evidence used to arrive at the decision includes the quality apparent through the written material submitted and, in most cases, subsequent discussion with the course team. In the present context it should be noted that the validation decision is simply concerned with whether the course is adequate: it is a cut-off decision, and, so far as resource issues are concerned, the responsibility of a validating body is generally confined to the question of whether sufficient resources are, or can be expected to be, available to achieve the aims and objectives of the course. The validating body will not be concerned with the efficiency with which resources are being deployed.

At this stage it might be helpful to consider alternative forms of validation which are not primarily course-based. A validating body might licence or accredit institutions to operate courses within specified subject areas and for specified levels of study. This could be done on the basis of regular reviews of the academic strength of the appropriate areas of the institution but the difference between this approach and the one presently in use is that the institution could design and mount courses without the specific approval of the validating body. Thus the confidence of any accrediting or licensing body would be in the procedures and established reputation of the institution rather than in specific courses.

FUNDING BODIES

The work of both the UGC and the NAB can be divided into two aspects. One is concerned with the allocation of funds against a given number of students. The second aspect is the planning function which is concerned with the number and distribution of students for whom provision is, or should be, made in the system: an activity which has not hitherto been carried out in the public sector. (In order to avoid overlap with other contributions to this volume the emphasis in this section of this chapter will be placed on a public sector funding body and, in particular, on the likely style of operation of the NAB. At the time of writing little is known about the proposed modus operandi of the NAB and hence the section must be highly speculative.)

The planning function of the funding body may extend both to a consideration of the total number of places that should be provided for a given subject area and to decisions or recommendations about the way in which the student numbers and courses should be distributed between the institutions. In the case of the former, political considerations are likely to predominate, but the funding body may be able to provide significant information, especially if it works closely with professional bodies in the case of vocational areas. Broader political and regional considerations will also be present in decisions relating to the distribution of students between institutions but it is highly likely that a significant element in this process will be some kind of ranking of courses. Since this will apply in a period of contraction it is likely to result in the closure of some courses. Similarly, ranking would be required in a period of expansion if that is achieved by increasing the size of existing courses rather than by establishing new ones. Any ranking will need to take account of regional factors as it is unlikely that large areas of the country would be left without access to courses in major subjects. This point is especially relevant in the case of the public sector with its extensive provision of part-time education.

It is important to note, in the context of the allocation function, that NAB was established (in late 1981) following the inception of a unit funding system which was introduced for the first time for 1982/83. At that time the system was modified by the inclusion of the so-called 'further funding' which moderated the reductions suffered by those institutions with above-average costs per student. It is difficult to predict the period over which the transitional or interim arrangements will continue and when, if ever, a system of pure unit funding will be introduced. It is, however, likely that the proportion of the Advanced Further Education Pool devoted to further funding will be reduced over the next few years, resulting in a narrowing of the differences between institutional average costs in public sector institutions.

In the context of the present funding system it can be argued that if the average cost per student for a given subject (or strictly for a group of subjects which are funded at the same level) is higher than the national average cost per student for that subject in public sector institutions then one, or a combination, of the following conditions must apply:

a   The institution is one with historically high unit costs and is thus receiving, through further funding, more than it would under a system of pure unit funding.
b   The institution is receiving additional financial support from its maintaining local authority.
c   Students of the subject in question are 'being subsidized' by students elsewhere in the institution where the average cost per student is less than the national average.

It is likely that in the future the first two of these factors will decline in importance relative to the third.

In the discussion document on the subject of the Interim National Body issued by the DES in October 1981 mention was made of the point that the Interim Body 'would open the long-deferred process of developing non-formula criteria for the distribution of AFE resources' (Paragraph 7). There must be considerable doubt as to the extent to which a national body concerned with some 400 institutions and working to a tight time-scale could depart to any significant extent from a formula-based approach. Thus, although the discussion paper refers in Paragraph 6 to the need to adopt a more discriminatory (non formula) system of resource allocation to take account, inter alia, of justifiably high cost courses, this could still be achieved by using a formula-based approach which, for example, assigned a higher weighting factor to students on such courses.

The implications of the above are that:

a   When ranking courses the main focus of attention will be a comparison of 'benefits' given equal costs rather than a comparison of costs. However, the NAB may be concerned if it identifies a course which has abnormally high costs resulting from an undue degree of cross subsidization within the institution.
b   There will be a need for an academic input to the derivation of formula used to distribute funds, including the identification of the legitimate needs of high cost courses.

If it is assumed that cost differentials are minimized because of the application of a formula-based method of allocation then the ranking of courses will be made by comparing benefits or outcomes. For this purpose certain quantitative factors may be used, including:

a   The quality of the students who join the course as measured by such factors as 'A' level scores. However, this is not very helpful in the public sector where many institutions recruit a high proportion of mature students who do not possess conventional entry qualifications.
b   The quality of the output of the course as measured by such factors as drop-out rates and the classes of degree awarded. This is superficially a more appropriate criterion, but it does have limitations. It is not obvious that the needs of the country are best served if institutions all strive to achieve success in terms of the factors identified in this paragraph. For example, a course which recruits a high proportion of mature students or students from groups who are poorly represented in higher education may serve a more useful social function than a course which recruits middle-class school-leavers even if the average degree class of the latter group exceeds that of the former.
c   The above suggests that there may be some value in developing

a measure of 'added value' — one which combines measures of the quality of the student intake and of the output of the course.
d   The relevance of a course in terms of preparing students for their careers could be measured in terms of the employment record of students but it must be remembered that such statistics are often extremely difficult to obtain.

A more important factor in the ranking of courses is the qualitative judgement concerned with the educational experience provided by the various courses. In practice it is likely that courses will be ranked on the basis of a vector which includes certain quantitative elements together with the qualitative judgements. The next section of this chapter will be devoted to the extent to which validating bodies can, with their present style of operation, provide inputs to a process of the type described in this paragraph.

Before moving on attention must be paid to the question whether courses should be ranked or whether comparison should be made of the total provision in a given subject area, which in the case of public sector institutions often covers a very wide range including sub-degree, degree, postgraduate, professional and post-experience short courses. Since one of the strengths of the public sector institution is the range of its courses it would be extremely unfortunate if separate rankings were made for different levels of courses. This could lead to decisions whereby institutions would be restricted in their range of courses which would be undesirable in that the opportunity of students to transfer between courses in the same institution would be restricted. Another danger of such an approach is that since staff and resources are usually employed over the whole range of courses the decision to, say, remove a degree course from an institution might result in the closure of an excellent sub-degree course.

THE VALIDATING INPUT TO FUNDING
Clearly, validating bodies are interested in many issues which are also the concern of funding bodies, including the quantitative data referred to in the previous section, as well as in the assessment of education experience offered by courses. However, there is a significant and substantial difference between the foci of interest of funding and validating bodies. As has been argued earlier, funding bodies will have to be concerned with ranking decisions while validating bodies are concerned with cut-off decisions. To observe this distinction is not to say that those concerned with validation could not, or indeed do not, take a view about the comparative standards of courses. However, any rankings that are currently made by validators are made on unsystematic and (formally at least) covert bases. If rankings were to become part of the output of the validation process significant changes in that activity would be required.

If it is accepted that the rankings should be made on the basis of the whole range of courses offered by the institution rather than by level of course, it follows that for many institutions more than one validating body would be involved. Further, the professional bodies may be able to provide the funding body with valuable information, especially with regard to the relevance of the courses. Thus, in the case of many institutions, no one validating body could provide all the information which might be seen as relevant to the allocation of funds.

To return to the development of a formula for funding decisions it was argued that there should be an academic input to the derivation of a formula used to distribute funds, particularly with regard to the identification of justifiable cost differentials between subjects. It is clear that a validating body such as the CNAA will not be able to offer very much direct help in this matter as it is not concerned with a comparison of the level of resource usage across subjects — or indeed within them.

ALTERNATIVE RELATIONSHIPS BETWEEN FUNDING AND VALIDATING BODIES

Since there is an overlap in the existing information needs of funding and validating bodies the question arises as to the extent to which the validating bodies might extend — or indeed restrict — their interest in resource matters and their consequent relationship with the funding body. There is obviously a wide continuum of possible degrees of strength in the links between funding and validation bodies. Some possible models will be outlined in this section.

Very Loose

    a No contact at all, the independence of the validating bodies is seen as the prime aim.
    b Informal contacts (which is likely to happen in practice even if no formal contacts are established) with all that this implies for inconsistency: the superficial or partial independence of the validating bodies is preserved.

Loose

It is possible to envisage many types of formal contact whereby each body does its own job but in a co-ordinated fashion. For example:

    a By ensuring that 'academic' members of the funding body have recent or concurrent experience of the work of the validating body and vice versa.
    b A common committee structure could be operated which would aid in the dialogue between the funding and validating body. The strength of the link could be increased if there were an overlapping membership between the committees of the two bodies.

Tight
The validating body could become the academic arm of the funding body by providing the academic input. The role of the validating body could be confined to the offering of advice and information with no involvement in the decisions of the funding body.

Alternatively the validating body could share in the decisions of the funding body. A validation body might well argue that if it is to service the funding body by providing it with academic intelligence then it has the right to play some part in the way it is used. This view has been adopted by the CNAA but it is not altogether clear why this should be unless it is thought that the funding body does not have the capacity to interpret what it has been told. Indeed, it could be argued that in many ways it would be better if validation bodies confined themselves to the proffering of advice and took no part at all in the actual decision making. This would aid their relationships with their client institutions, which would otherwise be likely to be harmed if the validation body were seen to be a party to, what will inevitably be, from time to time, harsh decisions made by the funding body.

Very Tight
Validation and funding are carried out by the same body; either the funding body would incorporate the validating body or vice versa.

THE CONSEQUENCES FOR VALIDATING BODIES
In this section will be discussed the effect on the work of validation bodies (in the context of their present style of operation) of the different degrees of relationship identified above.

Loose Links
It is unlikely that the existence of loose links would have a significant impact on the work of the validating body. There may be some difficulties if some members of the validation 'visiting parties' were also associated with the work of the funding body in that they might be perceived to hold a more powerful position vis à vis the other members of the visiting party. Staff of institutions might also feel inhibited when dealing in the context of validation with those whom they believe to have a strong influence over the future funding. There may also be accusation of unfairness and inconsistency if some visiting parties included members who were concerned with the work of the funding body and some did not.

Tight Links
The establishment of links which could be characterized as tight or very tight would be likely to have a significant impact on the work of the validation bodies.

Relationships with Institutions
Institutions might well be expected to be highly defensive in their relationships with the validation bodies, especially in a period of retrenchment. There is a danger that institutions will try to hide their weaknesses and not share with the validating body their own assessment of their problems. Certainly the concept of partnership in validation as developed by the CNAA is likely to be placed under severe strain. While it may be expected that the changes in the relationship that are likely to flow from the establishment of tight or very tight links between the funding and the validation bodies could have an adverse affect on the validation process it may be possible to take certain steps to minimize them. It may be possible to separate the strict validation process from the involvement in activities relating to the funding body. The two forms of activity have different time-scales in that course approval and reapproval is a relatively short-term exercise while decisions that would be taken by the funding body are likely to be taken over a far longer period. It may be possible to maintain the partnership between the institution and the validating body in respect of the validation activity on the assumption that the sort of appraisal that forms the focus for course review visits is unlikely to have a direct impact on the advice tendered by the validation body to the funding body. The extent to which such a separation is actually possible, or would be seen as credible by institutions, must be in question.

Consistency
It was argued earlier that validation involves a 'cut off' decision: that is that it is concerned with the question of whether this course is good enough without any overt consideration of 'how good is the course relative to others'. The decisions that will have to be taken by a funding body are inherently ranking decisions: 'with a given level of resources which institution is offering the best (in terms of the chosen critera) courses'. Thus consistency will be of far greater importance in the work associated with funding than with validation. In the latter case consistency may be necessary at the accept/reject boundary but this is much easier to achieve than a consistent set of judgements covering a wide range of levels. The subject boards and committees of the CNAA and the analogous committees of the other award-making validation bodies do strive to achieve consistency but there must be doubt whether they would be able to satisfy the more stringent conditions of consistency referred to above. In order to achieve 'consistency for and in ranking' it may be necessary to involve fewer people in the activity, to which, in consequence, they would have to devote more of their time. Alternatively, or additionally, the validation body would have to strengthen its own central processes in an attempt to ensure that its various specialist groups were demonstrating a consistent approach to the evaluation of courses standards.

Concentration of Academic Power

If one or more of the validating bodies became the academic arm of the funding body, or if a combined funding/validation body were established there would be a danger that academic power might be concentrated in too small a group which could result inter alia in the stagnation of academic development. The risk could be minimized if the business of the funding/validating bodies were conducted openly and if there were a real opportunity for interaction between institutions and the funding/validating body. It must also be noted that a validating body need not be monolithic and that it is possible for a range of views to co-exist within it. While it is not necessarily the case that a combined funding/validating body will become too prescriptive in its approach, there is a real danger that a prevailing orthodoxy evolved by such a body might impede academic development.

A related drawback of a tight, or very tight, form of association is that there would no longer be a validating body independent of the funding body which could promote the legitimate needs of institutions where academic or social criteria rather than resourcing criteria were paramount. There have been instances where the CNAA, not least because of its independent status, has been able to influence the attitude of local authorities in their role as funding bodies in respect of the resource needs of institutions. The establishment of a national body for the public sector with, it is to be hoped, the development of a more rational basis for the distribution of funds might reduce the risk that individual institutions will suffer disproportionately in the matter of resource allocation. There may, however, still be an advantage in there being a national agency which has credibility and which can challenge the view of the group responsible for the allocation of funds.

CONCLUSIONS

In assessing the comparative advantages of the different possible types of relationship between funding and validating bodies attention must be paid to the question of costs, both as they affect the national agencies and institutions, and the need to guarantee and enhance academic standards and to foster academic vitality.

The needs of validating and funding bodies for quantitative information overlap to a considerable extent and there is an obvious need to rationalize the collection and publication of data. At the same time it is important to ensure that data for universities and public sector institutions are prepared on a comparable basis to aid trans-binary comparisons.

Short-term Developments

A strong case can be made for the view that, in the short term, validation and funding should be organized as entirely separate activities. This argument is based on the view that many public sector institutions are still at the stage where they need to sustain an open, self-critical and honest dialogue with validation bodies in order to become fully mature, and that such a dialogue is likely to be impeded if the validating and funding processes are closely allied. Although this view is an attractive one it is likely that the balance of advantage lies in there being some formal contacts between the funding and validating bodies. Such contacts could aid both processes but it is likely that the greatest benefits would accrue to the work of the funding body. Those concerned with validation not only have the opportunity to take a view on the comparative strengths of different institutions but have also developed a frame of reference within which to judge a variety of institutions and hence could provide a valuable qualitative input to the deliberations of the funding body. In the case of the NAB such contacts could best be established by ensuring that a high proportion of the members of its 'third tier' have current or recent experience of validation despite the possibly inhibiting effect that this might have on the relationships between validating bodies and institutions.

There are considerable differences between the needs of a validating body operating at the level of the course and those of the funding body, and hence in the short term, while validation continues to be centred on courses, it would not be sensible, or perhaps feasible, to establish tight or very tight links between funding and validating bodies.

The Medium and Long Terms

The way in which validation should evolve is a matter of current controversy. For example, the CNAA is undertaking an inquiry into its longer-term development. As public sector institutions mature, justification for validation of their courses by an external agency will become less persuasive and there would be considerable advantages, not the least of which would be cost savings, in replacing course-based validation by a system of accreditation. This should still involve a regular peer group review of its work over a range of subjects but an accredited institution would not be required to obtain specific approval for its courses from a validating body. Institutions could be accredited for the whole of their work but, given the varying rates of development and different degrees of strength of subject areas within all institutions, it might be more appropriate for accreditation to be granted in respect of different subject areas within institutions. If such a development took place it is possible to envisage a situation where an increasing number of institutions would be accredited for the whole or part of their work while other institutions continued to be subject to validation on a course-by-course basis.

A similar development might be observed in the planning aspect of the work of the funding body if, in the public sector, individual course approvals are replaced by what has been termed 'programme approvals' whereby an institution would be given the freedom to decide what courses, in terms of level, mode of attendance, etc., it wished to mount within the appropriate subject area. The institution would be restricted either by an explicitly stated target for student numbers or by means of a limit implied by its level of funding. The freedom of an institution to mount courses within its agreed programme could be made subject to it receiving the necessary approval from the appropriate validating body in which case validation would continue to be operated as a distinct activity. However, if the validation process developed in the way suggested above, the differences between the decision required by the funding and validating bodies would become so slight that it would be difficult to justify their separate operation. The funding and validation roles could be merged if the 'programme approval' made by the funding body carried with it the grant of accreditation to the institution for the given subject area. This would reduce both duplication of effort at the national level and the problems presently experienced by institutions arising from the diversity of external agencies with which they have to contend. These considerations lead to the view that, at some stage, the validating bodies should be merged with the funding body. The timing of the change would obviously depend on the emergence of the developments of the type envisaged here and the pace at which they occur.

The above proposal leaves the question of how to deal with those institutions which were not judged to be at a stage where they could be accredited. In part the problem would be reduced through the passage of time but it is probable that many smaller institutions, or those with only a very small proportion of advanced work, would continue to require a course-based validation approach. This problem could be overcome by the combined funding/validation body retaining a section which would validate courses from such institutions. An alternative and, probably, a better one (depending on other developments in the management of public sector higher education) would be to adopt a regional approach whereby validation of all courses in local institutions would be carried out on behalf of the national body by the accredited institutions.

One obvious — but contentious — implication of the arguments outlined in the paragraph above is that there seems to be no reason, other than the sheer scale of the operation, why universities should not be treated in the same way as public sector institutions. The developments envisaged for public sector institutions would mean that the funding/validating body would share many of the characteristics of the UGC although it is hoped that it would operate in a far more open fashion. Thus, given the convergence in the methods of funding and academic oversight it would be easier than it is under the present arrangements to remove or to shift the binary frontier.

8

RESOURCE ALLOCATION WITHIN UNIVERSITIES

by Geoffrey Sims

INTRODUCTION

In any industrial enterprise it is possible to determine the cost of the production of any product and this, when related to market forces, will determine its selling price. The need to sell at an acceptable price may sometimes result in a downgrading of the product quality but clearly, if the quality is too poor, it will not be saleable anyway.

The forces which define the finance available to universities can seldom bear any readily assessable relationship to the quality of the product which emerges and in many cases the cost of the product to a future employer is only loosely related to its quality. The university system is thus largely at the mercy of whatever current national economic policy is being pursued as regards its overall level of finance — which must in the end have some influence on the quality of its product. The chain of communication between the individual university department trying to bring out the best in its students and the corridors of the Treasury is not unlike those vast windy passages which intervened between the small brain of the dinosaur and its nether regions, where messages frequently got lost with the resultant extinction of the species.

The immediate link between government and the universities is the University Grants Committee. The University Grants Committee indeed shoulders the difficult task of advising government of real needs on the one hand and, on the other, of distributing to its supplicant universities the significantly lesser sum of monies allocated. Contrary to much contemporary press report the University Grants Committe, through the media of a good data base and a conscientious and effective system of visiting committees, is for the most part well informed about the abilities and needs of the departments of individual universities and, notwithstanding the sometimes apparently surprising advice offered to its customers, usually has better defences for its decisions than might be suspected from the parochial arguments advanced by its critics and attackers.

In times past allocations were made to universities through the University Grants Committe on a quinquennial basis allowing each university, in discussion with the University Grants Committee, to produce a development plan for its next five years of operation. The quinquennial system gave universities time for adaptation, for it allowed for the inevitable inertia arising from the three-year basis of most degree courses, whilst at the same time offering sufficient flexibility to allow any institution to incorporate provision for unforeseen new needs. Increases in academic staff salaries were separately funded and it was a straightforward matter to undertake coherent academic planning within the boundary of a reasonable financial horizon. Perhaps in the long period for which the system persisted universities may not have been sufficiently alert to obvious national needs. Perhaps it was also true that they tended to 'look too longingly at the past whilst backing reluctantly into the future' — but the basic system afforded them every opportunity to exercise their initiative and imagination.

In more recent times the economic complexities of the nation have seen not only substantial decreases in resources available, but increasingly these have been the subject of annual announcement (on one occasion after the end of the session to which they referred). Further, the imposition of strict cash limits, in a sector where 'product prices' cannot be increased and where salaries are determinned by a process of 'free' collective bargaining, has tended to move the majority of universities into a position where coherent academic planning has been superceded by the substitution of short-term survival strategies. In consequence new developments have had to take second place to redundancy policies and neither the traditional 'community of scholars' nor the protagonists of 'change to meet national need' have found much room for manoeuvre, let alone comfort.

GOVERNMENT AND ADMINISTRATION

The traditional machinery of government enshrined in the charter and statutes of a typical university consists (in England) of the court (usually a large body meeting only once or twice a year), the council, responsible through a finance committee for all financial matters, and a senate, whose terms of reference relate solely to academic matters. There is usually a majority of lay members on both court and council to satisfy the need for public accountability whilst the senate is made up entirely of 'academics'. Financial power then resides mainly in the council, though the days when a senate could take any major academic decision without regard to financial consequences are long past. Furthermore, it is not unknown for a court at one of its rare assemblies to seek to impose constraints on the operation of the council, making its responsibilities for the day-to-day conduct of affairs extremely difficult to carry out. Such decisions are uncommon, but if they affect for example investment policy or personnel questions, though they are not usually mandatory on the council they can nonetheless be inhibitory on its freedom of action. The role of such 'occasional' bodies in university government must surely be in need of redefinition when those held responsible for university management cannot properly discharge their ordinary functions without such restriction. The court nonetheless fulfils a valuable role as a commentator on university affairs, for those who attend its meetings are already interested in the university's affairs. Courts are often unduly large however and a meeting with even 50 per cent attendance must be accounted good. One consequence of this is that it is possible for the court to become a vehicle for pressure group activity of a kind which is not necessarily desirable. This is not to disparage in any way the principle of lay participation in the operation of other university bodies, such as the council and its sub-committees, where the leavening of experience from other spheres of endeavour is as invaluable as is also the indispendable independence of mind which it can bring to bear.

The finance committee, or its equivalent, then will usually recommend a primary division of the university income to cover essential costs concerned with maintenance of the fabric, rendering it habitable both in terms of climate and safety, allocating funds to welfare needs, the Union of students, and to the administration. The residue is then available for academic purposes and, lest this should seem to imply a wrong order of priorities, it should be stressed that, in present times, the real direct academic need is usually so great that there are few universities where maintenance and minor works provision is remotely adequate and short-term economy will lead to serious problems in the longer term. Further, in many universities the administration has been cut to the bone at a time when there are very strong arguments for expanding it to meet the vastly increased loads arising from financial stringency*. Indeed it is probably true to say that to over-economize on administrative expenditure certainly prejudices not only adequate management of the fabric and services, but also seriously affects the ability of the academic community to make optimum use of its time, let alone maximize its resources.

If it is assumed that the university administration is competent and enlightened, it will have done everything possible in the face of the opposition to see that all possible economies in the energy system have been achieved and that wherever savings are possible or services can be improved, an optimum investment in computers and their associated software will have been made to facilitate matters. This will have been done using the advice of informed academics (more committees to service), university 'co-operative' O & M units and, where necessary, outside consultants. It is to be hoped also that finance directors are wise enough to recognize that capital investment today can facilitate recurrent saving tomorrow (though some, like Treasury officials, appear still to find this concept anathema). It is further to be hoped that they have made good use of debt-collecting facilities, the short-term money market, and investment advisers (if there is any money to invest).

FACTORS IN ACADEMIC RESOURCE ALLOCATION
The crucial question then arises of how to allocate in the best interests of

---

* 'Sims' paradox': The smaller the funds available for academic purposes the greater is the amount needed to administer them equitably.

the 'academic institution' and its future 'health'. Academic 'health' is not an easy property to define in any absolute way and there are many academics who are inclined to argue that what is done already almost by definition constitutes health, whilst other courses of action, however desirable, could only imperil rather than improve it.

Since the Robbins Report, we have been committed to plan our course provision in such a manner that we can respond to qualified student demand, and, even though there are those who would not unreasonably argue for variants of the Robbins principle, its status in resource allocation and, at the same time, its defence is still to be found in the force of student preference. The time when students applied to read particular subjects, without regard for job prospects after graduation, had started to pass a decade ago and now the pattern of student application is very sensitive indeed to the likely job market. We witness the ever increasing demand for places for electronic engineers and computer scientists and the sharp decline for courses in sociology and the traditional, literature-based courses in single Honours modern languages. The obverse side of this coin however shows a huge demand for dual studies in languages with business studies, and with economics, law, politics, etc. — all combinations which point clearly towards broad modern career pathways.

The basis for allocation then has to take account of likely trends in demand as well as the protection of conventional strengths. There is thus a strong case for some body within the allocation path assuming a primary role for both estimating likely demand and reconciling it with academic respectability — a pragmatic approach perhaps, but in my view a proper one. The count of academic respectability is, as always, related to the research/professional competence within the university's command, for if a university cannot offer quality based on real strength the students it will attract would be better off in some other kind of institution.

The degree of latitude for manoeuvre in this situation is not so great as may seem apparent and the operation is thus difficult. On the one hand, typically, some 75 per cent of the university's budget is spent on salaries (mostly on tenured staff) and attrition in recent years has left little room for readjustment in the detail of the non-staffing budget. With present policies then, and the distorted staff age profiles which we have inherited from the heady expansion of the 60s, it is easy for this stage of the process to become one of fine tuning at the fringes.

DETERMINATION OF INSTITUTIONAL SHAPE
Whatever the difficulties of the time it is essential that the university should have some form of strategic plan. During the last few years it has often been the case that the need to react pragmatically to new financial limitations has largely obscured longer-term goals. Though it would be untrue to suggest that at departmental level initiatives have not been taken, many institutions have not felt able to give sufficient

thought to the measures necessary to safeguard the shape of the institution in the longer term. The primary means of securing economies has been through the freezing or lapsing of staff vacancies wherever these have occurred and clearly 'chance' is not a good arbiter in planning matters, not least because those people most likely to move to other posts are those in disciplines where there is a strong market demand (which contrarily is also a primary reason for maintaining such departments' strength) or those who are the most lively and able in other sectors. Such response has been largely forced on many institutions, but is in every sense the most damaging course that could be followed for the general quality of the university.

Academic freedom is often invoked as being imperilled by contraction, as is university autonomy. The author values both, but there is no reason why the former, properly interpreted, should be at risk. A university's automony on the other hand is always likely to be restricted to some extent in times of scarce resources. Most university staff will accept that autonomy will not be absolute all the time, but will defend it as a right, if it is seen to be permanently endangered.

At a time of diminishing resources and contracting student numbers then, it is likely that the planning machinery, appropriate to times of expansion, will prove insufficient, for whilst it is possible to achieve academic expansion with a fairly light hand on the tiller, contraction needs to be 'managed' both positively and sympathetically.

Contraction is always difficult, particularly within successful institutions. Decisions may have to be made about courses to be discontinued, reductions in staffing, or even departmental closure. There are no magic solutions to the problem of which path should be followed unless there are conspiciously weak activities, whether measured by student demand and quality or by staff achievement. Indeed, if such areas are evident they must reflect some degree of mismanagement of the institution in the preceding years.

Contraction must thus be achieved as far as possible by general consent and the ways in which such consent is sought, as well as the areas in which contraction is to be achieved, will vary greatly from one institution to another. Occasionally, existing machinery may be adequate, but more often than not the final decision will have to be left in the hands of some elected or nominated group charged with recommending areas for diminution or growth to the senate. Any such group needs all of the goodwill it can command and thus extensive consultation is necessary, as is openness about the criteria used. Contrary to popular academic self-perception, departments do not always face every aspect of change as thoroughly as they might and to challenge any department with the task of producing structured answers to questions about its future intentions and previous achievements generally induces a concentration of minds not often otherwise in evidence! Producing the answers can even be a stimulus to the department and may well throw new light on the position and prospects it has both within and outwith its own domain. The digestion of this kind of information at university level can be a lengthy exercise, but it may well provide a sound basis for short- and middle-term strategies which after discussions with deans and heads of department may well be acceptable to the senate.

The problems of staff reduction which inevitably follow can offer a host of difficulties depending as already suggested upon the status of their contracts, any redundancy schemes available, and many other factors, particularly if sudden changes become necessary. Given some continuity of national policy for the system as a whole, together with a return to longer-term planning, the residual problem should become manageable. Sadly the era in which we live has not blessed us with either of these preconditions and what is now seen by some as the over indulgence of the 60s has been followed by the present hangover.

APPROACHES TO RESOURCE ALLOCATION

Academic decisions having been made about the institutional shape, the difficult problem of achieving a fair and appropriate distribution of resources must be faced. There are broadly two basic approaches to this task. One is to make a per student capita allocation to faculties (or corresponding departmental groupings) and leave the detailed distribution to deans and heads of departments. Such virement puts the responsibility for a proper balance between academic and supporting staff and between departmental grants and other expenditure where it is best judged — in the departments themselves. It does not obviate the need for some central university involvement, however, as contracts of employment must be with 'the university', as must research grants and contracts, and indeed this will be true of all agreements where legal questions relating to liability or indemnity are at issue. It is furthermore likely to be ineffectual when times are really hard, as faculties tend to close ranks at these times and are in consequence unlikely to inflict hardship on their fellows.

The other approach works entirely through systems of central committees which relate to specific expenditure heads (academic, technical, clerical staff, departmental grants, equipment provision, and so on). This kind of machinery is at best imperfect in getting the expenditure balance between subheads right for any one department — but it does relate central policy for each staff group more directly to the appropriate trade union interest, which is always of importance. As a departmental head, it may not always get you quite the right answer, but as it is clearly not your fault you can always blame the central administration instead. This can often be therapeutic for departments, though it is hard on the administration! It does however offer a system of day-to-day control from the centre which may be advantageous in time of contraction.

Generally speaking all systems of resource and allocation control in universities have their disadvantages and all share a tendency towards being cumbersome. The more decentralized systems do however offer the prudent departments a more direct incentive to save and thereby solve their own future problems with less 'angst' than attempts at solution through a more central system. The question of incentives is crucial and the right to create reasonable departmental reserves to assist with day-to-day problems (eg extension of temporary research appointments, provision of emergency secretarial help, or conference and travelling expenses) can be a significant help. It must be recognized however that incentives to prudent housekeeping can bring embarrassment in their train for when government looks at university 'reserves' in their agglomerated form, whether related to equipment or other heads of expenditure, and sees substantial unspent balances, it is convenient for it to conclude that the system is over-financed. Without hesitation I would refute this conclusion for it is many years since most universities had as much as the equivalent of two weeks recurrent expenditure in their bank accounts as a contingency reserve: governments would do well to realize that a university with a turnover of perhaps £35m (excluding trading activities) is a major business and needs to be allowed to function in like manner. Few businesses not about to enter the hands of the liquidators could run on this level of reserve — even with benevolent bank managers, an aid which universities can seldom rely on in an essentially non-profit making business.

RESOURCE ACQUISITION

What then of university entrepreneurial activity? Opportunities for earning are available to most professional discipline areas within the university system, though the degree of opportunity varies markedly according to the location, size and competence of the university and of the talents and dispositions of the individuals available. Most non-University Grants Committee income of this sort clearly involves a commitment by the university to deliver the advice, results, design, etc. contracted for on a time-scale that seldom relates to the traditional academic patterns. A balance thus has to be struck between this kind of activity and the fundamental commitment of the university to its teaching and other long-term work. A limit needs to be set on the amount of staff time that can be given to such activities, though the setting up of university companies and advisory units may overcome most of these problems through the self-financed employment of supplementary staff who are able to supply degrees of professionalism which universities cannot always easily offer from normal 'academic' resources. It is in most cases the breadth of the departmental base to which such activities can relate which limits their scope. As this base is increasingly narrowed through retrenchment the opportunities too are reduced, for the difference between accepting such responsibilities in a department with a student/staff ratio of 10:1 is radically different from facing the same request at a student/staff ratio of 14:1, where tutorial groups have significantly increased in size, decreased in efficiency and there are other primary activities demanding precedence. Indeed, which of us has not seen the erstwhile colleague who, in his own pecuniary interests, has not been carried away into the 'other world' with subsequent problems for his primary employers: another reason for approaching with care the problem of balance between intra-mural and extra-mural activity.

It is further true that within the climate of the UK the attitude of industry to corporation tax often leads to an unwillingness to pay more than marginally costed sums for services from universities to those continued existence it already feels it contributes extensively. This is not a counsel of despair for, speaking as one who for more than two decades has been heavily involved in promoting this kind of activity, experience teaches that you win some and you lose some and the winnings are seldom likely to be that great. The main dividend from the activity which is of inestimable benefit is the two-way transfer of awareness and reality through the portals of both university and industry.

RESEARCH FUNDING

Most of this chapter has been concerned with resource allocation in relation to the teaching responsibility of the university. That there remains a fundamental responsibility laid on each member of staff to advance knowledge in his own area of scholarship is something which suffers a total eclipse in an era where student numbers and the per capita 'unit of resource' appear to dominate discussion of the financing of the system. Again the narrowing, through retrenchment, of the departmental base often leaves the university embarrassed that it cannot supply that part of the dual support system which is expected to match, and render viable, those projects for which the research council system and other contractors provide part finance. Few universities now manage to retain research funds of a size which can cope with the sophistication of modern laboratory-based research, and large grants awarded to universities through the outstanding abilities of certain of their staff can often prove a major headache.

Universities differ widely in their approach to internal research funding. Some do not have designated research funds, others do, while some allocate departmental and equipment grants on a scale calculated to make a realistic contribution to the university part of the dual support scheme. Internal research funding has suffered greatly from the present long period of financial stringency as it has almost always been sacrificed to preserve the more immediate demands of teaching.

In the author's view it is necessary to preserve some such central fund, both for the encouragement of innovation and for a variety of related purposes, eg:

    i   To fund arts-based work for which there is no other grant source.
    ii   To provide 'start-up' funding for new staff or new projects for

which outside funding is not yet merited or available.
iii To fund internal costs associated with adaptation of premises for research purposes.
iv To enable part costs of equipment and its installation costs to be funded (usually arising from part research council funding).

The above implies the need for some machinery for vetting the real costs to the university of acceptance of any research grant or contract. Even with industrial contracts, where realistic overheads can be charged, it is rare for all capital costs to be met through the contract. With research council funding no overheads are chargeable and equally grants from trusts and foundations seldom cover the real costs of research. Few universities, though they may have an 'overheads' policy, have tackled the full range of problems implicit in these comments. The task is a difficult one because any attempt to set a limit on the total sums of money to be made available for supporting inadequate grants will oblige the university to monitor, and then choose between, grant applications either at their inception or at some later stage. The most obvious 'later stage' is when a grant offer is actually made to the university (department), and departments which have won grants do not expect to be thwarted by their own universities in what they not unnaturally perceive as their hour of success.

Such judgements are always difficult, if not invidious, and may frequently prove to be wrong. The associated problem of provision of premises and their adaptation is often catered for through a separate minor works budget, where UGC rules allow for quite substantial expenditure (up to 3 per cent of the recurrent grant available to the university). In practice few (if any) universities are able to spare a sum of this order and, particularly in the modern specialist or high technology areas, research contracts may have to be turned down because they cannot be housed.

Perhaps the most serious of all of our present problems is our general inability to offer career prospects to able research workers beyond the immediate post-doctoral stage. Imaginative research council schemes have only produced a slight amelioration of the problem, the previous solution to which was predicated on the likelihood of a university post arising, in due course, either from retirement or through expansion. Particularly at a time when science-based research continues to provide new foundations for new industries it is a matter of great concern that whilst the universities contract and industry remains in recession, there is little recognition that partial preservation of the research council budgets alone is insufficient to retain more than a very narrow base of research personnel to serve the years ahead. Possibly the best partial solution, which would in no way compromise the senior fellowship and special replacement schemes offered by some research councils, would be for each university to provide funding for a number of research posts into which academic staff could be seconded for fixed periods. The posts would be allocated internally on a competitive basis and temporary replacement staff allocated to the departments involved. At the present time however few universities could afford a scheme of this kind — indeed many existing, previously well endowed, research fellowships can now only be offered on an occasional basis due to the present insufficiency of the original endowment and the inability of the university to top it up to a reasonable level.

CONCLUSION

Some of the concerns expressed above will be of transient significance, but they need to be faced and not merely left with the pious hope that they will disappear soon enough to cause no harm. We are currently facing at least a decade in which there will be a minimal input of new university teachers and the stifling of a generation of research workers. The place of non-science-based subjects in the universities is further prejudiced because of the growing demand for 'job-qualified' graduates, coupled with an ability to generate self help of the kind enjoyed by other university groups. The universities are acutely aware of these problems but, against the background of a non-existent higher education policy, no system of internal resource allocation can, in the face of possible substantial staff redundancy at all levels, deal adequately with these problems. We shall still continue to adapt and to innovate, but universities have always been about the future, just as the future is also a concern of much of our commerce and industry. Even here, though, with policy control largely in its own hands, industry has not infrequently found itself faced with seemingly insoluble problems, the consequences of which have been all too sadly apparent in the last few years. We have no desire to emulate industry in this regard.

The sole policy which determines our present path of contraction appears to involve only a basis of numerical factors — whether attached to student numbers or to unit costs. Traditionally universities have stood for broader objectives and, in the more socially responsive mode to which they have adapted, remarkably, during the last decade, they deserve a better reasoned argument in support of their future existence than they or any of our recent governments have addressed so far.

SUMMARY
1 The concept of the 'unit of resource' needs re-examination as not all necessary university activities are student number-related.
2 Government must provide for a return to quinquennial (or at worst guaranteed triennial) funding.
3 Implicit in 1 is the need to provide adequate provision for the teaching activities of the university as well as for complementing the non-university component of dual funding.

4 To ensure that research is firmly rooted in a stable university base all universities must:

   i Take a positive approach to research policy (which implies the necessity of a research committee in each).
   ii Be able to identify the real costs of carrying out research so that proper budgetary provision can be made.
   iii Have a conscious research allocation policy which makes provision for assisting innovation also.
   iv Evolve means of offering career prospects for able research workers.

   iii and iv will be difficult to achieve in the absence of adequate overall funding or plainly defined national research policy.
5 Universities should both encourage and regulate entrepreneurial activity which relates to its primary research and teaching work.
6 Universities will need to evolve new acceptable internal machinery for central control of academic policy and expenditure. Such machinery could take many forms but the more free-running approaches to administration are less likely to succeed in times of contraction.
7 Universities should seek to achieve more flexible staffing structures whilst accepting the need for the retention of some form of tenure for the majority of staff.
8 Incentive policies to encourage efficiency in the management of academic departments must be evolved. A study of existing systems should be carried out with a view to encouraging good practice.
9 Government should allow universities to carry adequate reserves both for 'good housekeeping' purposes and to encourage innovation, not least in relation to the needs of industry and other 'consumer' interests.
10 Universities should set up means, where they do not already exist, of guaranteeing that maximum efficiency is achieved in non-academic areas through clear plans for energy conservation, use of modern data processing techniques, and administration generally.

REFERENCE
CUA (1976) Staff/student ratios and their use *Proceedings of the Conference of University Administrators* pp. 21-38

9

STRATEGIES FOR SURVIVAL

by John Fielden

The topic of this chapter is the institutional approach to allocating resources. It is not directly concerned with UGC criteria and Pooling Committee or National Advisory Body norms, although they inevitably have a major impact on institutional attitudes and processes. This chapter will look at current influences for change and will investigate their implications. It will also speculate on the institutional requirements for survival and growth over the coming decades.

Since resource allocation is the framework within which an institution tries to achieve its goals, the style and substance of resource allocation procedures play a key part in allowing an institution to be effective. If for example an institution imposed a rigid and severe staff/student ratio approach on all academic planning, with no provision for qualitative judgements about exceptions, there would be an immediate impact on internal performance and behaviour. Institutional effectiveness would suffer.

PAST AND PRESENT MODELS

It is no easy task to classify styles and methods of resource allocation in institutions. There are several difficulties:

— Informal and unofficial resource allocation mechanisms are often more influential than the formally agreed procedures.
— Resource allocation is rarely a rigid once-off exercise, as different categories of resources and increasingly volatile flows of funds require continual decision making.
— Some internal decisions which are in effect resource allocation decisions are not recognized as such. Acceptance of external research contracts can involve an institution in significant internal financing.

The cumulative effect of these factors is to lessen the significance of the formal budget exercises, since greater changes so often occur outside the conventional budgetary process.

Despite these problems it has been possible to make some generalizations about styles of resource allocation (Moodie and Eustace 1974; Fielden and Lockwood 1973). The most helpful interpretation is to consider all institutions' resource allocation systems as ranging somewhere along two separate spectra; the dictatorial to the participative; the qualitative to the quantitative. These can be overlaid upon each other as shown here

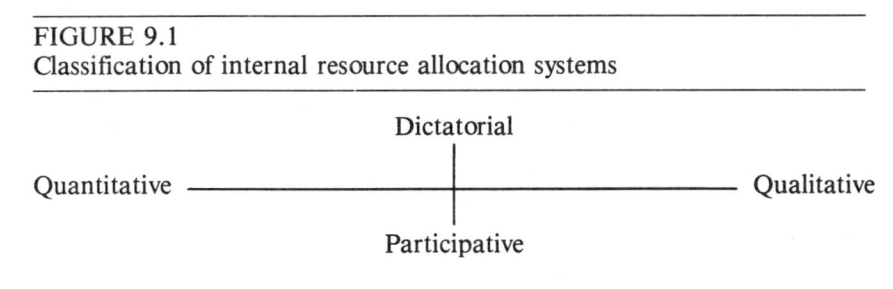

FIGURE 9.1
Classification of internal resource allocation systems

```
                     Dictatorial
                         |
Quantitative  ———————————+——————————— Qualitative
                         |
                    Participative
```

in Figure 9.1. Study of this can lead to some surprising conclusions. A hurried analysis might suggest that institutions with firm, almost dictatorial leadership preferred quantitative formulae-based approaches to resource allocation or that the participative style automatically ensured a qualitative bias in decision making. Observation, however, suggests that exactly the opposite is true. Highly participative groups find it difficult or impossible to reach consensus about the quality of competing bids and tend therefore to welcome such quantitative aids as can be accepted as fair to all. The principles of 'equal misery' and across-the-board cuts typify this style. In contrast, the powerful director or vice-chancellor can protect the weak department, where he identifies some concealed potential, at the cost of a numerically better-endowed department. Away from the bluster of a competitive committee room most senior academic staff will recognize the need for a leadership prepared to take difficult value judgements. The leader need not be the institutional head; it is not unknown for some vice-chancellors to allow a well-respected senior colleague to take on this role when he is sure that their values and priorities are shared.

The tools and techniques of resource allocation have not varied widely in the 1960s and 1970s, and there have been few changes in the basic options. The widespread administrative use of computers led to the declaration of many false dawns for computer-based models and planning systems. In practice, however, the most sophisticated aids have been locally developed formulae (of varying complexity) used to assist in the allocation of staff and departmental grants. Several polytechnics have followed the example of the Pooling Committee and used mechanisms based on contact hours, teaching load and class size, the elements identified in the influential Pooling Committee document of 1974. In very few cases however have the judgements and conclusions of the formulae been allowed to stand without a qualitative overlay, and special cases have usually proliferated.

INFLUENCES FOR CHANGE
If this has been the position over the last two decades, covering the full range of circumstances between optimistic expansion and demoralized contraction, is there any reason why resource allocation should be any

different in the next fifteen years? Are there any special features which will affect institutional behaviour and mechanisms for distributing resources in the 1990s?

It is suggested that there are a number of crucial and influential factors which will significantly change the style and approach to resource allocation. Although one cannot place any weighting on the relative significance of these factors, taken together they could mean an entirely new environment inside the institution.

Financial pressures are clearly the most important external factor, yet institutional resource-allocation systems have survived them until now. However, they have recently moved on to a new scale of severity requiring radical reappraisals of existing provision rather than tinkering at the margin. What would happen if pressure continued at this level or even moved on to a higher scale of intensity, fuelled by demographic factors and national unit cost bases for allocation? Inside an institution these pressures have already produced the following results:

— A random, ad hoc element to planning as sudden retirements or staff departures produce welcome and painless savings, which it is only too easy to accept. The best resource-allocation practice would be to reject some of these fortuitous gains by filling posts in areas of agreed development.
— Severe distortions in the age structure of academic staff have already been identified in many institutions. Not only has this serious implications for research and the regeneration of teaching material, but it will also produce problems of internal morale and performance.
— Directly related to the question of a declining research capability (since an ageing staff must usually be less productive than a broadly mixed age group) is the topic of staff/student ratio and teaching load. Will it be necessary for universities to abandon the assumption that all staff undertake a similar and significant research function and move to the polytechnic model in which research time is separately budgeted and controlled?
— Declining allocation of internal funds for the replacement of research equipment in real terms may well match the decline in research capability. Unless external private or research council funds can provide such equipment some research may not proceed. Since research councils seem resigned to an expectation of level funding at best, there is every chance that their equipment buying power will fall. Trends in equipment sophistication will push up the average cost of each item in real terms; this probably means that a fixed budget is able to buy fewer items. Or will higher education follow the pattern in defence spending, where instead of man being equipped, sophisticated equipment is being manned?
— Although the polytechnics have long had their development

monitored by regional advisory councils, the extent of regional initiatives taken has been insubstantial. Common sense would suggest that more centrally determined course approvals at the AFE and non-university levels must produce economies. Trans-binary co-operation in a regional context is not common, unless imposed by central agencies as a requirement for central funding. Sadly, the instances where it occurs are rare enough to make news. (See project descriptions of the National Development Programme in Computer Assisted Learning in the Final Report of the Director (Hooper 1977).)

— The difficult economic decisions required by polytechnics and universities do not emerge easily from decision-making processes and structures developed for the age of participation and attempted collective agreements. Although pressures for extension and 'democratization' of these processes have long since died off, counter pressures to streamline the procedures have not yet been successful. Perhaps this factor will cause internal decision-making processes to change to reflect widespread impatience with tortuousness and delays.

There is a resulting need for two decision-making models in every institution; a formal leisurely process devoted to deciding on the core funding and a speedier ad hoc mechanism for responding to major commercial or external opportunities, where time is of the essence.

— Resource allocation in the institution is greatly influenced by — and is almost a mirror image of — national funding decisions. Thus, a reduction in funds to universities flowing directly from the UGC has already focused attention on overseas students as a market. Fees are a controllable variable and substantial fees can make life less unpleasant. Central decisions by, say, the UGC and the MSC are now affecting institutions more directly than ever before. On the one hand there is a firm indication that cuts and economies are expected, while on the other there is a provision of liberal funding, which it would be folly to ignore. The cumulative effect of these changes is to reduce the influence of the senate or academic board in setting strategic academic objectives for the institution. They can orchestrate a response to external sticks or carrots, but the scope for creative planning is being reduced.

— At a time of serious unemployment students give more thought to their degree choice than they do in periods of full employment. It is therefore to be expected that 'market pressures' will be evident where employment potential is high at the end of the degree course. The institutional decision-makers must weigh up the part they wish such courses to play in their portfolio. Should they get an increasing share of resources because of the strong demand or

does the overall academic strategy imply a less substantial role for the temporary 'cash cow' (Sizer 1981).
— A final, but significant, influence on institutional structures and decision making arises from the effect of the financial pressures on academic entrepreneurs. Those who have ideas which require finance and who fail to get it internally or from recognized research council or trust sources inevitably look elsewhere. The range of innovative approaches with industry and commerce is already substantial. This topic will be explored further in this chapter, but out of the entrepreneurial drive of the enthusiast arise new questions about institutional resources and some rethinking of the way they should be controlled and allocated.

The effect of these factors on institutional structures and systems during the 1980s and 1990s will be profound. It is unlikely that resource allocation will be as unified or as corporate a function as in the past. Before this argument is developed further, it would be sensible to define the broad requirements for institutional survival by describing what a successful institution will have achieved.

A STRATEGY FOR SURVIVAL
The keynote word for institutional survival has been and will continue to be 'flexibility'. Flexibility will be needed in several senses:

— In attitudes, expressed as an openness to new proposals, which may challenge conventional structures or approaches but which will aid the prosperity of the institution.
— In resource-allocation techniques and procedures since, as has already been shown, the environment within which resource decisions have to be taken is volatile and sometimes time-constrained.
— In structures and powers, with an acceptance of possible risk-taking by people to whom decision making has been delegated. Formal structures may remain, but as endorsing bodies, holding individuals to account for their decisions.

There are ten ways in which an institution can exhibit this flexibility. Some require considerable changes in structures and procedures, while others need no prior preparation and are already operational in some institutions. A successful institution will:

i   Encourage entrepreneurs to be entrepreneurial. This can be a matter of attitudes and systems. Although in the last resort it may be necessary to warn an individual that his ideas overstep the limit of what is desirable or seemly for the institution to become involved in, there should be few filters at the initial stages of entrepreneurial enthusiasm. Such an approach can be time consuming for administrators, but their convenience is not a major factor in planning the academic future. The most common source for entrepreneurial attention will be private sector companies and the institution should at an early stage agree some overall guidelines as to the style and manner of its involvement in purely commercial undertakings.

ii Develop internal mechanisms and services which can help the entrepreneur. These can range from the ability to understand the corporate environment to the formal establishment of research companies. The latter can be either unique to the project or an umbrella organization for all staff members which allows profits to be shared between the participant and the institution as a whole. Another simple area where academic staff may require help is in the production of technical reports and proposals to outside commercial standards and quality levels.

iii Actively promote its skills and facilities in the outside world. Good examples of this at present are the plethora of science parks being developed by many academic institutions, in conjunction with local authorities in some cases. Institutions are investigating a wide range of promotional mechanisms linked to regional development bodies, industrial development companies, local authority joint committees, or trade and industrial exhibitions. If an institution wishes to make industry aware of its capabilities and research experience there has, in today's environment, to be an element of salesmanship involved. Industry at large is not sufficiently aware of higher educational structures and practices to know how to go about tapping their resources, even where these have been identified. There is therefore room for some active promotion. Such effort should not only be directed at industry; the public sector is equally in need of such services.

iv Promote funding and staffing mechanisms which enable it to retain flexibility. The institution has an obligation to seek to remain innovative and be able to fund new academic developments. It must therefore adopt all the tools and techniques which make this possible. Among these are short-term appointments for staff and rewards for departments which agree to forego security in this way.

v Develop and maintain a long term institutional strategy for the academic core of the institution. There will be several disciplines which it is agreed to maintain as a constant. In some cases these will be subjects which do not lend themselves to entrepreneurial flair, as the opportunities for external sponsorship are limited. The institution should seek to offer these some guarantee of funding (without allowing complacency) from central sources.

How can an academic organization reach a degree of consensus on this favoured core? Even if it does, following the guidance given by Sizer (1981), is it right that the favoured subjects should be wholly cushioned? Might one find two cultures along side each other — the arts core and the entrepreneurial sciences?

Is it right that chemists, say, should be forced to scavenge in the market place just because there is some industrial money around to support chemistry research? Or should one give all disciplines a guaranteed minimum funding, leaving them to seek their own development money? In this event some subjects would never be likely to expand.

Answers to questions such as these can only be given by each institution itself since they involve a local balance of academic criteria and value judgements.

vi Encourage continual evaluation and self-appraisal. Whether this is by external peer groups or by internal self-analysis is not crucial. The important fact is that the zero base concept is adopted at intervals for each of the main activities of the organization. Higher educational institutions are most reluctant to arrive at harsh judgements about their constituent elements. Like a tree with many branches, they try to feed sap into a rotten branch. Such a branch may fall and damage other healthy ones; it would be better for the whole if it were cut out.

The verdict of the evaluation exercises should be incorporated in the strategic thinking and regular resource allocation exercises referred to. The more flexible an approach has been to staff tenure and other funding the easier it will be to make a change of direction. Other aids to flexibility are provisions for staff retraining and voluntary early retirement.

vii Incorporate cost-effectiveness criteria in the evaluation and review of academic performance. Senior academics and administrators have been ambivalent about using unit costs or cost criteria in academic decisions. While accepting that the world outside makes wide use of cost information, because there is very little other basis on which to compare institutions, they have shrunk from too obvious an emphasis on cost criteria in internal resource allocation. However quantitative the formulae there is always ample opportunity for qualitative overlay. This hesitation about cost criteria has almost become a ritual; costings are produced only to be discarded. Is it not time that they were accorded their own weight? How often does an academic board say: 'That is a fine course but we cannot afford it because it is too expensive'?

Once the world of costing is entered we can find several useful concepts:

- Incremental cost, the extra cost to an institution of a course of action.
- Opportunity cost is also particularly worthwhile as it describes the cost of a lost opportunity — what might have been gained from an alternative use of the same resources.
- Sunk cost, a favourite term of government economists, graphically relates to past costs. Decisions for the future can often forget sunk costs and concentrate solely on future flows of taxpayers' money.

If these three definitions are brought to bear on institutional decision making in an intelligent way, they can vividly illuminate resource-allocation decisions.

viii Emphasize that management skills are valued in the academic community. It is by now almost a cliché to say that managerial talent is not the key factor in academic promotion. However, this is not the same as ignoring it altogether. Where two equally able candidates differ only in their management capability, clearly the better manager ought to be favoured. There is a limited supply of geniuses and an individual who can manage complex research projects capably deserves to succeed. A head of department or senior academic with management skills will automatically acknowledge the importance of the criteria and factors for survival that have been listed. He will appreciate the significance of costing, he will wish to retain flexibility in the deployment of his own resources and will himself evaluate the performance of his subunits. Thus, a vice-chancellor or director who appoints a manager of this calibre will have a valuable ally in the battle to retain flexibility in the use of resources.

ix Encourage appreciation of market disciplines. Recent government decisions have made it clear that academic institutions have no divine right of existence. In order to survive they should be aware of all their markets; the community, the students and their parents or advisers, and employers. Yet how many British institutions embark on institutional research in the American sense? Are polytechnics aware of their catchment area? Do they know why students choose them? Do universities know why they rank where they do on the UCCA form? Is not one model of survival the one that tailors an institution's offerings to satisfy the wants of the market it has identified? Or aims to convert the market to wanting what it can provide? Even if no self-respecting senate would ever endorse this approach wholeheartedly, does it not have much to teach those who wish to survive and prosper?

x Streamline its decision-making structures and processes. Reference has already been made to cumbersome participative planning and resource-allocation systems which equalize misery or very thin slices of happiness. Such systems are unlikely to be capable of responding promptly and flexibly to the broad range of resource opportunities that will arise. Decision making has to be simplified. This should take three stages:

— The establishment of strategic guidelines by the supreme academic body concerning the academic shape of the institution and areas for growth and contraction.
— Delegation to specified individuals of powers to allocate or withdraw resources, approve contracts and agreements within the broad guidelines.
— Identification of a formal, very small subcommittee of three or four individuals to act as a sounding board for those with delegated powers. This subcommittee should be free to meet at very short notice during vacations and term time.

Individuals and subcommittees to whom powers are delegated are in the last resort accountable to the body which gives them their powers. Academic board or senate should be realistic in the way it calls to account those to whom such authorities have been given.

The ten points described would represent a startling change, if they were all implemented overnight. The operative word, again, should be 'flexibility'. The objective of all the ideas is to enable the institution to respond promptly to change. Not all will need to adopt these proposals, some may have got far beyond them already.

IMPLICATIONS FOR PARTICIPANTS

The future, as described above, is likely to be less secure and predictable for most participants. There will also be more complexity in financing and funding relationships and it may be difficult to define lines of accountability and control in some instances. It should, however, be dynamic; change will be a fundamental element in academic planning and there will be opportunities for new development.

A brief review of the likely impact on each of the key participants will illuminate the scenario.

For students the changes should be beneficial. Their education may be more relevant than hitherto if the market lessons have been learnt and of more consistent quality if evaluation criteria can be consistently applied to the process of learning. Those teaching staff who are engaged in entrepreneurial activities with the outside world may bring an understanding of its problems to their teaching, but there is a risk that they may be distracted by the demanding timetables of industrial clients.

A significant number of changes in the role and status of academic staff could influence their support. They would have a changed tenure and less job security. They might enjoy institutional funding for their teaching activity only and even in this there would be pressures of performance review and accountability. There would be reduced involvement in formal, institutional decision making and resource allocation, but a very broad scope for seeking external funding for research. The institution would back promotional initiatives of this kind and there would be personal rewards and incentives if the individual were successful.

The academic leadership would adopt a positive style. While external agencies would themselves probably be dirigiste, the in-built flexibility of response would offer the leadership a chance to overcome these constraints. Despite these advantages it may be difficult for the director or vice-chancellor to remain fully informed on all the developments in the institution. The greater freedom for entrepreneurial staff to seek external sources of funding could lead to apparent loss of 'control' and it would be necessary for the academic leadership to find some means of monitoring what is going on. The leadership role would be difficult if it were desired to restrict some entrepreneurial activity, since, without the control provided by finance, the powers available are somewhat intangible.

Administrators will have to service a greatly changed decision-making structure. They will also need to develop improved reporting and information systems to match the delegated authorities and devolution of decision making. If people are given power over resources, they will require specific information to help them manage those resources. The control and reporting systems may not change as regards the academic core subjects, although there may have to be some mechanisms for recording the outcome of self-appraisal or evaluation exercises. In one area administrators can expect to provide a new category of service. This would be in relation to company formations, international negotiations, commercial accounting and taxation advice, and many other topics resulting from the industrial involvement of the institution.

How realistic is the prospect that has been described? Is it a management consultant's dream (nightmare to some) or might it be the way forward? Taken individually the steps are not dramatic and none are improbable, but put together they imply a greatly changed environment. There will also be many other solutions for individual institutions which have not been outlined. Can the scenario be reconciled with Sizer's pessimistic concluding quotation from the Carnegie Council (1980) that 'the internal constituencies are more likely to be united around doing nothing than doing something'?

REFERENCES

Fielden, J. and Lockwood, G. (1973) *Planning and Management in Universities* London: Sussex University Press

Hooper, R. (1977) *The National Development Programme in Computer Assisted Learning. Final Report of the Director* London: Council for Educational Technology

Moodie, G. and Eustace, R. (1974) *Power and Authority in British Universities* London: George Allen & Unwin Ltd.

Sizer, J. (1981) Assessing institutional performance and progress. In Wagner, L. (Editor) *Agenda for Institutional Change* Guildford: Society for Research into Higher Education

TERMS OF EMPLOYMENT

by Peter Knight

The prime question which has to be answered by an analysis of the terms and conditions of service for academic staff must be: how can those terms and conditions be changed in the 1990s so that:

a   the quality of education received by students is improved,
b   the quantity of education at advanced level is changed 'appropriately',
c   the efficiency in cost terms is improved,
d   the acquisition of knowledge is enhanced?

If that is the central question that this chapter is designed to answer preliminary analysis indicates that the results will be depressing.

There may be difficulty in acknowledging that the terms and conditions of service of academic staff have a significant impact on the scale and scope of higher education. This problem seems to arise from the fact that public debate, particularly about the level of salaries, does not usually concentrate on the educational consequences of the issues. The debate, at that level, could be regarded as the rather ritual posturing by the representatives of employers and employees that is intended to influence the negotiations that always occur in a more private manner. Yet it must be accepted that the aggregate effect of several salary settlements that, say, reduce higher education salaries would be an inexorable lowering of the quality of the service by reducing its ability to compete for able employees. Conversely, successive high settlements would increase the unit cost and may cause the government to take action to reduce the quantity of higher education available. Such changes tend to be slow and subtle in their effect rather than immediate and obvious. Nevertheless, over a period of years the terms and conditions of academic staff could have far-reaching consequences for higher education.

INERTIA

A single basic premise must now be emphasized because it is upon that premise that the argumentation will be developed. That premise is that in all questions of salary and conditions of service there is a massive inertia. Change is exceptionally difficulty to achieve because the existing terms and conditions of service, even if totally inappropriate, make the negotiators on both sides prisoners of history. We are paid what we are paid because our predecessors were paid what they were paid. There is little rationality in any pay structure. A rate of pay is 95 per cent history, 5 per cent destiny. The opportunity for rational analysis or for logical approaches is restricted to a very small amount of adjustment at the margins.

One factor which encourages and enhances the natural inertia of the system is the edifice of employment law that has been created over the past three decades. All concepts of employment law are general concepts. They do not have written into their statutes and schedules a phrase that says 'except for the academic staff of Giggleswick University'. Employment law governs the relationship between employers and employees and is as applicable in the most refined university college in the land as it is applicable in the smallest, most reactionary, independent company. It may be inconvenient, it may be misunderstood, it may be inappropriate, it may be counter-productive, but it is the law and it applies to professors, vice-chancellors, lecturers and all other employees. The very fact that it is written as a general statement means that it will restrict and preclude actions which might otherwise have been in the interests of a developing system of higher education.

HISTORY

Universities

If it is accepted that the prime determinant of the existing system is the historical constraint that has acted upon it, then it is interesting to look at the different historical developments of the university sector as against the public sector. Such a study may indicate why sectors have different characteristics in relation to pay and conditions.

The universities owe their origin to private enterprise. They were created at various times in the development of the country by individual trusts and endowments. Consequently, the characteristics of the system in the early part of this century were that there was little, if any, uniformity in staff and salary structure as between one university and another. Salary levels reflected the size of endowments and the fees that could be charged. The fees that could be charged were determined by market forces and the number of potential students who could be enrolled.

The University Grants Committee was appointed at a time when it was decided to increase considerably the state aid given to university education. From its formation in 1919 until the end of the Second World War the University Grants Committee monitored the level of academic salaries. However, it never advocated that those salaries should be standardized between institutions for to do so would have been regarded as an unacceptable attack on the individual autonomy of the universities.

Consequently, in 1930 it was reiterating the opinion:

'... we have expressed on previous occasions, adverse to any general scheme applicable to all university institutions and providing for uniform fixed salary scales in automatic increments. Each university or college must be free to decide for itself what is best suited to its own needs and resources and it is not only natural but desirable, that the size, wealth and standing of different institutions should be reflected by difference in salaries.' (Cmnd 3866)

A fine statement for university autonomy and for what is colloquially known in the terminology of industrial relations as 'plant bargaining'. Except, of course, for the fact that while the salary levels were fixed in each plant it is unlikely in the extreme that there was any bargaining in terms of a collective discussion between employers and their employees.

Ideals founder on the rocks of pragmatism and after the Second World War the less well endowed universities found that they were unable to offer appropriate salaries without substantial government money. There were discussions between the University Grants Committee and the Treasury in 1946 as a result of which the UGC specified a standard rate for the professorial salary. The Committee wrote in 1946:

'There can, in the judgement of the Committee, be no justification for the utilisation of a university of a largely increased Exchequer grant for the purpose of raising salaries beyond the level which the Treasury are prepared to subsidize.' (Cmnd 2267)

This was a complete reversal of their previous policy. That reversal owed its origin to simple market forces. If universities were still free to offer any salary that they thought appropriate then there could be 'poaching', whereby the best endowed institutions might be able to bribe away from the less well endowed institutions their most able staff by offering them higher salaries. If poaching develops then it can quickly become self-fuelling. As able staff enhance the reputation of an institution and such enhancement leads to more endowments then such endowments lead to an increased ability to poach even more staff from other colleges. Consequently, the concept of a standardized rate of pay was inevitable.

In 1948 the Spens Committee (Cmnd 7420) reported on the pay of consultants and specialists working in the universities and introduced a standardized salary scale. In 1949 a new basic salary framework covering all other academic staff was announced. This was the first time that scales of salaries had been laid down nationally for all principal grades of university teachers.

It is interesting to note that once the concept of a national pay system had been accepted it was introduced with considerable speed and competence. Only the universities of Oxford and Cambridge and the pay of clinical staff remained outside the system. The system not only specified the pay, it also specified a maximum proportion of senior posts (ie senior lecturers, readers, professors) to lecturer posts. Failure to have specified such a ratio would have led, once again, to the dangers of poaching as a well endowed institution could have offered more promoted posts.

There is a secondary, but significant effect in the introduction of a national salary scale. Let us assume that previously the rates of pay of individual lecturers had been determined both by the ability of the employer to pay and the market forces prevailing at the time. In these circumstances lecturers who were not able to gain employment in outside industry and commerce would presumably be cheaper then those who could be offered attractive alternative posts. Hence a lecturer in a marketable subject, say physics, should have been paid more than a colleague in a less marketable discipline such as ancient Greek. A national salary scale removes the effect of such market forces from the system and individual colleges are obliged to pay the same amount of salary to all lecturers irrespective of their discipline. This creates the concept of a rate of pay of a university lecturer. Yet the subjects upon which a lecturer is practising his profession will receive substantially different rates of pay in the outside community. This dilemma creates a tension within the pay structure that is probably more significant in the public sector than in the universities but it is worth noting that it was only postwar that it became apparent within the universities.

The university scales are interesting. First, they have always had equal pay for men and women. It would be pleasant to think that such an egalitarian concept was introduced as a matter of principle; but its origins may lie in the fact that there were very few female academics. This is a complete contrast with the situation in the public sector. Secondly, the basic university lecturer scale is exceptionally long (Appendix). In fact, it is probably the longest single scale in the whole of public employment. It is largely age-related, with extensive use being made of an age-tie point, usually at age 26. Such a scale is unimaginative, plodding and designed to discourage creativity and to eliminate incentives. It is a scale for time-servers. It is inescapable that once appointed to that scale individuals will creep up to the maximum with only minor variations in the speed at which they achieve that goal. The only opportunities for rewarding merit remain in promotion to a more senior post. It is surprising that in a community that is meant to encourage initiative and reward creativity the basic salary scale should be such as to discourage such activities and to provide the minimum possible opportunity for rewarding them.

An interesting discussion can be had about the basic question as to why university lecturers are paid the amounts of money that they are. That phrase is not meant to imply over or under payment. It is simply asking what rationale there is for the existing level of pay. The rationale is notionally based on the concept of a 'fair comparison'. As market forces have now disappeared some other mechanism is necessary to fix the rate of pay. The Priestley Royal Commission on the Civil Service (Cmnd 9613) reported in 1955 that in relation to the pay of civil servants there could be a principle of 'fair comparison': that

'... the jobs thought to be compared must be found to be capable of reasonably close comparison in the sense that the duties, responsibilities, conditions of service of the one, exhibit, if not an identity with, at least what can rightly be called a similarity to those of the other.'

In relation to university teachers the National Incomes Commission (Cmnd 3866b) stated that:

'... a principle which it thought was proper in looking at university salaries... (was) ... the competition of several occupations for recruits from the same sort of supply ... were obliged to look at the salaries offered by the others in order to judge what, in the context of the relevant circumstances of the whole field in which the competition operates, was required to restore the balance between several competitors.'

The basic principle being established here is the concept that in order to recruit able staff one needs to pay the same amount as one's competitors. The idea was now established, without challenge, that there was an industry called the universities and that there was a pool of potential recruits from which employees might be selected and in order to remain competitive an appropriate rate of pay needed to be offered.

There is an underlying attitude in all these debates. That is that one needs to pay university lecturers the sort of salary that will, largely, insulate them from the vulgarities of everyday life. While they will never be rich, they should not be poor, because if they are poor, they are unlikely to be able to discharge their duties. You cannot expect men to think great thoughts on small salaries. This is an interesting attitude, particularly as it does not extend down to research workers on limited-term contracts within the university system. It is the concept of a gentleman's salary for gentleman's work. All the parallels quoted tend to be from other types of gentlemen's jobs: ie higher administrative grades within the civil service.

This cynical analysis can be further supported by the fascinating contrast between the universities and the public sector. At no stage in the discussion on pay is there any debate about the duties which should be undertaken in order to justify that pay. Those duties are 'understood'. There are very few occupations in which such an understanding exists. One might be tempted to say that the closest parallel is with members of parliament. Now it is arguable whether or not members of parliament are provided with a salary that is sufficient to insulate them from everyday life. They may well be significantly underpaid, particularly by international comparisons. Nevertheless, the concept of terms and conditions of service for members of parliament in determining their pay is clearly inappropriate.

Whether it remains inappropriate for 30,000 university academic staff is a radically different matter.

With the exception of the standardized university superannuation scheme, all other matters, except for pay, are the responsibility of the individual university. Obviously, in some areas such as sick pay, or maternity leave, there are statutory provisions and there is some uniformity between institutions. Nevertheless, the basic principle is that conditions of service, if specified at all, are matters for plant bargaining in each individual university, in a situation where the universities usually decline to bargain.

Public Sector
The public sector of higher education has developed from technical education and teacher training; in their turn these owe their origins to developments in, or deficiencies in, the school system. The origin of the existing salary structure is the salary structure that existed in primary and secondary schools as long ago as 1925, when the Burnham Committee was instituted to determine the pay of teachers. That committee has, from time to time, undergone various changes in its statutory base and different committees have been set up to deal with particular types of teachers. For instance, there have been separate committees to consider agricultural education, and there was a committee, the Pelham Committee, which considered, on a non-statutory basis, the pay of staff in teacher training colleges. The Pelham Committee was merged with the Burnham Further Education Committee as recently as 1976. The existing situation is that the Burnham Primary and Secondary Committee determines the pay of school teachers and the Burnham Further Education Committee governs the pay of staff in further education colleges, agricultural colleges and all public sector higher education institutions. The word 'colleges' is used loosely in referring to the remit of these committees. The committees determine the pay of teachers. Whether those teachers happen to be teaching advanced work in a particular college is not a matter for the committee and, except in unusual circumstances, is not likely to be a prime determinant of the pay of the individual.

In contrast with the university scales the scales that have applied in further education have been standardized as national scales from as long ago as 1925. It was in that year that the Viscount Burnham wrote to the secretary of state stating that:

'I strongly recommend:
1 The Board of Education shall ensure that no local education authority shall gain financially by paying salaries on a basis lower than the appropriate standard scales.
2 No part of such sum shall be applied towards so increasing the salaries of classes of teachers as mentioned in the report that would be tantamount to altering the operation of the scales'. (Burnham Committee 1938)

So for over fifty-five years there have been standard national scales operating in the public sector. Those scales did not provide for equal pay and it is to the eternal shame of the public sector that it was not until 1961 that equal pay was finally introduced. Naturally, equal pay was hard to introduce simply because there was a high proportion of women teaching in primary education. This is clear evidence of the way in which a feature of the primary and secondary scales largely determines the characteristics of the further education scales even when that particular feature is not relevant to further and higher education. The local authorities would not concede equal pay in further education simply because of the consequences on primary and secondary pay.

It is not only in the details of the pay structure that the effects of the primary and secondary scales are felt. The single greatest determinant of the level of pay in the Further Education Burnham Committee is the offer that is made and accepted by the Primary and Secondary Committee. It is political reality that the Management Panel will not make an offer in the FE Committee that is greater than the offer they have made in the Primary and Secondary Committee. Primary and Secondary leads in determining the size of the global sum. That is a fact simply because the size of the salary bill in primary and secondary education is of the order of £4.5 billion whereas the size of the salary bill in further education is slightly less than £1 billion. Given the inter-relationships between the two committees, Primary and Secondary makes the running. Further Education can only tinker at the edges. Hence it is self-evident that the salaries of lecturers doing advanced work in the public sector are primarily determined by the nature of the negotiations for the salaries of schoolteachers. That particular market force is overwhelming and cannot be ignored. It would be tempting and politically expedient to leave an analysis of the public sector hastily, without discussing the question of conditions of service. Conditions of service is a general term that relates to many matters that are uncontentious. For instance, questions of an appropriate scheme of sick pay, sensible pension arrangements, the amount of notice that is required on leaving a post are all matters that should be reasonably specified in the relations between an employer and an employee. Where the concept of conditions of service treads on sensitive ground is in the arrangements that exist in the public sector under the Conditions of Service Agreement which was negotiated in 1974 and 1975 (National Joint Council 1975). It is unlikely that any comparable document exists within the university sector. The most significant clauses in it are: 6.2, defining the working year; 7.1, defining a maximum of ten sessions; 7.3, defining the working week of thirty hours; 7.9, defining the maximum class contact hours per week; 8.2, defining a class contact hour; 8.3, introducing the concept of 'remission' of teaching; and 9, determining payment of overtime.

This agreement specifies, as one of its most contentious provisions, the maximum class contact hours that a lecturer can be required to teach in any one week. The idea of such an agreement would be completely alien to the university sector especially as the maximum lecturing hours that are required in the public sector are in excess of the lecturing hours that are usually expected within the universities. In contrast, the vacation periods in the public sector are substantially longer than they are under the arrangement for university staff. When this agreement was concluded there was a feeling that it was alien to the basic processes of higher education.

It is difficult now to separate legitimate objections to the arrangements from the political rhetoric that surrounded them at the time. It is certainly true that the agreement had its origins in the way non-advanced further education operates rather than in the style which many people would wish to see in advanced further education. It is equally true to say that the existence of the agreement has prevented class contact hours for lecturers in both non-advanced and advanced further education from being unreasonably increased. For the basic grades of Senior Lecturer and Lecturer Grade II the hours required are of the order of 15 — 20 per week. Those figures would represent the norm in many institutions. It can be argued forcibly that a lecturer who is teaching those hours, and an institution that is so requiring him, is not operating in a sensible or an efficient manner. A desirable characteristic of higher education, as it is offered by the university sector, is for students to be taught significantly less time in the week than their public sector counterparts and for the university staff to teach correspondingly less hours. Such a provision would enhance the quality of education offered in the public sector. Once maximum hours are specified there is pressure to ensure that staff are teaching those hours. A college management that is sufficiently courageous to try to prevent hours reaching the maximum is laying itself open to charges of inefficiency. For it would be easy to show that the staff were 'under-utilized' if they were only teaching 50 per cent of their maximum hours. Yet it is quite clear that teaching styles can be adopted so that greater emphasis is placed on the preparation of lectures, seminars and tutorial work and that consequently the overall efficiency of the operation is not jeopardized. The day when the Conditions of Service Agreement becomes an irrelevancy in advanced further education should be welcomed. It is to be regretted that all the evidence suggests that that day is a long way off. A recent report of the District Audit Commission laid particular emphasis on the question of maximum hours and seemed to suggest that there was something indecent in colleges not having their staff operating absolutely at the maximum. This was despite the fact that other, more sophisticated measures of efficiency, such as student staff ratios showed that the colleges concerned were operating in a perfectly satisfactory manner.

The main limitation of the Conditions of Service Agreement is that it specifies only that which is measurable. The prime characteristics of an academic's job relate more to what is not measurable rather than to what is.

It relates to the quality of the teaching, not necessarily the quantity, and it relates to the ability to carry out research and academic administration. A lecturer who discharges his commitments under the Conditions of Service Agreement, even if operating at the maximum class contact hours, and doing nothing else, is not contributing to the institution in the way that one would hope. I repeat, that the Conditions of Service Agreement, while infinitely valuable as a trade union bargaining tool inhibits the sensible development of teaching styles in public sector colleges and prevents the academic staff concerned from having a professional and rewarding outlook on work.

FLEXIBILITY
In both the university and the public sector the salaries and conditions of service of the academic staff are often characterized as rigid and inflexible. It is often superficially thought that greater flexibility would lead to a more enriched and vibrant system. Envious glances are cast at the United States where there is often free bargaining on an individual basis between the academic and the university over the appropriate rate of salary; tenure largely does not exist for junior staff; academic appointments are not regarded as permanent and there is a greater mobility between younger academics in the various institutions than there is in this country. So, does flexibility as portrayed by the system in the United States offer us real opportunities for change? Before embracing flexibility with too much enthusiasm it is worth pausing for a moment and appreciating that our own system already contains employment opportunities that are characterized by such flexibility, particularly in relation to the treatment both in the universities and the public sector of research workers. The research worker, whether at doctoral or post-doctoral level, is in a situation where if he is not actually occupying a lectureship then he has no career structure. The rates of pay are depressed because the groups concerned are in no position to bargain and agreed terms and conditions of service are largely non-existent, so that individuals can be exploited, if that is not too vulgar a word, and will have little redress. As was said of many slaves in previous centuries — they actually enjoy it, so it's probably good for them.

The present arrangements for the employment of research workers have grown up with the institutions. It was previously regarded as a perfectly sensible way of ensuring that the most able undergraduates remained with their discipline for a further three years or more in order to obtain their doctoral degree. Then after a discreet interval of post-doctoral work they moved on to a full-time academic appointment. Inevitably there was an element of weeding out in this process. Some students fell by the wayside because of their inability to maintain the appropriate academic standard. Others decided that they were either not suited to or did not wish to pursue an academic life and obtained jobs in other areas of employment. Nevertheless a substantial number went on to tenured academic posts. The first signs that the system was beginning to fail occurred when more and more researchers were finding themselves in the position where they had to move from limited term contract to limited term contract at post-doctoral level and their chances of obtaining secure employment were receding with each move. As the situation in relation to new posts got worse it became clear that this career structure, or lack of one, was an employment trap into which one should not move. Now the chances of gaining a permanent appointment at the end of either a doctoral or a series of post-doctoral appointments are vanishingly small. Hence we have moved to a situation where the students who are attracted into these appointments are only those who are not able to obtain outside employment.

In other words the lack of a secure career structure is filtering out of the system the most able people, whereas previously the flexibility of the system kept the most able in. Flexibility is a disincentive to the most able, who can always find better and more secure opportunities elsewhere. Given the structure of employment in the 1980s the continued use of limited term contracts for people of ability is an appalling way of providing employees for the research function. One cannot help but wonder whether, particularly in the physical and engineering sciences, the greater use of technicians or graduate assistants would not be a better way of ensuring that the same volume of research was done, albeit by a smaller number of academics.

A study of the duties carried out by research students would lead a neutral observer to question whether they were students receiving instruction, or whether in reality they were employees carrying out certain duties that happened to be prescribed in an unusual way. For if the conclusion that they were employees were valid then they should not be paid a grant but should be paid a wage. Surely any impartial and dispassionate analysis of the system would conclude that the research students were not students — but employees who happened at the end of a limited term contract to gain a doctoral degree. Interestingly the difficulty that the public sector has experienced in getting research students from the research councils has led them to use the research assistant posts. Research assistants are, in the majority of the polytechnics, used in exactly the same way as research students. Able graduates are appointed to the post with the expectation that in two or three years they will leave having undertaken the work that is appropriate to gain a higher degree. They are, of course, required to undertake a small amount of teaching and demonstrating duties in addition to their research but that amount is often nominal. Consequently, in the public sector, the people who are being employed in research are employees and they are paid. It is equally worth pointing out that at the conclusion of their limited term contracts they may well be eligible for and receive redundancy pay.

It would be wrong to give the impression that the public sector is in a more honourable position in its treatment of research workers than its university counterpart. The same general problem continues to occur in relation to the level of salaries. Prior to the study by the Clegg Commission of job comparability of lecturers, the rates of pay of research assistants were determined locally. Whenever the rates of pay are determined locally for a group which is poorly organized, the effect is that the level of pay is depressed. In many areas the research assistants, who presumably would have good first degrees, would receive less than their degree and qualifications would entitle them to in school teaching. The Clegg Commission was rightly appalled at these arrangements for local bargaining and as a result made a recommendation that a national scale should be introduced. Inevitably that national scale is substantially less rewarding in terms of salary than the graduates would attract if they were appointed to the lecturer scale. Nevertheless that salary is still substantially greater than the amount of income that research students would receive as a result of their research council grants: a differential that can be acutely felt in departments where research students and research assistants are working side by side.

The pattern of employment of research workers gives us evidence of the ultimate flexibility. There is no evidence that the quality of research is in any way enhanced by such flexibility and a genuine concern must be that the line between flexibility and abuse of people's goodwill is a very narrow one; and it is one which I think we have crossed in dealing with research students. The job of a research student is demonstratively that of an employee, not that of a student.

INTERNATIONAL COMPARISONS

In any discussion of higher education policy it is usual to study the international comparisons to see what can be learned from other country's mistakes. However, when it comes to questions of salary and conditions of service such international comparisons are almost irrelevant. A survey of the systems that exist around the world will demonstrate those where there is free bargaining between the individual and the university; those that are characterized by a hire and fire mechanism; those where the lecturer is only paid for the hours that he actually happens to teach and for the rest of the time he must produce his income in other ways; and those where there are formal rates of pay, predefined career structures and reasonably stable forms of employment. The most significant fact that has to be accepted is that systems that are created in other countries are created out of the attitudes and framework of law of those countries. It would be impossible to pick up the practices in the United States and to transplant them wholesale to this country. Whether they were good or bad is irrelevant, they simply do not fit into the forms of employment which we operate. The system of employment law, which is not designed specifically with university and polytechnic lecturers in mind, has tremendous inertia. If you try to create within it a bubble in which higher education is isolated from its effects and if the consequence of that operation is that the terms and conditions of service in higher education are less attractive than those in outside industry, then the most able lecturers will leave for the more stable forms of employment offered outside. Hence the quality of one's employees will fall and consequently the quality of the system will fall. Hence your local framework of employment law is absolutely final in determining the room for manoeuvre that is available in any particular circumstance.

MYTHS OF EMPLOYMENT LAW

It must further be emphasized that the framework of employment law within this country, when coupled with the general attitude and expectations of people in white collar employment, is not noted for its flexibility. This is not simply a matter of party political argument, although there are changes of degree with changes of government. There is a general attitude in this country that makes it difficult for a public employer to act in a cavalier or entrepreneurial manner towards his employees. Hence it is exceptionally difficult for such an employer to operate a system of hiring and firing almost on a whim, which would be the characteristic of higher education in some other countries. This is not an argument about tenure which is a particular interpretation of an unusual set of contractual arrangements. It is to say that even if tenure did not exist the universities would be exceptionally hard pressed to dismiss lecturing staff. Similarly the polytechnics do not find it easy to dismiss their academic staff other than for exceptional cause. The concept of hire and fire does not exist in this country for professional employees and if it were introduced as a way of enlivening the employees in higher education then quite simply the best would leave, the worst would try to stay.

If this is a depressing analysis there are isolated glimpses of hope. It has been argued that it is hard to sack academics. Putting questions of tenure to one side for the courts of law to resolve, we are left with the question, 'Why is it difficult to sack academics who are incompetent?' The answer is often not hidden in employment law, it is hidden in the attitudes of employers and employees. It is difficult because nobody has tried it, and it is difficult because people misunderstand the provisions of the law. There is a general principle of common law which provides that no one can be forced by law to work and no one can be forced by law to employ. If you dismiss an employee without good reason, no court in the land can require you to re-employ him. What a court can do is to reward the employee with compensation and for the employer it is a question of judgement as to how much he is prepared to pay in order to get rid of a particularly inept or obstreperous individual. Hence if a polytechnic director were so minded, and received the backing of his governing body and local authority as appropriate, he could walk into the staff room one day and say, 'Dr Bloggs, or Professor Higgins, get your cards, you are out of the college as of now.' A situation which would not be too surprising for his American counterparts would certainly leave him swinging gently in the breeze on the front page of the *Times Higher Education Supplement*. Let us ask ourselves the question, 'Could he actually do it?' The answer is that if he were acting as the employer, yes he could. He could summarily dismiss without cause. There would then be a grubby and unpleasant battle through industrial tribunals and the net result would be that if the director failed to demonstrate good cause he would be instructed to re-employ. At that stage he could still turn round and say, 'No, I will not obey the instruction to re-employ.' The industrial tribunal would then be able to award to the staff concerned only compensation for loss of employment. There is no power in law for a tribunal to oblige the employer to take staff back. As the compensation in such cases is not particularly large in relation to the salary that academics attract, it may well seem an attractive proposition for employers to pursue. Needless to say the circumstances described would be somewhat unusual in the placid world of higher education and the union representatives of the individuals concerned may have something to say about it. However, it is worth emphasizing that the process of dismissal can occur and indeed has occurred in a number of cases. There have been dismissals for just cause and dismissals for unjust cause but they have largely been dealt with quietly and without any attendant publicity. They are very much the exception, not the rule.

WHAT CAN BE DONE?

It has been a basic contention of the arguments presented in this chapter that the terms and conditions of service of academic staff on both sides of the binary line are exceptionally difficult to change. Change is inhibited both by the inertia of the status quo and by the stultifying framework of employment law. The single example of flexibility, as it is applied to research workers, casts discredit on both the universities and the public sector as responsible employers. The question must now be asked whether or not there is any hope of a change in the system that would improve the provision of higher education in the 1990s.

An ideal system of employment could be defined as one where the individual employees had security yet were encouraged to change their jobs frequently; where the rates of pay represented a just reward for the levels of skill and responsibility deployed and yet were economic; where the system was lawful in that it was within the framework of employment law but that framework was recognized as a support for the system rather than an inhibitor.

It might be possible to introduce improvements that would achieve these objectives by changing the attitudes of mind of the staff and their employing colleges. For instance, on both sides of the binary line emphasis is often placed on the quality of research when considering questions of promotion. Such an emphasis tends to ignore other more desirable features of employees' experience. Now suppose that the emphasis were removed from research and that the key to promotion were to have recently spent two or three years in industry, commerce or the professions. If that were the guiding attitude of mind then there would be a positive inducement to staff to seek contracts outside the institution. Security could be provided by the college seconding the staff either on salary, or even on salary with an element of enhancement, to recognize the contribution that that experience would make to their ability to teach when they returned. So a simple system whereby salary is enhanced by, say £1,000 for the first year spent in industry, then £2,000 for the second and third year would be a considerable inducement, at comparatively small cost, for individuals to seek employment and broaden their experience.

Undoubtedly, a number of the people so employed would find the outside work so stimulating that they would prefer to continue their career there rather than return to academic life. While the loss of such people would be a loss to the system, nobody is irreplaceable and a vacancy would be created for another appointment to be made. In making such an appointment emphasis could be placed on the desirability of bringing somebody into the institution in mid-career rather than continuing to recruit at the traditional level of post-doctoral experience. There would be nothing unlawful in such a process. All that would be required would be a change from the traditional attitude with its undue emphasis on research experience. There would be a number of technical details that would have to be tidied up. For instance, pension arrangements can often be an inhibition to such provisions. Once again, if the will were there such problems could be overcome.

Clearly such arrangements for temporary transfer to outside employment are more relevant to some disciplines than others. For the arts and social sciences there may be little external opportunity other than teaching in primary and secondary education. One suspects that such an option might not be particularly attractive to many academics. It should be recognized that for these disciplines it is not so important to maintain contact with outside professional interests. In these areas invigorating exchanges could be arranged between institutions and perhaps between countries. The problem once again is that the system offers no incentive for such activity. An incentive in salary would be an assistance. An incentive that recognized such a move as enhancing one's promotion prospects would be an encouragement, and simple provision like assistance with the expenses associated with moving and rental of accommodation would be an added advantage. The net cost of all these provisions would, when compared with the individual's salary, be small. Yet the net effect of introducing such arrangements would be to change the existing attitude of mind within the system as a whole. Such exchange experiences would be broadening. They would give to individual academics a wider perspective and understanding than they could achieve at present. One suspects that if the way to promotion for an Oxford don relied on him having had to spend two years in a nearby polytechnic as a Lecturer Grade II then the polytechnic would have to put up a barricade to keep out the applicants. Such exchanges would lead to a greater understanding of the values and attitudes within the sectors than exists at the moment.

The concept of job exchange or long-term secondment within the security of one's full-time employment is used all too rarely. Its introduction could significantly improve the quality of many academics and could provide at least one mechanism whereby there was a voluntary movement of people out of academic life into other forms of employment. The bad feature of academic life on both sides of the binary line is the idea that it is a job for life. In this respect the concept of tenure in the universities is a disgraceful anomaly which should be removed at the earliest opportunity. Security is one thing, academic freedom is necessary and should be defended, but the idea that those two objectives can only be achieved by a guarantee of a job for life is completely unacceptable in the current age.

Before leaving such a proposal it is worth emphasizing that the single greatest change that needs to take place in order to have a significant effect is a change in attitude towards the criteria for promotion. As long as research effort is regarded as the primary criteria there will be no change of this kind. The over-emphasis on research ability has a deadening effect on teaching ability. It is to be regretted that there are many signs that suggest that the public sector is making the same mistake as the university sector in this respect. Research work is important, and is significant in assisting the academic standard of the college, but to use it exclusively, as many do, to determine the promotion prospects of staff is an exceedingly bad employment practice.

There are comparatively few changes that are either needed, or could be made in the salary structure that would have a significant effect on the nature of higher education. The general level of salaries is adequate when compared with the salaries of comparable professions. That doesn't mean to say that one could not make a persuasive argument for a few more pounds here or a few less pounds there. It is to suggest that the general level of pay is appropriate and defensible. There are minor irritants and differentials which are strongly felt. Nevertheless, their removal is not likely to have a significant effect even although such problems should be resolved. In particular, the levels of pay in the public sector should be made to mirror the levels that the universities attract. In terms of its long-term consequences it does not matter if that was achieved by increasing public sector pay or decreasing that of the universities. The general principle is that there should be no differential between them. The existence of the differential, however small, is an irritant, not an assistant, to sensible transfer between the sectors. It must be stated that the only long-term way in which this can be guaranteed is for the pay of lecturers in advanced further education to be separated from the pay of lecturers education colleagues. Such an action will break the tie with the school scales which has been a deadening hand on the scales available for higher education. Strangely, this very effect may come about, not because of pressure from the higher education sector, but because the development of tertiary education for the 16 to 19 age group will require the pay of lecturers teaching non-advanced work to be more closely tied to the pay of primary and secondary teachers. Such a change will not be easy but the pressures that exist at the moment seem to be making it inescapable.

In relation to changes in employment law it is difficult to see any proposals which would have a significant or constructive effect. As has been mentioned before, one cannot isolate academic life from the general framework of employment law. The consequences of so doing would simply be to make it less attractive to work in higher education and probably to drive the most able exployees into other activities. Hence those who wish to argue that flexibility may be a saving grace are mistaken simply because they have failed to recognize that flexibility is a disincentive for employment and will dissuade staff of the highest calibre from entering higher education.

CONCLUSION

Radical changes in pay and conditions will not provide a credible structure for higher education in the 1990s. If general agreement is reached on the nature of the provision in that decade it must then be accepted that the employees who will provide it will be on terms and conditions of service not drastically dissimilar from those that operate at present. Some improvements can be made but these are more in the attitude of mind of the colleges and their employees than by fundamental changes in the salary structures. The hope that should be expressed, whether realistically or in vain is hard to determine, is that over the next few years the universities and the public sector will grow closer together in the principles and attitudes that determine their terms and conditions of service. Such similarity can only enhance the interchange between the sectors. In no way need it be viewed as weakening the essential distinctiveness of the two sides of the binary line.

REFERENCES

Burnham Committee (1938) *Scales of Salaries for Teachers in Technical and Art Schools* July, p.23

Cmnd 2267 (1964) *Report of the UGC on University Development 1956-62* February

Cmnd 3866 (1968) National Board on Prices and Incomes, Report 98 *Standing Reference on the Pay of University Teachers* December, p.4

Cmnd 3866b (1968) National Board on Prices and Incomes, Report 98 *Standing Reference on the Pay of University Teachers* December, p.6

Cmnd 7420 (1948) Spens Committee *Report of the Inter-Departmental Committee on the Remuneration of Consultants and Specialists* May
Cmnd 9613 (1955) Priestley Commission *Report of the Royal Commission on the Civil Service 1953-55* November
National Joint Council for Teachers in Further Education (1975) *Conditions of Service for Further Education Teachers in England and Wales* ('The Silver Book')

APPENDIX

COMPARATIVE SCALES

It has been exceptionally difficult in the past to provide a meaningful comparison between the university lecturer scales and the Burnham further education scales because of the different settlement dates; from 1982 both sectors will settle on 1 April each year but at the time of writing neither group has concluded its negotiations.

Scales at 1 March 1981

University			Public Sector		
	Increment	£		Increment	£
Lecturer	0	6,070	Lecturer II	0	6,012
	1	6,475		1	6,387
	2	6,880		2	6,753
	3	7,290		3	7,116
	4	7,700		4	7,470
	5	8,105		5	7,818
	6	8,515		6	8,205
	7	8,925		7	8,556
	8	9,335		8	8,952
	9	9,750			
	10	10,106	Senior Lecturer	1	9,324
	11	10,575		2	9,702
	12	11,000		3	10,116
	13	11,425		4	10,539
	14	11,855		5	10,917
	15	12,305		6	11,295
	16	12,860			
Senior Lecturer/	0	12,305	Principal Lecturer	0	10,509
Reader	1	12,860		1	10,896
	2	13,190		2	11,277
	3	13,635		3	11,712
	4	14,075		4	12,090
	5	14,515		5	12,477
	6	14,960		6	12,861
	7	15,410		7	13,245
Professor: minimum		15,730	Head of Dept. V: minimum		12,942
: maximum		18,480	Head of Dept. IV: maximum		15,432

11

SOME RADICAL PROPOSALS

by Alfred Morris

This final chapter presents nine proposals which arise out of a personal interpretation of the papers presented to the SRHE Leverhulme seminar on resources and their allocation. Most of them are idiosyncratic and the product of lateral thinking. It is doubtful whether the authors of the seminar papers would agree fully with the proposals and certain that the references made in this chapter to earlier chapters of the monograph do not amount to a summary of their content.

POLICY ANALYSIS AND THE DES

In 1973, Heclo and Wildavsky spent a year researching the expenditure process as it actually operates in British central government. They paid particular attention to the Public Expenditure Survey Committee (PESC) and wrote that '... What is needed is not somehow to hold the Treasury back, but to enhance the ability of operating departments and the Cabinet to compete with its judgement. ... The present and growing danger is that macro analysis of the economy is tending to overwhelm micro analysis of policies. ... Up till now, the macro tail has wagged the micro dog; it is time that both acquired a place up front where the barking and gnashing of teeth take place' (Heclo and Wildavsky 1981, pp.380 and 383).

Heclo and Wildavsky identified the weakness of British political administration as its sacrifice of substantive rationality (policy results) to maintaining its communal culture. In many ways, the University Grants Committee is the epitome of that culture and the following passage, written in 1972, is still pertinent:

> '... How can the UGC's efficiency of procedures, relevance of information and validity of values be intelligently debated by the academic community and by society while such secrecy is maintained? ... We are entitled to know more about decision making processes and techniques within the Department of Education and Science and the University Grants Committee. ...' (Morris 1972)

The remedies Heclo and Wildavsky prescribed emphasized the need for multiple, independent and external evaluation, and criticism of Departments of State and their policies. In particular, they proposed that each department be required to spend a small proportion of its budget on sponsorship of external evaluation. No doubt they would extend that recommendation to include bodies such as the UGC.

In Chapter 2 of this volume, Booth writes about the roles of the Department of Education and Science and the Treasury and emphasizes the small number of people involved in their negotiations over policy proposals and PESC. Booth forecasts that the attention which the DES can devote to particular areas of policy is likely to decrease in the foreseeable future. Notwithstanding its 'Departmental Planning Organization' (which includes a financial models and operational research unit) the DES capacity for conducting major policy studies is severely inhibited. The overseas student fees issue is used by Booth to demonstrate the difficulty of reconciling the overlapping policies of two departments when each is primarily concerned with the impact on its own expenditure programme.

Booth's analysis when set in the context of Heclo and Wildavsky's research into the public expenditure process, invites Proposal 1.

Proposal 1

a *Within PESC there is a need for an improved quantitative and demographic perspective and for a more sophisticated and extensive set of DES models of the higher education system, which should be available to outside bodies for analysis using alternative assumptions.*
b *More information should be available to outside bodies on DES discussions with other departments such as Employment and Industry, and the impact of DES policy changes on the budgets of other departments should be estimated and published.*

One of the most powerful allies that a lobby can hope to enlist is the Treasury. They have every reason to regret that macro economic management may so overwhelm micro analysis of policies as to produce effects on individuals and institutions which are plain daft. If external analysis can identify departmental policy effects which are not congruent with macro economic objectives, then it is the treasury that is most likely to welcome and act upon that analysis.

By way of example, the government is currently funding the considerable cost of purchasing the surrender of tenure in the universities in order to quicken the pace of their contraction. As reflected in the DES budget, the chosen policy makes economic sense both in terms of the discounted return on the pattern of incremental cash flows and in terms of the 'pay back' period. But this ignores the effects of the policy which will be reflected in the budgets of other departments: the reduction of government income from taxation and national insurance, the increase in social security payments as a consequence of a reduction in staff and student numbers, and so on. The design of a comprehensive cash flow model suitable for evaluating the economic effects of this policy choice and the quantification of the data with an acceptable degree of accuracy, are not matters of great technical complexity. But the DES has few staff and little incentive to attempt such analysis.

Is it naïve to suppose that resource allocation decisions will be changed if superior techniques and more sophisticated analyses are introduced? It may be that the reasons for the forced contraction of higher education have little to do with levels of public expenditure or demographic trends. Perhaps it is of the nature of politics that the true strategy is rarely stated and to subject policy to critical appraisal in terms of a government's stated objectives is to tilt at windmills. But Wildavsky is no newcomer to the concept of political rationality: his thesis is subtle (Wildavsky 1974).

No amount of external policy analysis can guarantee improved decisions because there is rarely a sufficient concensus as to the objectives in terms of which those decisions are to be appraised. What external policy analysis can do is improve the capacity for intelligent budgetary choices. A budget is a set of goals with price tags attached, it records the outcome of a political struggle and is best thought of in terms of a preference function determined by a collision of competing forces. The budgetary process is one in which the participants start with a perception of what is, choose between an identified set of alternatives, and seek to move towards some alternative state on the basis of predicted consequences: this is why alternative analysis is so important. It can improve perception of what is, extend the identified set of alternatives and refine predictions as to consequences. Without changing people's values, their decisions can be changed and improved with the quality of information available to them.

EXPERIMENTATION WITH INCENTIVES
One way of categorizing the competing forces which collide to determine policy in higher education is as 'supply side' as distinct from 'demand side'. The first volume in this SHRE Leverhulme series deals with higher education and the labour market, the second with access to higher education. Those monographs are about possible patterns of demand. In Chapter 3 of the present volume, on privatization and the market mechanisms in higher education, Maynard reminds us of supply side rigidities: there is an existing stock of academics whose interest lies in seeing that the consumer prefers what they as producers are equipped and inclined to offer. Maynard argues that, regardless of ideology, the obstacles to change and the more efficient use of scarce resources are very similar: what are needed are experiments with incentives and rewards to use resources efficiently and there is scope for this in both public and private institutions.

In Chapter 4 Woodhall suggests that the experience of other countries which operate loans schemes provides some valuable lessons. Woodhall points out that there are few Western countries without some form of student loan scheme; there is no evidence that loans necessarily deter low income students or women; and, if loans are provided by commercial banks, this would reduce public expenditure and the public sector borrowing requirement.

The chapters written by Maynard and Woodhall invite Proposal 2.

Proposal 2
To encourage efficiency and innovation in higher education, there should be experiments with incentives and rewards made possible by modest price differentials between and within institutions (through tuition fee levels) and loans schemes are needed for that purpose.

The case for incentives and rewards and the role of price differentials is identified by Maynard, but how can price differentials be introduced? Woodhall describes how for mandatory award holders a tuition fee is at present set at a level recommended by the Secretary of State for Education and Science and is paid to institutions by local education authorities which then recoup ninety per cent of the cost from central government. The tuition fee for mandatory award holders could be abolished with an initial and compensating increase in the quantum of the UGC recurrent grant and the Advanced Further Education pool so that neither students nor institutions need suffer financially as a result. Institutions could then be encouraged to determine their own modest levels of tuition fees for mandatory award holders, to vary these from subject to subject to reflect the interplay between costs and student demand, and be allowed to retain the proceeds. It would be for the student to meet the cost of these tuition fees and most institutions would choose to negotiate loans schemes with the major banks in order to attract both students and fees.

The administrative costs of implementing this proposal should not be high and would largely be borne by the banks: they are eager to attract students as customers and are aggressive in their competition to do so. For institutions, the task of collecting tuition fees paid by banks rather than by local education authorities on behalf of students, presents few problems. As to the incidence of bad debts, they will be a feature of any loans schemes but are likely to be minimized if it is the institution rather than the state which both evaluates the credit risk and has the incentive to follow up defaulters.

Complexity, prospective unpopularity and the lengthy 'pay-back period' have deterred successive governments from implementing a loan scheme. The higher education community itself has been nervous of the idea of student loans: in part because of fear that loans will deter student applications and also because it has never been convinced that any cash generated by such a device in the longer term would supplement public spending on higher education rather than be diverted to other purposes. The proposal set out above is rather different: the prime purpose is to experiment with incentives and rewards through price differentials;

government does not feature in the scheme, and it is for each institution to decide whether it wishes to charge a modest tuition fee to mandatory award holders and is in a market position which will allow it to do so. If the level of tuition fee varies from subject to subject, so might the income of departments: that could provide the incentives and rewards for institutions to compete not necessarily in terms of lowering their unit costs, but rather in terms of offering courses for which students are prepared to pay a premium.

It does not follow from Proposal 2 that central government's per capita expenditure on higher education should be reduced or that the survival of institutions should depend on their ability to generate tuition fee income. What is intended is that the flow of supplementary private funds into higher education should be increased by giving institutions an incentive to offer what students want and are willing to pay extra for. Would the proposal prove to be a Trojan horse used by the government to reduce, as distinct from redistribute, its own per capita support for higher education? It seems doubtful; in this case the Trojans do not need a horse. Higher education has little to lose other than its lack of confidence in the willingness of students to contribute directly to the cost of their courses.

One danger of Proposal 2 might be that the most prestigious institutions will concentrate on attracting the better-off student. But market mechanisms are subtle, the ability of an institution to charge a premium reflecting its prestige will soon be lost if it lowers its entry standards. It seems unlikely that the tuition fee premium charged by even the very prestigious institutions for their most sought after courses will exceed a few hundred pounds per annum and Woodhall's research suggests that there is no evidence that loans necessarily deter low income students. Even so, in the first years of operation of such a system it might be advisable for the NAB and the UGC to issue guidance on fees policy. For example, they might specify a level up to which income generated from fees will be disregarded in assessing the grant requirements of institutions and recommend that part of the proceeds be used for initiatives designed to complement the present system of financial support for students.

GRANTS, LOANS AND INTENSIVE COURSES
Woodhall identifies some of the most widespread criticisms of the present system of financial support for students: the means test, the unfair distinction between mandatory and discretionary awards, the absence of a comprehensive system of support for sixteen to nineteen-year-olds, and discrimination against part-time students and non-advanced education. Woodhall also reminds us of Blaug's argument that '... the present grants system is perhaps the least efficient method conceivable of increasing working class participation in higher education' (Blaug 1972, p. 296).

The attractions to government of a centrally administered loans scheme of the sort envisaged by Woodhall — not linked to price differentials as in Proposal 2 — include its potential use as a mechanism for a series of marginal adjustments in order to redistribute spending within the student support budget and meet the criticisms made by Blaug and others. By way of example, from Table 4.1 in Chapter 4, we learn that the number of holders of mandatory awards in 1979-80 was 323,000: that is loans averaging £300 per student, when repaid by those students would have raised about £97 million. In the same chapter we learn that the cost of abolishing the parental contribution in 1979-80 would have been £94 million; alternatively, the cost of providing means-tested educational maintenance allowances for all pupils over the compulsory school-leaving age was estimated in 1978 to be £100 million for England and Wales.

If loans are linked with price differentials in the form of tuition fees as in Proposal 2 above, it will be the institutions rather than the government which raise say £97 million of private funds to supplement public spending on higher education. How will the pattern of spending of that amount differ as a result? Whilst the DES might see educational maintenance allowances as its priority, the institutions will surely be more selfish. But, particularly with guidance from the NAB and the UGC, the self-interest of institutions might coincide with what the DES regard as socially desirable objectives such as increasing access to higher education for disadvantaged and under-represented groups. Maynard suggests that contested outcomes are empirical issues and best resolved by experimentation.

Both Maynard and Woodhall see loans as more than a mere mechanism for redistribution of resources. Maynard states what he describes as the liberal view of the beneficial effects of student loans: the questioning of existing supply side structures and then the evolution of alternatives:

'... university institutions which teach for three years but seem to use capital and labour indifferently over long vacations and which inhibit the division of labour ... might be challenged by institutions offering two-year degrees and different resource-use patterns.' (Chapter 3, p. 64)

A recent statement of the case for fewer enrolments on traditional three-year degree courses and for increased provision of two-year courses to considerable numbers of people at present excluded from higher education is advanced by Carter (1980). Lord Robbins told a select committee of the House of Commons that Carter's proposals were imaginative (Fifth Report, Vol. II, p. 430). Carter's case is stronger when set in the context of the marked decline since 1972 in higher education opportunities for school-leavers with less than two 'A' levels (Fulton 1981, p. 50). Information on the extent and costs and benefits of students — particularly in the non-university sector — starting courses but failing to complete them might provide the strongest support of all for Carter's view that '... at least twenty per cent of those at present taking first degree courses, would gain more benefit in terms of personal development and contribute more to the community, if they could leave after two years without the stigma of failure or of leaving work half done' (Fifth Report, Vol. II, pp. 425/426).

An earlier seminar in the SRHE Leverhulme series discussed proposals by Cane for alternative two-year courses and Wagner both referred to Carter's views and asked why the traditional ninety weeks of study for a degree course cannot be compressed into two academic years (Wagner 1982, p. 19). This leads to Proposal 3.

Proposal 3

a Public expenditure on student support should be redistributed so as to encourage wider participation and reduce the dominance of the three-year full-time degree course.

b The DES should identify the extent and costs and benefits of students starting courses but failing to complete them.

c The NAB and the UGC should invite proposals for more intensive courses — and earmark funds to support experiments with two-year degree courses in particular — and the DES should express its willingness to amend the mandatory award regulations correspondingly if this is necessary.

If the student support system is to be the mechanism by which the dominance of the three-year full-time degree course is to be changed, how can it be done? Carter would limit the mandatory award to the first two years of study and suggests that those who proceed to a third or subsequent year should borrow to enable them to do so. Fulton suggested that credit transfer is arguably the single reform which could have the greatest effect on demand levels and called for the present system to be replaced '...with a system of "educational entitlement" whereby every citizen is entitled to support for his or her education or training regardless of its level. Such support would comprise an age-related maintenance grant and remission or reimbursement of fees, for a maximum of four years full-time or its part-time equivalent after the compulsory school-leaving age of sixteen. This entitlement should be supplemented with a system of state supported loans, available for further periods of education or training as desired...' (Fulton 1981, p.30). Carter and Fulton would use the student support system as the mechanism for reducing the dominance of the three-year full-time degree course and both would rely upon a comprehensive and government-supported loan scheme of the sort discussed by Woodhall. Theirs are radical proposals which go much further than the sort of experimentation with tuition fees and loans proposed above. Is it necessary or wise to go so far?

In the case of two-year degree courses at the University College at

Buckingham, the DES has shown that it is willing to be flexible by modifying the student support system, presumably on the basis that its concern should be with the cost per graduate rather than the cost per student year. The NAB and the UGC should follow the DES example and fund the institutional costs of some experimental two-year degree courses for which the estimated cost per graduate is no higher than that of comparable three-year courses. Maynard is surely right that contested outcomes are best resolved by experimentation: in this case the experiment would test the feasibility of more intensive degree courses.

As regards steering some students away from three-year degree courses towards two-year courses leading to TEC or BEC or similar awards, the answer may well be to act on the supply side by reducing the proportion of degree to sub-degree level courses available. One way of doing this would be for the size of the university sector to be reduced more than that of the non-university sector, in which most of the two-year sub-degree level courses are concentrated and in which more of the degree courses are modular in form and suited to credit transfer arrangements. Because the DES exercises direct control over course approvals in the non-university sector, it is not a difficult matter to adjust the balance between degree and other places available in the polytechnics and colleges. The DES can also use its controls over courses in the non-university sector to encourage more modular courses and credit transfer arrangements. Given the scope for experimentation using the existing course approval powers of the DES, it seems unwise and unnecessary to introduce wholesale reform of the student support system based on a full-scale government supported loan scheme.

ALLOCATION BETWEEN SECTORS

The use of market mechanisms in Proposals 2 and 3 is limited to experimentation with some element of incentive and reward as distinct from determining the very shape of higher education. It follows that the balance between university and non-university sectors must be centrally planned. What are the factors that should determine the balance?

The distinctive characteristics of the university (the 'U') sector of higher education are the scale of its postgraduate work and research effort, which is reflected in the close relationship between the 'U' sector and the research councils and in the dual support system by which a substantial but unspecified part of the UGC grant is for un-earmarked research purposes. University students are, for the most part, mobile, and because of the dual support system it makes sense for whatever monies are available to be spread between universities on a basis which is dominated by judgements, subject by subject, as to excellence as perceived — in particular — by the research councils. It follows that resource allocation in the 'U' sector should be dominated by a national focus.

As to the 'non U' sector, the colleges and polytechnics, its distinctive characteristics in comparison with the 'U' sector are:

— It caters for twenty per cent more students.
— The scale of its sub-degree level work.
— The scale of its part-time work.
— A pronounced vocational bias.
— Much greater emphasis on mature students.
— Much greater emphasis on working-class students.
— Its predominantly regional catchment areas.
— Only a minority of students arrive direct from school.
— A high proportion of students arrive from further education.
— A substantial proportion of students have work experience.
— Strong commitment to sandwich education.
— Students have lower 'A' level grades.
— Substantial provision for entrants without two 'A' levels.
— Courses tend to be broader and more are modular.
— Quality control is external and by peer group review.
— Lecturers have poorer degrees, more work experience; more have trained to teach and they tend to put students and teaching before subject and research.

The chairman of the National Advisory Board for Local Authority Higher Education, Christopher Ball, told the Council of Local Education Authorities at their 1982 annual conference that '... higher education in the scope of the NAB is local and regional in emphasis rather than national...' and went on to list other distinctive characteristics as: the range of advanced and non-advanced work, the mixture of attendance modes, teaching comes first, cost effectiveness, responsiveness to need, and external validation (Ball 1982). Some of these characteristics are reflected in Tables 11.1, 11.2 and 11.3 whilst others are identified in published material (CDP 1981, p. 12; Fifth Report Vol. III, pp. 550-558; Fulton 1981, Chapter 2).

Because of its distinctive characteristics, an appropriate approach to the planning of course provision in the 'non U' sector would be to:

1. Identify the primary catchment area of each institution in terms of home-based (and particularly part-time) students — this is an exercise in which considerations such as transport lines are of great importance.
2. Identify the demographic trends — not just age cohorts but the socio-economic and ethnic profiles — which will affect demand for higher education in each catchment area; this will soon demonstrate that national trends disguise marked regional variations.
3. For each catchment area, plan: first, that part of course provision

which is not 'portable' (that is, all part-time courses and provision for full-time and sandwich students who prefer to be home-based); last, provision for the 'mobile' element of full-time students — an exercise in which the volume of provision for the 'portable' element at any one institution is designed to cement the part-time and home-based provision into an economical unit.

Contrast the approach advocated for the 'non U' sector (a basis determined primarily by forecasting regional demand for non-portable,

TABLE 11.1
Student numbers in higher education 1979/80: United Kingdom (thousands)

	'U'[1]	'Non U'[2]
BY TYPE OF COURSE		
Postgraduate	49	13
1st degree	248	129
Other	4	81
BY AGE[3]		
Under 21	179	112
21 and over[4]	121	111
FULL-TIME	301	223
PART-TIME	31	171
TOTAL	332	394

1 Excluding the London Graduate School of Business Studies and the Manchester Business School
2 This includes maintained and assisted colleges in England and Wales, Education Authority day colleges in Scotland, Stranmillis College of Education, and education/authority and library board colleges in Northern Ireland. Only those institutions which run advanced courses are included, except in Scotland where the coverage is just those institutions which run full-time or short full-time advanced courses. Also includes direct grant and voluntary colleges in England and Wales, central institutions and colleges of education in Scotland, and voluntary colleges of education in Norther Ireland
3 Ages as at 31 August
4 If all postgraduate students are 21 and over, the figures for full-time undergraduate students are 72:98 for 'U' and 'non U' sectors respectively

Source Based on a background paper for the SRHE Leverhulme seminar on resources and their allocation prepared by the DES, 1982.

part-time and full-time home-based students) with the approach advocated for the university sector (research council influenced assessment of excellence on a subject by subject basis with students regarded as mobile). This leads to Proposal 4.

Proposal 4
University resource allocation must be dominated by a national focus: provision in the 'non U' sector — colleges and polytechnics — should be dominated by a regional focus.

In a nutshell, the binary line may be imperfectly drawn, but for resource allocation purposes it exists and has a rationale: it separates a research-led sector funded through the dual support system (and which needs a national perspective) from a sector which needs a regional perspective and either is or could be led by the patterns and policies of schools and

TABLE 11.2
Student numbers by subject: full-time, sandwich and part time:[1] United Kingdom (thousands)

	'U' FT/SW	'U' PT	'U' Total	'Non U' FT/SW	'Non U' PT	'Non U' Total
Education	11	4	15	46	16	62
Medicine, dentistry, veterinary, health, etc.	35	2	37	8	10	18
Engineering, technology	37	1	38	36	47	83
Biological, mathematics, physical	70	3	73	21	15	36
Business, professional, vocational	17	1	18	47	43	90
Social science	63	3	66	28	38	67
Arts	62	4	66	38	3	41
TOTAL	296	19[2]	315	223	171	394

1 For the universities these are student load figures which reflect the teaching load on departments rather than the subject of study of the students. The total is lower than the total university numbers in Table 11.1 because the student load figures exclude students who are away from the university for all or part of the year and those who are on self-financing or externally financed courses

The public sector figures represent the subject of study of the students and so are not directly comparable with the universities figures. Student load figures are not available for the public sector

2 The universities student load figures for part-time students are calculated on a full-time equivalent basis, and so the student load numbers are much lower than the actual numbers shown in Table 11.1

Source Based on a background paper for the SRHE Leverhulme seminar on resources and their allocation prepared by the DES, 1982.

TABLE 11.3
Student entry to full-time and sandwich degree courses: 1978/79 degree courses

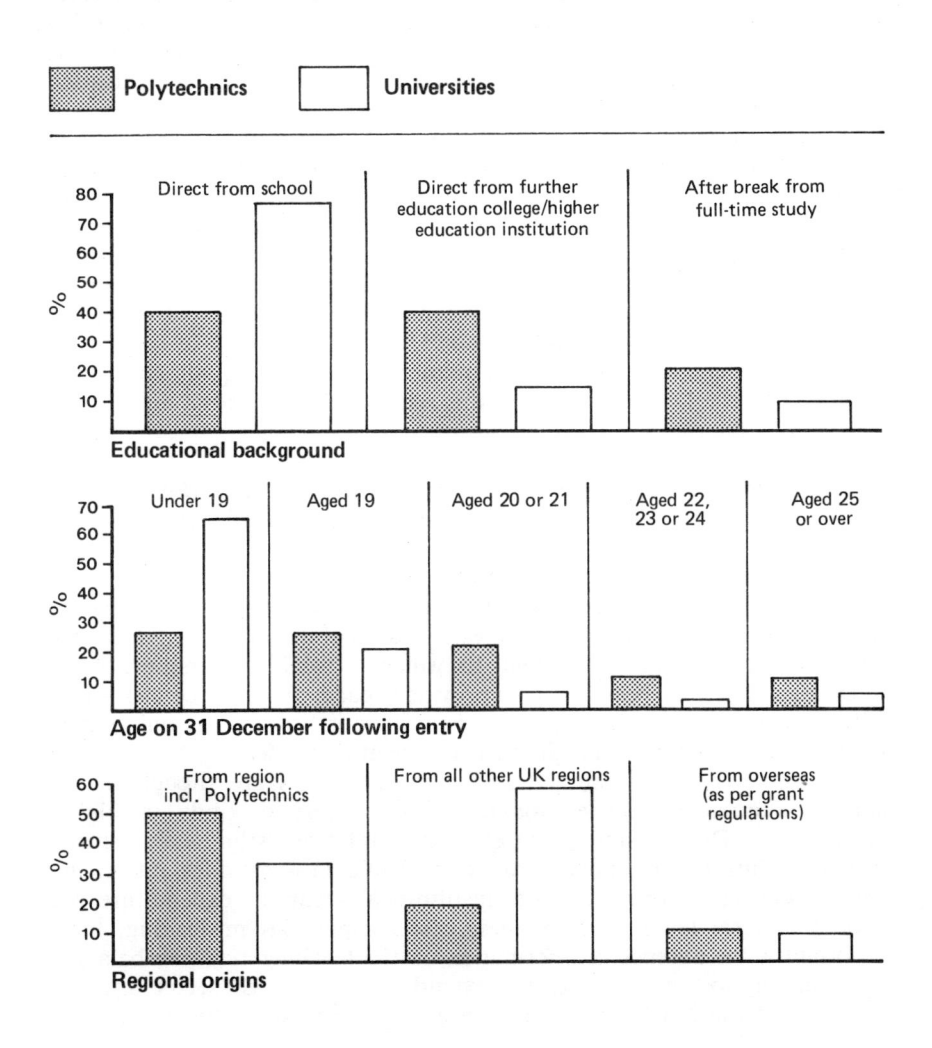

▨ Polytechnics   ☐ Universities

Educational background

	Direct from school	Direct from further education college/higher education institution	After break from full-time study
Polytechnics	40	40	20
Universities	77	15	10

Age on 31 December following entry

	Under 19	Aged 19	Aged 20 or 21	Aged 22, 23 or 24	Aged 25 or over
Polytechnics	27	27	23	12	12
Universities	65	21	7	4	4

Regional origins

	From region incl. Polytechnics	From all other UK regions	From overseas (as per grant regulations)
Polytechnics	50	20	12
Universities	34	58	10

Note The contrast between polytechnics and universities would be even more marked if part-time and sub-degree level students were included

Source CDP 1981

further education colleges. The case for local authority influence — as distinct from control — in the higher education colleges and polytechnics is for a seamless robe which may not exist but is a feasible and desirable garment. It is one in which to swaddle those upon whose greater participation the future of higher education depends: the groups identified by Farrant, particularly those who gain five or more 'O' levels and in some cases 'A' levels too, but then turn their backs on higher education (Fulton 1981, p. 50).

Who is to decide the balance between the 'U' and 'non U' sectors and how is it to be done? Surely this is the role of the DES? Because of tenure, the optimum financial strategy for higher education may be to minimize labour costs per unit by filling the universities to capacity and then determining the size of the 'non U' sector as a residual. Alternatively, university capacity could contract in line with its primary client group — the population of eighteen and nineteen-year-olds with two 'A' levels — whilst provision in the 'non U' sector expanded in proportion to increasing demand from its more mature and less well qualified clients. In order that the DES can perform this role we make Proposal 5.

Proposal 5
The DES needs to form a view on how far what the 'U' sector does or could provide is a suitable substitute for provision in the 'non U' sector.

There is a view that the nation should not prefer nor can it afford to make available to an increasing proportion of the population the sort of education at present provided in the universities. Lord Robbins wrote, '... I cannot sufficiently emphasize the extent to which I think universities, while accepting expansion, have failed to provide broader first degree courses...' (Fifth Report, Vol. II, p. 424). What is at issue is how far the universities are prepared to modify what they are and what they offer.

To whatever extent the 'U' and 'non U' sectors are thought to be suitable alternative vehicles for provision of certain kinds of higher education, the DES must weigh carefully their relative costliness: in terms of avoidable, future and opportunity costs. Table 11.4 provides interesting comparisons of historical average institutional recurrent expenditure per student. Several factors render these cost comparisons misleading, most important is the absence of information on the teaching/research balance. The dual support system does not extend to the 'non U' sector and the chairman of the NAB sees little chance of it doing so in the foreseeable future (Ball, 1982)

As long ago as 1969, the Committee of Vice-Chancellors and Principals undertook an inquiry into the use of academic staff time because '...Those concerned with national research policy were anxious to know what proportion of university expenditure should be regarded as relating to research.... The UGC also has a legitimate interest in the use of staff

TABLE 11.4
Unit costs (£)[1]

	Universities[2] (GB)	Maintained sector[3] (England and Wales)		
		Polytechnic	Other	All
Medicine/dentistry	5,664	-	-	- -
Lab/workshop-based subjects[4]	3,814	2,997	2,571	2,832
Classroom-based subjects[5]	2,145	2,141	1,837	2,038
All faculties[6]	3,183	2,633	2,297	2,509

1 At 1979/80 outturn prices
2 Excluding the Open University
3 Relate to estimate of advanced courses in maintained sector
4 ie technology and engineering, science, maths, health, architecture, etc.
5 ie social, administration and business studies, education, languages, etc.
6 For voluntary colleges the all faculties unit cost was £2,069

Source Based on a background paper for the SHRE Leverhulme seminar on resources and their allocation prepared by the DES, 1982.

time, in order that they might gain a fuller understanding of the relative costs of undergraduate and graduate work, and of different subject groups, in the different universities' (CVCP 1972).

Proposal 6
To provide a crude but useful proxy for the quantum of the UGC recurrent grant which is for earmarked research purposes, the excess of universities' present expenditure over a normative undergraduate teaching cost (based on idealized polytechnic expenditure levels) should be regarded as support for research and postgraduate work.

In Chapter 5, Moore identifies seven alternative financial models for the future funding of universities. Moore's model 'C' involves an attempt to separate the funding of research from the funding of teaching and he asks, should the system continue to allocate research money primarily on the basis of undergraduate numbers, or should money for undergraduate teaching be separated from that for postgraduate and research activities? Interestingly, Moore illustrates the idea by suggesting that 85 per cent of recurrent grant to be attributed to undergraduate teaching. This would produce a rather similar result to using the average 'all faculties' unit costs of the polytechnics shown in Table 11.4, though normative undergraduate teaching costs would be somewhat lower because based on an idealized level of utilization of polytechnic capacity.

Any basis for measuring the funding of research and postgraduate work implicit in UGC grants which wins general acceptance will beg a question first posed in August 1971 to the Secretary of State for Education and Science (Mrs Margaret Thatcher) in a report from Sir Frederick Dainton of his study on the support of scientific research in the universities:

'...Should there be greater concentration of Research Council selective support in certain universities and departments? ... Should there be establishments — whether universities or other institutions of higher education — which undertake little or no research?' (CSP 1971)

A minority report of a House of Commons Select Committee on the Funding and Organization of Courses in Higher Education, published in 1980, included the following:

'We considered and rejected the idea of a redefined binary line in which institutions with substantial income from the Research Councils, and to which the 'dual support' system was thought crucial, would be funded by a similar body to the UGC ... we are convinced and recommend that 'dual support' should apply to departments rather than to institutions. ... The present system locates decisions on UGC financed research where it is most difficult to exercise it on a discriminatory basis; that is, at university level.... If the national interest and considerations of timeliness and promise are to hold much sway ... decision making needs to be at national level, and its exercise on a cost conscious basis ought to be influenced to a far greater extent by the Research Councils. ... We recommend a transfer to the Research Councils, of that part of UGC grants which is attributable to research. ...' (Fifth Report)

Any answers to Dainton's question or any recommendation along the lines of that in the Select Committee minority report are matters for the SRHE Leverhulme seminar and monograph on structure and governance. For resource allocation purposes these matters are critical to any assessment by the DES of the relative costliness of the 'U' and 'non U' sectors as alternative vehicles for provision of certain kinds of higher education.

ALLOCATION WITHIN SECTORS

Given that it is part of the role of the DES to determine the balance of resource allocation between the university and non-university sectors, by whom and how should the balance within sectors be determined? In the university sector, it has been asserted that there is need for a predominantly national focus. Consequently there is little need for change except that the UGC might concentrate on funding only undergraduate work. In the non-university sector, the assertion that there is a need for a predominantly regional focus supports the case for local authority influence — though not necessarily control — over a schools and further education-led cluster consisting of the higher education colleges and polytechnics. This begs the question, 'How might the influence of local authorities — and through them that of schools and further education colleges — be increased even though their control of higher education institutions is loosened or ended? The answer might be found in the following proposal which is intended to ensure that schools policies and curricula begin to shape the entry requirements for higher education rather than the reverse.

Proposal 7
A small but significant proportion of the AFE pool should be allocated to local education authorities on the basis of a formula which favours LEAs with low higher education participation rates. The monies should be earmarked for use by LEAs to support particular courses with quotas of studentships to be filled by applicants with either non-standard entry qualifications or no entitlement to a mandatory award.

Proposal 7 identifies a direct and practical way of implementing that part of Proposal 3 which called for public expenditure on student support to be redistributed so as to encourage wider participation and reduce the dominance of the three-year full-time degree course. Carter, Fulton and Wagner have each stated the case for change: this proposal identifies a means of achieving it and, significantly, it does so at the level of resource allocation within sectors by local education authorities. In Chapter 6, Pratt argues for apportioning responsibility for resource allocation in the public sector on the basis of who is best able to formulate problems and who to propose solutions. Underlying Proposal 7 is the conviction that chief education officers are well placed to formulate the local problems which inhibit access to higher education and that the 'non U' sector is well placed to propose solutions to those problems. The proposal also meets other requirements identified by Pratt: it is apt, supportive of educational purpose and statutory arrangements, invites both public scrutiny and attempts to develop new techniques for measuring educational effectiveness, and it is likely to prove politically acceptable. If Proposal 7 were accepted it could turn the 'problem budgeting' approach advocated by Pratt into a reality because it would put every chief education officer in the land in the position of advising local education authority members on how to spend earmarked monies on supporting higher education initiatives which related directly to local problems or complemented local schools and further education policies. If the UGC chose to follow a similar procedure to that recommended for the AFE pool it could blur the binary distinction in a constructive manner and the prospect of extending their influence into the universities might provide a political carrot sufficient to wean LEAs off the notion that they need actually to control their own institutions of higher education.

Lewis, in Chapter 7, discusses the relationships between a funding body and an academic validating body such as the Council for National Academic Awards, the Technical Education Council or the Business Education Council. A distinction is drawn between the cut-off decisions made by validating bodies such as the CNAA, where the prime criterion is that the standard of awards should be comparable with those of the universities, and ranking decisions which are not their concern and are only made by them on unsystematic and covert bases. Lewis lends support to a plea by Pratt when he stresses the importance of qualitative judgements concerned with the educational experience provided and suggests that there may be some value in developing a measure of 'added value' which combines measures of the quality of the student intake and of the output of the course. Only when the maturity of public sector institutions calls into question the need for their courses to be validated by an external agency does Lewis envisage the point being reached at which the funding and validation roles should be merged.

One important development which Lewis anticipates is that individual course approvals in the 'non U' sector, may be replaced by programme approvals whereby an institution is given freedom to decide what courses it wishes to mount within a specified subject area. That development surely calls for the NAB first to give the 'non U' sector guidance on the nature of the planning process in which it wishes them to engage and then to concentrate on appraising those plans.

ALLOCATION WITHIN INSTITUTIONS

Chapter 8 by Sims and Chapter 9 by Fielden take us into planning and resource allocation at institutional level: by and within colleges, polytechnics and the universities. Central to Sims' theme is the case for each institution to develop an academic plan whilst Fielden lends support to the need for careful selection of cost concepts appropriate to the choices confronted. Both authors are sensitive to the growing impact of market forces and Fielden asks how many British institutions embark on institutional research in the American sense.

It is instructive to read the chapters by Sims and Fielden with Proposal 2 in mind: that price differentials between and within institutions, through tuition fee levels, be encouraged. Implementation of that proposal on a basis such as that described would demand skills, concepts, techniques, and above all institutional research of a kind few institutions fully comprehend.

The chapters by Lewis, Sims and Fielden provide the background for Proposal 8.

Proposal 8

a Validating bodies' judgements as to the 'ranking' of departments or courses should not dominate resource allocation by bodies such as NAB.

b NAB should encourage and allocate resources on the basis of plans grounded in institutional research into: catchment areas; demographic trends affecting student demand and employers' needs within those catchment areas; an ethnic and socio-economic profile of students; research into what factors influence student choices; and student feedback on course content, teaching standards, etc.

Given the supply side rigidities referred to earlier and constraints such as tenure, it is a logical corollary to Proposal 8 that planning should be concentrated on identifying the marginal but compounding capacity for change which will arise as posts fall vacant and thus make possible a reshaping of the institution, and on determining how to harness that marginal capacity for change to introduce new courses or make significant modifications to the curriculum.

SUPPLY SIDE RIGIDITIES

The penultimate chapter of this monograph is by Knight, who writes about the terms and conditions of service of academic staff. They are the principal resource with the allocation of which this monograph is concerned and in the economic sense they have become less scarce. Table 11.5 provides a reminder of the numbers involved.

Knight suggests that there are unlikely to be radical changes in pay and conditions in higher education in the 1990s. Academic staff will be employed on terms and conditions similar to those that operate at present. But it is interesting to reflect on Knight's chapter with Proposal 2 in mind: that there should be experiments with incentives and rewards made possible by modest price differentials between and within institutions through tuition fee levels.

It may be true that there will be no abandonment of uniform salary scales in favour of plant bargaining. But, as Knight reminds us, before 1949 there was no scale of salaries laid down nationally for all principal grades of university teachers: this because salary levels reflected the fact that institutions charged fees in accordance with their wealth and standing. If Proposal 2 were implemented it could be that institutions would choose to channel their fee premiums into bonuses or sabbaticals or similar rewards which varied between and within institutions.

Regardless of pay and conditions, it has been clear for a decade that government and higher education were set on a collision course, as the following extract from a paper written in 1973 makes clear.

'...If the stock of tenured academics continues to rise in almost direct proportion to student population, then a collision course will be set. Even before the plateau of sufficiency is reached, inflexibility in redeploying aggregate resources will provoke a major clash over objectives. Arguments about whether we should seek to satisfy 'manpower demand' or 'student preference' will be submerged in popular agreement that the one priority which the nation will not allow for its massive expenditure on higher education is that of distributing the student population to match an inflexible academic pattern. ... To obtain greater flexibility in redeploying resources, future appointments to tenured posts must be restrained to encourage the substitution of alternative resources capable of more rapid and less costly redeployment. Otherwise the considerable cost of selectively redeeming, or tolerating, excess academic capacity will need to be met.' (Morris 1973)

The costs referred to in that extract are being met now and are best measured in terms of tens of thousands of 'student exposure years' foregone.

Complete control over the size and subject distribution of the academic population could be obtained by the government insisting that in future the decision to create, or refill when vacant, any academic post which is to be a charge on state-supplied funds should be approved by the NAB or the UGC. The relationship between higher education institutions and state in respect of academic staff could be like that between institutions and private benefactors including charitable trusts.

In practice, effective control over the size and subject distribution of the academic population can be obtained with a minimum of bureaucratic interference by voluntary acceptance of a modified version of the approach described above. This leads to Proposal 9.

Proposal 9

a Both the NAB and the UGC should collect and publish rolling five-year forecasts of the number and subject distribution of academic posts likely to fall vacant.
b Both the NAB and the UGC should publish broad 'supply side' guidelines regarding the distribution between subjects and institutions of academic posts as they fall vacant.

Banished to a desert island with the task of predicting the subject pattern of higher education course provision in 1990 and allowed only one file of information, the wise man would ask for the file of pension scheme data on lecturers. The following extract regarding university staff illustrates why this is so.

'... The expansion of the university system in the 1960s and the early

TABLE 11.5
Teaching staff numbers in higher educatin 1979/80 (thousands)

	'U' (GB)	'Non U' (E & W)
Universities[1]	34.3	
Open University	0.9	
Polytechnics		16.9[2]
Other maintained establishments		60.8
Total full-time staff	35.2	77.7[2]
Part-time staff	6.3[3]	13.2[4]
TOTAL	41.5	90.9

1 The university figures refer to teaching and research staff paid wholly from university funds. If those who were partly financed and not financed are included then the full-time totals is 43.4 thousand
2 The public sector figures relate to maintained, assisted and grant aided establishments in *England and Wales* only, in March 1980. They include staff undertaking both advanced and non-advanced work. At the polytechnics staff employed on advanced teaching represent almost all of the teaching staff. At the other maintained establishments a much lower proportion of staff will be teaching at advanced levels
3 Including 5.2 thousand for the Open University
4 These are full-time equivalent numbers of part-time teaching staff in maintained and assisted establishments (not grant aided) in England and Wales, in January 1980

Source Based on a background paper for the SRHE Leverhulme seminar on resources and their allocation prepared by the DES, 1982.

1970s has resulted in an age distribution of staff significantly different from that required in a steady state situation in which, for example, about twenty five per cent would be expected to be aged 55 or over. This means that in normal circumstances relatively few would be expected to retire in the next few years and correspondingly few recruited ... the age of staff varies considerably between academic departments. Overall, staff in medical, arts and social studies departments tend to be younger than those in engineering, technology and other science departments. ... Compared with an overall age distribution in Great Britain with a mean of 42.5 years and fourteen per cent aged 55 or over, individual university distributions ranged from one with a mean of 37.7 years and with only two per cent aged 55 or over for a predominantly medical university, to one with a mean of 45.6 years and with twenty two per cent aged 55 or over for a largely technological institution. ...' (UGC 1982, p. 9)

Will the guidance in Proposal 9 as distinct from dictates regarding the redistribution of academic posts be sufficient to reshape the supply side of higher education? There is the example of the UGC:

'... The UGC enjoys an especially subtle authority derived not from the exercise of legal powers but from influence allowed by universities. A university is not required in any legal sense to follow UGC guidance but politically rational behaviour involves only exceptional and considered disregard for such guidance... .' (Morris 1974, p. 43)

The example of the UGC is where what Heclo and Wildavsky described as the communal culture of British political administration shows its strength.

The first proposal in this chapter called for an improved quantitative and demographic perspective and for a more sophisticated and extensive set of DES models. One of those models could be of the academic stock and designed to identify the scope for change which will arise as posts fall vacant and thus make possible a reshaping of higher education. Whether higher education is shaped by guidance or by dictate, such a model could help identify the answer to a key question which will recur throughout the next decade: 'To what extent is it necessary to intervene with compulsory redundancy or voluntary premature retirement schemes?'

CONCLUSION

The proposals in this chapter may appear to be an odd mixture: incentives and rewards through tuition fees on the demand side, and central intervention on the supply side to influence the shape and size of the academic stock. But is a mixed economy such a stranger? Maynard makes the point that the problems faced by 'socialists' who adopt a collective ideology, and by 'liberals' who adopt a market ideology, are very similar!

The thesis that underlies the nine proposals in this chapter is simple, if not naïve: decisions can be changed and improved with the quality of information made available, both analysis and experimentation should precede radical change, the use of incentives and rewards is not synonymous with a private or market approach, and intervention on the supply side may be more effective in reshaping higher education than attempts to stimulate and influence patterns of demand.

PROPOSALS
1 a Within PESC there is a need for an improved quantitative and demographic perspective and for a more sophisticated and extensive set of DES models of the higher education system which should be available to outside bodies for analysis using alternative assumptions.
  b More information should be available to outside bodies on DES discussions with other departments such as Employment and

Industry, and the impact of DES policy changes on the budgets of other departments should be estimated and published.

2   To encourage efficiency and innovation in higher education, there should be experiments with incentives and rewards made possible by modest price differentials between and within institutions (through tuition fee levels) and loans schemes are needed for that purpose.

3   a   Public expenditure on student support should be redistributed so as to encourage wider participation and reduce the dominance of the three-year full-time degree course.
    b   The DES should identify the extent and costs and benefits of students starting courses but failing to complete them.
    c   The NAB and the UGC should invite proposals for more intensive courses — and earmark funds to support experiments with two-year degree courses in particular — and the DES should express its willingness to amend the mandatory award regulations correspondingly if this is necessary.

4   University resource allocation must be dominated by a national focus: provision in the 'non U' sector — colleges and polytechnics — should be dominated by a regional focus.

5   The DES needs to form a view on how far what the 'U' sector does or could provide is a suitable substitute for provision in the 'non U' sector.

6   To provide a crude but useful proxy for the quantum of the UGC recurrent grant which is for earmarked research puposes, the excess of universities' present expenditure over a normative undergraduate teaching cost (based on idealized polytechnic expenditure levels) should be regarded as support for research and postgraduate work.

7   A small but significant proportion of the AFE pool should be allocated to local education authorities on the basis of a formula which favours LEAs with low higher education participation rates. The monies should be earmarked for use by LEAs to support particular courses with quotas of studentships to be filled by applicants with either non-standard entry qualifications or no entitlement to a mandatory award.

8   a   Validating bodies' judgements as to the 'ranking' of departments or courses should not dominate resource allocation by bodies such as NAB.
    b   NAB should encourage and allocate resources on the basis of plans grounded in institutional research into: catchment areas; demographic trends affecting student demand and employers' needs within those catchment areas; an ethnic and socio-economic profile of students; research into what factors influence student choices; and student feedback on course content, teaching standards, etc.

9   a   Both the NAB and the UGC should collect and publish rolling five-year forecasts of the number and subject distribution of academic

posts likely to fall vacant.
b Both the NAB and the UGC should publish broad 'supply side' guidelines regarding the distribution between subjects and institutions of academic posts as they fall vacant.

REFERENCES
Ball, C. (1982) The seven principles of LAHE *Education* 160
Blaug, M. (1972) *An Introduction to the Economics of Education* Harmondsworth: Penguin
Carter, C. (1980) *Higher Education for the Future* Oxford: Basil Blackwell
CDP (Committee of Directors of Polytechnics) (1981) *The Polytechnics: Vision into Reality* London: CDP
CSP (Council for Scientific Policy) (1971) *Report of a Study on the Support of Scientific Research in the Universities* Cmnd 4798. London: HMSO
CVCP (Committee of Vice-Chancellors and Principals) (1972) *Report of an Enquiry into the Use of Academic Staff Time* London: CVCP
Fifth Report (1980) *The Funding and Organization of Courses in Higher Education* HC 787. House of Commons Fifth Report from the Education, Science and Arts Committee, session 1979-1980
Fulton, O. (Editor) (1981) *Access to Higher Education* Guildford: Society for Research into Higher Education
Heclo, H. and Wildavsky A. (1981) *The Private Government of Public Money* London: Macmillan
Morris, A.C. (1972) The UGC and the mystery of the quinquennial cake *Times Higher Education Supplement* 41
Morris, A.C. (1973) Flexibility and the tenured academic *Higher Education Review* 6 (2)
Morris, A.C. (1974) *University Planning and Organization: Background Papers* University of Sussex
UGC (University Grants Committee) (1982) *University Statistics 1980* Vol. 1. Cheltenham: Universities Statistical Record
Wagner, L. (Editor) (1982) *Agenda for Institutional Change in Higher Education* Guildford: Society for Research into Higher Education
Wildavsky, A. (1974) *The Politics of the Budgetary Process* Boston: Little, Brown